The Irish Girls

M.C. Ryan

ISBNS
PARENT : 978-1-78237-595-1
EPUB: 978-1-78237-596-8
MOBI: 978-1-78237-597-5
PDF: 978-1-78237-598-2

A CIP catalogue for this book is available from the National Library.

Published by ORIGINAL WRITING LTD., Dublin, 2014.

Printed by CLONDALKIN GROUP, Glasnevin, Dublin 11

Dedicated to the Friends I've been blessed to have,

who are gone but always remembered

FOREWORD

2013 in Ireland was designated the year of 'The Gathering.' It was an appeal on behalf of the Irish Nation to the hundreds of thousands who left Irish shores over the last 150 years in search of work and a better life, to return again from the four corners of the world to re-trace their sometimes lost ancestry and reunite with all their relatives and friends.

With the whole world suffering an economic crisis in recent years Ireland once again like in the 1980s has seen a new wave of young and old leaving its shores in their thousands in the hope of finding employment elsewhere. I believe each and every person who has emigrated has a story to tell. My sister Maggie aged twenty and I aged eighteen left Ireland in the early eighties on what was to become a great adventure. We met people who we remember with great fondness to this very day. This is my story.

ACKNOWLEDGEMENTS

Thank you to my son Stephen and my daughter Grace who have been a constant source of love and support throughout the years in good times and bad.

Thank you Becky for taking such good care of Stephen

Thank you Sharon, even though we don't meet often enough, we are still as close as when we met all those years ago as teenagers
Thank you Dorothy for being such a source of encouragement and making me believe in myself at a time in my life when I felt everyone was against me

Thank you Ann for the happy times we shared together, you always managed to lift my spirits

Thank you Trisha for remembering me when most did not
Last but not least, a special thanks to Linda, my workmate and friend, 'you are a true blue'

I would also like to mention a 'new friend' Mary, a real lady who worked tirelessly with great attention to detail, typing and proof-reading my book. Thank you.

Contents

Chapter 1

Country Roads

The year was 1980. I was seventeen years old and living with my family in a small village called Cratloe, which was about fifteen minutes' drive from Limerick City, but in the County of Clare. Cratloe was an area of great natural beauty with its hills and forests, stone walls and winding country roads. The village, like many others dotted across the Irish landscape consisted of a eighteenth century church, a school, post office, butcher's stall, grocery store and of course a pub. There was also a newly built community centre which was a hive of activity as it served many purposes from GAA meetings to organised sporting events, cake stalls run by the Country Women's Association and the youth céili dance every Friday night, a disco it was not, but beggars couldn't be choosers.

My family's home was situated about a mile from the village and was sitting on the side of a hill with stunning views of the surrounding countryside. If you looked out the kitchen window, to the fore of the picture you saw green fields with herds of grazing cattle; if you looked to the left, as far as the eye could see was forest which changed colour with every season; to the right, on the horizon was the city of Limerick which was lovely to watch at night with its beautiful array of lights sparkling in the distance. The view from the sitting room window was just as spectacular with a half-acre of lawn bordered by a privet hedge and flower beds with distant views of a Medieval castle and the River Shannon meandering its way along as it had no doubt, since time began.

Cratloe was indeed a beautiful place to live and that fact hadn't gone un-noticed. It had become in the previous twenty years increasingly popular with people from the city who wanted a more relaxed environment and a slower pace of life. My mother was 'over the moon' when we moved there five years before. The house was an old farmhouse which had been extended, but because it still needed a lot of cosmetic work, she managed to buy it at a knock-down price. She was thrilled at the fact it had central heating and a 'real' shower. I personally didn't care about the central heating or the shower. All I cared about was the fact that 'Mam' had said that when we moved to the country we would have plenty of space for a dog and a cat.

I was one of six children and the second eldest: Maggie at nineteen was the oldest, then after me there were three boys, Michael, Robert and James, last but not least there was Barbra the 'baby' of the family at four years old.

When we moved to Cratloe Maggie and I continued to attend the same Convent secondary school in Limerick City, as Cratloe School like most country schools only taught primary level. I didn't care which school I attended, because I knew that either way I was going to hate it. Maggie, on the other hand, was happy not to have to change schools, because she was very popular and had a huge group of friends, but also because the teachers loved her. Yes, Maggie was an "A" student.

I remember my first day in secondary school. I was always very shy and naturally very nervous, but Mam warned Maggie to watch out for me and show me the ropes' so to speak, so I wouldn't be wandering around aimlessly like an 'Eejit.' So when we got to school with fifteen minutes to go before the bell rang, Maggie gave me the grand tour with all her gang in tow. Making our way through the crowds and what seemed to me, endless corridors, Maggie pointed this way and that to the classrooms, the Science Lab. the Gym and finally upon our arrival in the cloakrooms she pointed to the rows of lockers where I could hang my coat. The school was definitely twice the size of the Primary I had attended and I was relieved to have Maggie to show me around. I began to relax knowing that so far everything was going OK. 'Well Mary, any questions?' Maggie asked me just as the bell began ringing in our ears. 'Yes Maggie', I replied, 'see that machine hanging on the wall next to the toilets, what's that for?' Now Maggie scoffed, 'now girls, do ye see what I'm dealing with? She hasn't got a clue. Will you shut up Mary? Do you know anything? That's

a sanitary towel dispenser, you bloody 'Eejit' you.' 'Well how was I to know?' I blurted as she marched off.
I think that first day was a sign of things to come and as the years went by I was convinced that "Eejit" was my middle name. The teachers couldn't understand it. 'Your sister Maggie is such a pleasure to teach,' they would say, 'I don't know where they got you.' Every day was the same. 'Mary Ryan, why can't you be like your sister? What kind of an 'Eejit' are you?' It seemed that even when I was right, I was wrong.

One sunny spring day the art teacher Mr. O'Doherty decided it was too nice to be 'stuck inside' and brought the entire class outside to sit on the grass and instructed us to sketch anything we saw around us. I picked up a small branch that had fallen from a nearby apple tree. In pencil I drew the bark, the leaves and the delicate pale pink blossoms. I was really quite proud of myself when all my classmates agreed that mine was without a doubt the best. It was really pretty and I couldn't wait for the art teacher to see it. But he took one look at it, said it was so brilliant that I couldn't possibly have drawn it. 'What did you do Mary; bribe one of the others to it for you? You won't pull the wool over my eyes you know.'
A few months later, the same teacher asked the whole class to design a poster highlighting the dangers of drink. The whole school was taking part in the project and there would be prizes for first place and the runners' up. I couldn't believe it when I heard my name being called out over the crackly intercom system a month later as the over-all winner. Even Maggie was proud of me and was shouting to anyone who would listen that I was her sister. The art teacher Mr. O'Doherty however wasn't as pleased. 'Mary, that's a great slogan, "Delay the Day you Drink,"' he said reading aloud the slogan. 'Thank you Sir,' I replied delighted with the praise. 'Are you sure Mary you didn't read it in a magazine somewhere?' Mr. O'Doherty asked, bringing me down to earth with a bang. 'No Sir,' I insisted 'I thought it up myself.' I knew where I'd gotten the inspiration from, but I wasn't going to tell him. 'It seems Mary',

he said, 'that we have no choice but to give you the benefit of the doubt'. He then handed me a prize while muttering 'Well done' through gritted teeth.

I hated school and couldn't wait to get a job. Maggie loved school and couldn't wait to go to university. The only part of school I enjoyed was the walk to the bus stop in the morning and the return journey in the evening. When we first moved to Cratloe, Maggie and I would leave the house each morning at eight o'clock to walk the mile and a half journey to the bus stop which took about half an hour. But a few months later when I got to know the 'lie of the land', I told Maggie about a short cut I had discovered, but it meant we would have to wear wellington boots. 'Wellington boots Mary!' she roared, 'I wouldn't be seen dead in them.'

'Maggie,' I said, trying to persuade her, 'who in the name of God is going to see you at eight o'clock in the morning and the shortcut is only half the distance to the bus stop?' She finally agreed to give it a try and decided after the first morning that I was right.

It was a good idea. Instead of walking on the road, we walked along the railway track for about five minutes and then we climbed over a gate onto O'Donnell's land. There were always horses in the field and I would have happily stayed there all day just looking at them. Maggie was happy walking across the field also, but it had nothing to do with the horses. It was because she was able to smoke a cigarette without worrying that any of the neighbours would see her and report her to Mam. The wellingtons remained an issue though. She was afraid she'd run into Mr. O'Donnell's son Ron.

'I'll just die if he sees me in these', she'd say. 'Why Maggie,' I asked, 'do you fancy him?' 'He's alright I suppose,' she said coolly. 'Do you think he's good looking Maggie?' 'Not really Mary, but his family are very well off.' 'Has it not occurred to you Maggie, that a woman in wellies might be just what Ron is looking for?' 'What's that supposed to mean Mary? You're not making any sense.' 'Well Maggie, if you marry him you'll have permanent red marks around your legs from the wellies.'

'What on earth are you talking about Mary?' 'I'm talking about farmers' wives Maggie, God knows, there's enough of them around here, but I have yet to see one of them herding cattle in high heels!'

I could see the reality of the situation dawning on Maggie. You see she had a vision painted in her head of Ladies Day at the Galway Races and her there, dressed in all her finery, sipping champagne and eating oysters. She hadn't thought about the other three hundred and sixty four days of the year when she would be up to her knees in shit!

When we reached the main road we took our school shoes out of a plastic bag we'd been carrying, pulled our wellington boots off and slipped our school shoes on, put the wellies into the plastic bag, and hid the bag behind a bush for us to collect on our way home in the evening. Just as the bus was coming to a stop Maggie finally spoke, having been in deep thought.

'You know Mary, about Ron?' 'Yes Maggie, what about him?'

'I've just gone off him. You might be happy with that life Mary, but not me, no way!'

I knew that within a few years Maggie would be heading for the bright lights of the city and the nearest she would get to country after that would be listening to Kenny Rogers and Dolly Parton on the radio.

I knew that Limerick would be too slow for Maggie, not to mention Cratloe. Maggie wanted it all; she wanted to see the world. Maggie was right about me though. I loved the peace and quiet of the countryside. Every opportunity I got I would take off on long walks with my dog 'Rogue', sometimes the cat 'Kojak' would tag along. The neighbours thought it was hilarious to see the three of us strolling along together without what appeared to be a care in the world. I usually headed for the woods and could spend hours there. Our first stop was the lake where I'd practise skimming stones across the surface of the shimmering water, while Rogue desperately tried to retrieve them before they sank to the muddy bottom. I knew those woods like the back of my hand, every pathway and stream. I knew where to watch for foxes, rabbits, and every now and then I'd get lucky and see a deer. I just loved every minute of it and could sit there for hours without uttering a sound.

Once in a while Rogue would take off through the trees only to arrive back a few minutes later with a live rabbit in his mouth. Amazingly he never killed them; he just stood with his tail wagging at the speed of light with the petrified rabbit wedged in his jaws. I'd say 'Rogue, drop him!' and he would. It always took the poor rabbit a few seconds to react and make a run for it, as if he couldn't quite believe he was still alive. Rogue would just sit there and watch as the rabbit leapt over fallen branches and tree roots until he disappeared into the undergrowth. It was often dark when we turned for home but that never bothered me and if I had a tent and something to eat, I would have been quite happy to stay. I knew I had nothing to worry about as long as Rogue was with me.

Rogue had quite a reputation around Cratloe and everyone knew he belonged to me. He was a large dog and although he loved children he hated men, so much so, that he would give out a blood curdling growl if any tried to approach me or knock on the front door, even our postman Jack didn't escape and lived in constant dread of him.

When delivering to our house Jack's only consolation was that he was working in a remote area which meant unlike the postmen in the city who delivered their mail on bicycles, he drove a small post office issued van. If it wasn't for this I don't believe we would ever have received any mail. Each day Jack would blow the horn as he approached our house, signalling to whoever was home that he had mail. If nobody responded, Jack too terrified to exit the van would drive on, open the window and throw the mail out.

Our mail was often found weeks later sodden and saturated on the roadside or protruding from a nearby hedge.

Mam often complained bitterly about the state of my clothes when I returned from my adventures in the woods. 'How in the name of God am I going to get those clean?' she would say staring at the caked in mud or grass stains on my jeans. 'What on earth do you be doing up in those woods 'til this hour?' She would yell while pointing to the clock which hung on the kitchen wall. 'I thought you were lost Mary.' As time went by though, Mam complained less and less. She drew relief from the knowledge that she knew where I was and that while Rogue was with me I wouldn't come to any harm, which couldn't be said for Maggie.

Chapter 2

Saturday Night Fever

Maggie had gone on to attend university as expected. She had also managed to secure a part-time job in a local hotel, where she worked as a waitress and although her grades at university remained excellent she was socialising more and more with her friends. 'That one has fairly gotten her eye teeth,' Mam would say annoyed. 'I'll put a stop to her gallop though, one of these days.' But no matter how much Mam argued with Maggie, Maggie remained defiant.

The morning of Maggie's eighteenth birthday they had a huge row in the kitchen. I was hoping I wouldn't be dragged into the discussion, so I kept my head down trying to eat my bowl of cereal, while the two of them shouted like 'fish-wives' across me. It was enough to give a person indigestion. 'I've had enough of you Maggie and your gallivanting, coming home here at all hours,' Mam yelled. 'Mam, I'm eighteen now, it's my money and I'll do what I like with it,' replied Maggie smugly. 'Just 'cause you can't drink Mam,' Maggie continued, 'doesn't mean all of us have to take the pledge'. (The Pledge was a solemn oath to God never to drink). If Mam had more than three drinks, which she rarely did, she would be 'as sick as a small hospital' for days.

'Don't you dare speak to me like that Maggie? This is my house and as long as you're living here you'll abide by my rules, there's enough money being wasted on drink and you needn't think you're going out again tonight!' I thought they'd never shut up. 'I am so going out tonight Mam,' Maggie replied, refusing to give in. 'I'm meeting the girls in town later, they're treating me to a new outfit and tonight we're going to the disco in the hotel. The manager has given me tickets to get in free because it's my birthday.' 'Oh that's big of him Maggie, 'tis no wonder, you're there so often now, you must have "shares" in the place.' Maggie leapt up from the kitchen table refusing to listen to anymore. 'Oh happy birthday Maggie,' she muttered sarcastically to herself as she stormed out the door, in the direction of her room.

I was sitting there, scraping the remaining few crumbs of cereal from my bowl, silently relieved that for once it was Maggie getting the 'telling off' and not me. Mam was left talking to herself, something that we had grown accustomed to.

'The cheek of that one talking to me like that, if she knows what's good for her she'll come home here tonight, at a respectable hour. I don't know where I went wrong.'

I watched in silence as Mam scrubbed the plates so hard she was in danger of erasing the design from the ceramic. 'I have one daughter who is in danger of becoming a lush,' she continued 'and one daughter who doesn't want to go to school'. Here we go, I thought to myself, now that Maggie had retreated to her bedroom slamming the door, I was in direct line of fire. 'Can you blame me Mam?' I blurted. 'All the teachers hate me, just last week Mrs. Sadlier gave me a thousand lines to write "I must not yawn in class" and as if that wasn't bad enough, you attacked me when I told you I'd need two new work books just to write them. Mam I'm sick to death of them calling me an amadáin.' 'You are not an 'Eejit' Mary,' Mam offered in a more sympathetic tone. 'In fact, the teachers tell me you're brighter than Maggie. You just don't apply yourself to your work.' 'Oh sure Mam, if that's the case why did you tell me when you returned from my last parent-teacher meeting that Mr. McNamara suggested that you should sit down and maybe even consider having a double brandy before hearing his report?' 'Well Mary, I admit that was a bit harsh,' Mam said apologetically. This was my chance I thought as I could see that Mam was regretting telling me what the teacher had said. 'Mam, just so you know, as soon as I can get a job, I'm leaving school.' With that she went out to the back yard carrying the sweeping brush and muttering away to herself.

That night there was no sign of Maggie coming home. Seven o'clock, eight o'clock, each time the clock on the mantle-piece struck a new hour I'd hear Mam talking aloud to herself. 'I warned her, I warned that one, she needn't say I didn't.' With every hour that passed Mam's mood was getting worse and I wondered what if anything she was going to do? Maybe I thought she was going to sit up waiting for Maggie to come in. God, I could just picture Maggie tip-toeing across the sitting room floor in the dark half-drunk from the pints of Harp, passing Mam's bedroom door and believing she was home free; then out of the blue, Mam jumping out on top of her. It didn't bare thinking about. The rest of us wouldn't get a wink of sleep. It would be like listening to a bag of cats.

I had stayed in the kitchen all night; my schoolbooks spread out across the table as if I were studying, but I could think of nothing else but the scenario that could possibly unfold. At about 11.30 I decided to make tea.

I poured two cups, one for Mam and one for me. I cut two slices of the boiled fruitcake Mam had made earlier, put them on a plate and carried them into the sitting room to Mam who was sitting in an armchair beside the fire, hoping that the meagre offering of tea and cake would go some way towards softening her mood. Just as I was about to hand it to her, she jumped out of the armchair. I nearly dropped the cup in fright and watched in horror as the two slices of cake slid off the plate and landed in a crumpled heap on Mam's clean floor. 'Mary, I'll be back in twenty minutes,' she said, ignoring the mess on the waxed floor. 'What Mam?' I said, shocked; 'where are you going at this hour?' 'Where am I going Mary? Where am I going?' she repeated in case I hadn't heard her the first time. 'I'll tell you where I'm going; I'm driving down to that hotel to get her, that's where I'm going.' 'But Mam, Maggie will be in the night club now,' I said, hoping she'd see sense. 'I don't care Mary, I'll find her, she will think twice in the future about disobeying me!' Mam grabbed the car keys from the kitchen counter top, went out the door and into the car like a flash. I really began to feel sorry for Maggie at this stage, but all I could do was go to bed.

The next day was Saturday, so there was no school. I awoke with memories of the night before and wondered how it had ended. As I entered the sitting room, I could hear Mam in the kitchen telling the boys to finish their breakfast and to stop teasing Barbra. I snuck out of the sitting room, down the hallway to Maggie's room and knocked on the door. 'Come in,' I heard her say in a low, sorrowful voice. She was sitting on the edge of the bed smoking a cigarette and didn't seem to care if Mam caught her. 'Oh Mary I'm disgraced', she said woefully. 'She made a holy show of me, how am I going to show my face in that nightclub ever again? Everyone saw her Mary, bouncers, bar staff, my friends, not to mention the hotel manager!' 'What did Mam say to you Maggie?' I asked not wanting to hazard a guess. 'She didn't say anything Mary, because I saw her before she saw me and I hid under a table. I had been up dancing with all my friends having a great time, when I saw her coming in the door, Mary I thought I was seeing an apparition. I just couldn't believe my eyes.' 'Well that wasn't too bad Maggie,' I said offering a little consolation. 'I mean at least she didn't see you.'

'Not too bad, are you joking me Mary? Everyone thinks our mother is a crazy woman and could you blame them? Only a crazy woman would walk into a night club wearing a night-gown and slippers!'

Of course I knew that Mam wasn't crazy, but after realising that Maggie was in a worse mood than Mam had been in the day before I decided to keep this knowledge to myself.

Chapter 3

Jesus Christ Superstar

Mam was simply overwhelmed and had her hands full with six children and not a day went by without one of us getting up to some kind of mischief, like the time I told Mam I was going upstairs to my bedroom to study. She looked really pleased and must have thought she had finally gotten through to me on the importance of education. I didn't hear Mam walk into my bedroom an hour later, and in fact if the truth was told, I didn't hear anything at all for the next few days after the slap I got from Mam across my ear. "What's this?' she screamed and grabbed the piece of paper I had been writing on. 'Dear Sir,' she read aloud; 'can you please tell me how much you want for the goat? A goat!' she shrieked. 'You're supposed to be studying, Mary, not replying to an advertisement in the paper for a goat. I just don't believe it, I give up, I just give up.' On another occasion Mam said she was going to town to buy some groceries. She brought Barbra with her and left Michael in charge of Robert and James. I don't know where Michael went, but when she returned about an hour later, she found James who was six at the time, standing on the gable end of the roof, which was about twenty foot high, dressed in a 'Superman' costume with Robert behind him convincing him he could fly!

Then of course there was the time when Robert was going through, what we liked to call 'The Jesus Phase.' Robert had watched the movie 'Ben Hur' and had become fixated on Jesus. Yes, it was fair to say Robert was his number one fan. He was obsessed, he wanted to be Jesus. He walked around the house wrapped in a sheet and was praying night and day, and if that wasn't bad enough, he told Michael and his friends that he'd love to know what it would be like to be on a crucifix. Sure Michael and his friends were only too eager to help him out. They found two planks of timber in the shed, nailed them together in the shape of a cross and when Mam returned from town she was greeted by Robert who was tied onto the cross which stood in the middle of the front lawn. Jumping out of the car she roared across the garden, 'Robert will you get down from there before you hang yourself!' 'I can't Mam, I'm tied on.' Mam struggled to untie the ropes as Robert explained that he had wanted to try out the cross, but that Michael had wandered off with his pals and left him there.

'Oh my God, Michael,' she said later; as we sat around the table eating our dinner, 'how could you have done that leaving your brother strung up like that, anything could have happened. Ye won't be happy 'til ye give me a heart attack. I just can't leave ye alone for two minutes.'

Mind you, it wasn't long before Mam felt like stringing Robert up herself. She had often commented how strange she thought it was that Robert was so much bigger than Michael who was two years older than him; only to find out from one of the neighbours that each day after dinner, Robert would call to his friends' houses complaining that he was starving, so feeling sorry for him the neighbours would feed him again. 'We must be the talk of the neighbourhood,' Mam yelled. 'I'm disgraced; the neighbours will think I'm not feeding ye.'

Yes. Mam certainly had her hands full and she very rarely had any time to herself. One of her few indulgences was at the end of each day when the boys and Barbra were tucked away in bed. She would disappear for half an hour into the bathroom and have a hot shower. She was like a new woman when she exited in her dressing gown. 'Oh that is great,' she'd say, 'a shower is so relaxing'.

That was all to end when 'Kojak' the cat joined the family. Mam never liked cats and it took a lot of pleading on my behalf to get her to change her mind, so I was really surprised to see how Mam had 'taken' to him. 'Kojak must be a pedigree', she would say stroking his long haired black and white coat. She liked him so much he was allowed to wander freely about the house, contrary to our initial agreement when I got him that he would be kept outside. That is, until one evening when she slipped away to the sanctuary of the bathroom carrying her towel and precious toiletries under her arm. I could hear her humming a little tune to herself as she closed the bathroom door. Not more than five minutes had passed when I heard unmerciful screams. I ran to the bathroom believing Mam had either slipped in the shower or scalded herself with hot water. When I got there, Mam was coming out the door, one hand was holding a towel which she had wrapped around herself and the other she was using to wipe the shampoo from her eyes which ran down her face from her un-rinsed hair. 'I'll kill him, I'll kill him, that little shit,' she screamed. 'Who Mam? What's happened?' I asked half afraid to approach her.

'That mangy cat, that's who, he shit in the drain hole of the shower and I didn't notice until the shower tray began to fill up. I thought it was just hair that was blocking it, so I reached down to clear it. I'll kill him if he comes near me. I can still smell it on my hand', and she started to gag at the very thought of it. I decided to offer an explanation for Kojak's behaviour, afraid that Mam would give him his 'marching orders.' 'Mam,' I said, 'you know the way cats always dig a hole when they have to go the toilet, well Kojak must have thought that the drain was like a ready-made hole.' My explanation didn't help. 'Ready-made hole,' she screeched, 'he'll have a pain in his hole, if I catch him!'

It would be true to say it was never dull in our house. Mam had a pair of lungs like Pavarotti but who could blame her, we had her driven demented. We weren't the only thorn in Mam's side though and as she often sad 'I'd be better off if I was still a widow, because that useless excuse for a man I married is good for nothing.'

Paddy was Mam's second husband. Her first husband Jack was Maggie's father and mine, but he had died of a brain tumour in America where they had lived very comfortably for six years. After his death she returned to her family in Limerick where she met and married Paddy. He worked for Irish Shipping and could be gone for months at a time, so Mam was most of the time trying to be both mother and father. I often watched Mam in the kitchen sifting through the bills, trying to figure out how to make the money last until Paddy came home from sea with the next pay cheque. Each time Paddy was due home Mam would remain optimistic, hoping that this time things would be different, but sadly even when Paddy was at home he was still away, that is, he was away in the pub. Mam never got to see that cheque and when Paddy did decide to fall home from the pub, all hell would break lose.

Chapter 4

From Russia with Love

Mam and Maggie didn't speak for days after the nightclub incident, each believing that the other was wrong, and neither of them willing to back down. I became the 'go-between' when they needed to communicate. 'Mary will you tell your sister her dinner is on the table?' 'Mary tell Mam I won't be home until late, I have to attend a lecture at the university.' I was sick of it. On and on they went; they were worse than children. 'Mary tell Maggie a letter came for her today.' I picked up the letter and brought it to Maggie who was listening to Abba's Greatest Hits on her new stereo in her bedroom. She had bought it with her wages from the hotel; it had a record player, a cassette player and a radio. It was really her pride and joy and nobody was allowed to touch it. 'I'm telling ye right here and now, she warned the boys, 'if ye touch it, I'll be up for murder'; and as an added precaution she would lock her bedroom door if she was going anywhere. It was the only way to ensure its safe-keeping. 'As far as I'm concerned,' she said, 'I might as well be living with a shower of delinquents. I can't wait to get out of this house.' Maggie did have a point, just the day before when once again she adamantly refused to let the boys play with the stereo, in protest, they had cut all her bras in half!

I handed the letter to Maggie and returned to the kitchen to help Mam washing the breakfast dishes. Maggie almost put the heart crossways in both of us when she burst into the kitchen a few minutes later. She was jumping up and down like a lunatic and waving the letter in the air as she yelled. 'I'm going to Russia. I can't believe it, I'm going to Russia.' Mam forgot that they weren't speaking to each other and asked nervously, 'What do you mean Maggie you're going to Russia? And will you stop jumping around you'll give yourself a hernia.' 'I applied for a scholarship to go to Russia Mam and I got it, oh my God it's fantastic.'

Maggie was beside herself, so much so, that she plonked herself down on the kitchen chair and lit up a cigarette. 'I've so much to organise,' she said between puffs. I was waiting for Mam to attack her for smoking but she just stood there wringing the tea towel in her hands and looked as if she would burst into tears at any moment. She finally spoke. 'How long will you be going for Maggie?' she asked. 'Six whole months Mam, six whole months away from here!' Maggie could hardly contain her excitement.

'But Maggie, it's halfway around the world and you know those people are different to us, they're communists for God's sake.' 'Mam it's not as if I'll be living with them, I'll be staying with other students on campus, students from all over the world, it will be great Mam.' Mam didn't share Maggie's enthusiasm and was looking more upset by the minute and kept searching for a reason that would make Maggie change her mind and stay. 'Maggie, you realise you have an American passport and things aren't looking good between the Russians and the Americans at the moment. I mean you could be kidnapped!' Maggie had heard enough. 'Mam will you stop will you. Sure why would they kidnap me? We haven't a pot to piss in; they'd need a miracle to get money out of us.' Mam was running out of reasons but as a last resort said, 'Maggie, it's such a long distance and you'll be travelling with complete strangers.' 'No I won't Mam.' On hearing this Mam cheered up a little. 'Oh so your whole class is going Maggie?' 'No,' she squealed with excitement. 'I was the only one picked from the whole of Ireland.' With that Maggie leapt to her feet. 'I have to call everybody and tell them my good news.' I felt sorry for Mam. She was grey in the face and she was talking to herself again. 'The only one picked to go,' she yelled. 'The only one stupid enough to apply more like it, who in the name of God wants go to go Russia?'

Maggie left on her journey to Moscow sometime in the middle of June. There were no direct flights to Russia back then, so Maggie had to plan the whole trip herself with a little guidance from Aunt Maureen who worked for Aer Lingus. I really had to admire her bravery. Her plan was first to fly from Shannon to London, from London she would fly to Helsinki in Finland, from Helsinki to Poland by boat and finally from Poland to Russia by train.

On the day of her departure, all of us piled into Mam's car and drove to the airport to see her off. Mam never stopped asking questions and giving instructions from the moment we left the house, to the moment Maggie left us to board the plane. 'Have you your passport and plane ticket Maggie?' 'Yes Mam, you asked me that twice already.' 'Have you your money? Make sure and keep it safe. Don't be waving it around in front of people.' 'I won't Mam.' 'If you need to call home, tell the operator to reverse the charges.' 'I will Mam, thanks.' 'Will you call me when you get there Maggie, so I'll know you're ok?' 'I will Mam.'

'Will you?' 'Don't be worrying, I'll be fine, I'll be back before you know it.' Mam wasn't so sure. 'You're definitely coming home for Christmas?'

On and on Mam went 'til it was time to say our goodbyes. We watched Maggie as she went through the departure gates carrying a small overnight bag which Aunt Maureen loaned her on one arm, and under the other wrapped in tinfoil was a boiled fruit cake Mam had baked the night before.

When we turned in the direction of the car park I was carrying Barbra, Mam was crying and the boys, well the boys didn't' even seem to notice that Maggie was no longer with us. They were fixated on the planes that were landing and taking off. I don't know how we managed to get home safe that day. Mam could hardly see through the tears and she was trying to drive and blow her nose at the same time.

I got my summer holidays from school a few days later and reminded Mam that if I succeeded in finding a full time job I wasn't returning to school. I'd had enough. Maggie was a hard act to follow and the teacher's reminded me of that every day. I found work in a fast food restaurant in Limerick and every week was able to give Mam a few pounds towards the housekeeping. Michael, who had just turned twelve got a summer job as a porter in the same hotel where Maggie had worked. His aim was to buy a racing bike. But he always put a few pounds aside for Mam. 'Every little bit helps,' she'd say gratefully.

As the weeks rolled by, each time the phone rang at home, Mam would shout to whoever was nearest 'answer that fast, it could be your sister'. Mam was always expecting it to be bad news. Maggie had called every week since her departure two months before. The calls were brief because Maggie who had taken Mam up on her offer of reversing the charges, didn't want Mam facing a huge phone bill, what she did want was to reassure Mam that she was ok. Sometimes the connection was really bad and mam struggled to understand anything Maggie said, but she didn't complain because each time a call came, it put her mind at ease, and she would be in great form for days. I knew that despite all their arguments she really missed having Maggie around.

Chapter 5

We're all going on our Summer Holidays

I really missed her too, we were never really close, but with Maggie gone I was the only one there to listen to Mam if she was having a bad day. I'd come home tired from work and listen to a litany of everything that had gone wrong; 'the water's been cut off, the car wouldn't start, Rogue ate the Sunday roast'. 'A friend told me Paddy is back in Limerick for the last two days and is buying drinks for everyone in the pub. There would be nothing left for her to pay the bills. Mary what am I going to do?' It was a never ending story and with Maggie gone I felt there was no escaping it.

Each day when I finished work, I looked forward to getting out of the city and away from the noise. I couldn't wait to get back to the peace and tranquillity of the countryside. Sadly, when Mam was in one of her moods, the countryside took on a whole different perspective. Apples suddenly fell from the trees. The birds no longer pecked away at their feeder, instead took off and landed on the highest branches. The dog hid under the hedge. The cattle who a few moments before had been gazing dreamily over the fence got the 'scutters' and scattered, shitting themselves to the far corner of the field, and I'd bet any money that hens in neighbouring farms stopped laying!

There was no escaping it. The fact was Mam was living in denial. I don't know if she kept hoping Paddy would change or if it was that she just couldn't imagine a way out. But the reality was, each time Paddy came home, he was drinking more and more. And although he was a quiet man sober, his moments of sobriety were to say the least becoming less frequent. She just kept hoping that the next time Paddy arrived home things would be different. They seemed to have what could best be described as a love, hate relationship, and you always knew how Mam was feeling at any given time. If she loved him he was called 'your father' and if she hated him, he was called 'that fella!' 'That fella better not think I'm keeping dinner for him, if he has money for drink he has money for food.' 'That fella better not think I'm paying for the taxi again tonight.' 'That fella better not be expecting me to drive back down the road to pull his sorry excuse for a body out of the ditch!'

The previous time Paddy was at home, I was in the kitchen when I saw Mam drive into the yard. I knew when I saw her get out of the car there was something wrong.

She had a face like thunder on her, even 'Rogue' the dog copped it and though twice about jumping up to greet her. He jumped out of her way but not fast enough to avoid a swift boot in the backside. Mam entered the kitchen shouting about 'that fella' 'and the state he was in, what would the neighbours say?' Trying to calm her and not really knowing what she was talking about, I shoved a cup of tea and some biscuits in front of her hoping this would do the trick. In between sips of the tea and munching of biscuits there were outbursts. 'I can't take anymore, that fella is nothing but a long useless streak of misery.' Then another sip followed by a deep breath, 'I mean Mary, I thought I'd seen it all, but this takes the biscuit, I thought I was seeing things!' I finally plucked up the courage and asked 'Mam what are talking about?' 'What am I talking about? I'm talking about that fella who else? He's down by the bridge and he's fallen head first into the ditch. All I could see was his "eggs in a basket arse" and his knitting needle legs up in the air. He's so drunk I'm sure if you asked him his name, he wouldn't know it. I'm telling you Mary I nearly crashed the car.' 'Where is he now Mam?' I asked, not one bit shocked. 'Where is he now? He's probably still there, I wasn't stopping, he's a disgrace. Mary, he promised me faithfully he was going to town to buy meat for the freezer. I was looking forward to a nice bit of roast beef.'

Every now and then Mam's prayers would be answered and Paddy would stop drinking. On these rare occasions Mam was like a new woman. She never raised her voice; she laughed a lot and spoke of her plans to decorate the house. 'Your father', she would say, 'is very handy, he can turn his hand to anything once he puts his mind to it, painting and wallpapering'. She had a vision of how the house was going to look when it was finished and couldn't keep from smiling to herself.

Mam always looked ten years younger when Paddy was on the 'dry.' It wasn't that she minded him having a drink and she understood that Paddy looked forward to meeting his friends when returning from a 'stint at sea.' 'He was quite entitled to have a drink', she'd say, 'but surely he'd want to provide for his family first. It wasn't as if he had to choose, he was earning enough to cover both'. We were all a lot happier when Paddy gave up the drink, but Mam was the only one who actually believed it was going to last. Paddy giving up the drink was like the rain stopping in Ireland. It was never for very long.

It was during one of these 'dry spells' that Mam woke me one beautiful sunny morning to tell me, 'your father is taking the boys and Barbra away camping for a few days to give me a break'. 'Where to?' I asked, sitting up in bed. 'He's taking them to Kilkee, he says I look worn out and he says with the kids away I'll get a lie in, and a bit of peace. He's borrowed a tent and with the weather being so nice, the boys and Barbra should really enjoy it'. I must have looked at Mam funny or thrown my eyes up to heaven, because all of a sudden she was frowning. 'Now, Mary, have a little faith, your father hasn't had a drink in two weeks and he says it will be a good opportunity for him to spend time with the boys and of course he'll be starting that new job when he gets back. I've borrowed some money from Aunt Maureen, those seaside restaurants and amusement parks can be quite expensive. Michael was a bit reluctant to ask for time off from work, but the manager agreed he was due a few days and I know he's reluctant "to dip into his savings", but I reassured him there will be no need as I've given his father more than enough money.'

Mam fell for it hook, line and sinker. Yes, he took them all to Kilkee. Barbra was all excited waving goodbye to Mam and I from the rear window of the car. Michael told her he'd buy her a bucket and shovel and promised Robert and James candy floss if they behaved themselves. Michael told me, five days later, after returning from Kilkee in tears that his father had helped to pitch the 'two man tent' he had borrowed for the five of them. He told them all about his own camping experiences as a young boy, and didn't even get annoyed when Barbra announced a few hours after they arrived that she had lost one of her shoes on the beach. 'Barbra', he said, 'don't be crying, people don't wear shoes at the seaside and I'm sure Mam will buy you a new pair when you get home.' Michael told me it hadn't stopped raining once and while he and his brothers and sister were camped in the tent, trying to stay dry, their father was camped out in the pub. Michael said he'd never forget it as long as he lived, saying they were like sardines in a tin and he didn't know which was worse, sitting there each day hungry and waiting for their father to return with the fish and chips he promised he was going to get when he left the tent each morning, or putting up with his Guinness 'farts' when he fell in on top of them each night. Michael said that he didn't blame Mam for not wanting to sleep in the same room as him. That was the last holiday they had with their father. In fact it was the last time they ever agreed to go anywhere with him again.

Chapter 6

The Silver Tongue Devil

All of us hoped that somehow Mam would 'see the light', but she kept falling for his empty promises. He always managed to get around her and of course it was easier to believe him; the alternative was to get rid of him and spend years living on welfare. Mam was a very proud woman, and not someone who would take easily to living off the tax payer, so as the years went by we watched Mam face one disappointment after another. The home in the country that she had so loved when first moving in had become a crumbling wreck and each of Mam's days were spent worrying about the next. I often thought we would have been better off living in a 'poorer' part of town, where everyone was in the 'same boat', whereas, we were living in an 'upmarket area' and it was assumed that if you lived there, you must be 'well off.' I felt very sorry for the boys and Barbra especially as Christmas time; while their friends were spoilt for choice with the array of gifts they received, they on the other hand were lucky to get anything at all.

By the time I was seventeen any feelings I had for Paddy as a 'father figure' had long since been diminished and any feelings I did have, were of anger and resentment. This was compounded by the fact that any time I socialised with my friends in a pub, I was guaranteed to bump into one of Paddy's friends. They couldn't say enough about him. 'Oh Paddy is the salt of the earth' or 'he's one decent man, that's right, you'd never have to put your hand in your pocket while Paddy was around.' Yes indeed! They often saw Paddy buy a round for the whole pub. On and on they would go, and I'd have to bite my lip so that I wouldn't blurt out the truth, which was, that more often than not, when Paddy was buying drinks for everyone, his children were at home hoping he'd bring home some bread or milk. If I lived to be ninety I'd never understand it and often thought to myself that he hadn't an ounce of nature in him, and we couldn't blame the 'drink' all the time, because even in his brief moments of sobriety, he wasn't much different.

I remember several nights when Paddy would stay home, promising Mam that he would never drink again. But the truth was, he was either too sick from drink to consider having a pint or he had no money. We would all be there, gathered round the fire watching television, the boys and Barbra dressed in their pyjamas hoping that if they kept quiet Mam would let them stay up a little later.

Every time there was a break in the programme for the 'ads' Paddy would get up from his armchair beside the fire, go into his bedroom only to return a few minutes later with his mouth full of *Liquorice Allsorts Sweets*. We would all stare longingly hoping he would offer us one, but he never did. To this day, I've never been able to eat one of those sweets. Why does that surprise you? I'd find myself saying, 'if he's capable of stealing from his own child, he's capable of anything' and he was.

Michael, who was only twelve at the time, had been working part time in the hotel for the summer months. The work was far from easy. He was either carrying heavily laden suitcases for the guests or scrubbing pots in the unbearable heat of the hotel kitchens. He was determined to save enough money to buy that bike, so that he could cycle to school in the autumn, which in turn would save Mam on bus fare. Every weekend after finishing work, Michael would arrive home with his wages and a big bag of leftover food for the dog and cat. After giving Mam a few pounds he'd put the remainder into his chest of drawers in the bedroom he shared with Robert. 'I won't be long now', he'd say, proud of his achievement.

One morning after getting out of bed, I arrived to the kitchen to find Mam crying into her tea. Robert, James and Barbra were just sitting there looking at her. Nobody was saying a word. It wasn't like Mam to be crying, she normally put on a brave face, so I knew at once it had to be very bad news. 'What's wrong Mam?' I asked, handing her a tissue to dry her eyes. 'Oh Mary', she said between sobs, 'he's taken Michael's savings, every penny, it's all gone.' 'Where is Michael now?'

I asked, feeling sick to my stomach. 'He's gone to work with his eyes red from crying, he looks worn out. That fella came in at all hours last night and kept Michael and Robert awake talking shite!' 'Is he gone to the pub already?' I asked, unable to comprehend how someone could stoop so low. 'No, no,' Mam said, blowing her nose. He's in the boys' room snoring his head off. 'Please, please Mary will you go and wake him and ask him to give the money back, I know he won't give it to me.'

Mam didn't have to ask twice. As I walked through the sitting room and down the corridor to the boy's bedroom I pictured Michael facing another hard day at work with nothing to show for all his efforts.

I thought of myself and all the times I'd faced school with little or no sleep because I'd stayed up the night before to defend Mam; sitting in the classroom bleary –eyed and worrying if Mam was alright at home, only to be screamed at by the teachers for being 'lazy.' I didn't bother to knock on the bedroom door as there was little point, a bomb wouldn't wake Paddy when he was in a drunken sleep. I reached my arm out and shook his shoulder, careful not to stand too close in case he swung at me. 'Where's Michael's money?' I asked while continuing to shake him. 'Will you go away', he finally moaned. 'Leave me alone.' 'Where's Michael's money?' I said again, shouting at him now and shaking his shoulder even more. 'If you don't go away Mary, I'll kill you. My stomach is killing me from that burger I had last night. I think I have food poisoning.' 'Food poisoning, alcohol poisoning more like,' I screamed. Straining to open his eyes in the morning light, he sneered up at me and said, 'Will you go away Mary, you're mad. You'll die roaring like your father did.'

Everything was a blur after that. I remembered my mother saying that my father had died an agonising death, only a shadow of his former self, from a brain tumour. I remember reaching for a hurling helmet that was lying on the floor next to the bed and I didn't stop beating him across the head with it 'til my fingers bled. If I had killed him there and then I wouldn't have cared. 'The next time you take money from anyone in this house', I said, shaking with temper, 'I'll kill you stone dead.' 'Enough is enough' I said to myself and I knew by the way he looked at me that he knew I wasn't joking. I walked out of the room leaving him there shocked and holding his head.

I rarely spoke to Paddy after that, and if I did it was only out of necessity, not because I wanted to. He kept out of my way while I was around and even though he didn't drink any less, after that, he came home from the pub a much quieter man than he had ever been in the past.

Chapter 7

Barbra Ann

The summer was coming to an end and, it was time for children all over the country to return to school. The last two weeks of August was a busy time for any parent and Mam was no exception to the rule. Children were taken to the city to be fitted for school uniforms. The next port of call was usually O'Mahony's Bookshop on O'Connell Street, where parents and children stood in line armed with lists telling them which children needed what books. Then, if you hadn't pulled your hair out at that stage, it was off to Eason's to buy pencil cases and school bags. Some children would have new winter coats bought for them, but with Mam's limited resources she always hoped we'd get a bit longer out of our old one. 'There's absolutely nothing wrong with the coat you're wearing,' she would say, totally exasperated. 'Do ye think I'm printing money? Yes, I know your coat is three years old James, but it still fits you perfectly.' Mam was right. The coat did fit James perfectly. It wasn't that James hadn't grown in three years, it was just that whenever mam bough us any clothes, to ensure that she got value for money, she would buy them in a size two or even three times too big. If we questioned her judgement she always had a practical solution. 'Just roll up the sleeves,' she'd say, 'and it will keep your arms twice as warm.'

When I started secondary school the issue was my skirt. 'Mam, I can't wear that skirt, it's way too long.' It was stressful enough starting in a new school with a middle name 'Eejit', without looking different to the other seven hundred pupils as well. 'Mary, don't be ridiculous,' Mam said knowing I was about to burst into tears after looking at myself in the mirror. 'Turn the waistband over a few times and when we get home I'll move the button a few inches to stop it falling down. Mary you'll shoot up any day now and you'll be glad of the extra few inches.' Mam was right. I did grow quite a bit over the next three years and she often reminded me, 'Mary' she'd say, 'I bet you're glad I bought that skirt in the bigger size now. I have to say Mary; you got great wear out of it.'

At least Mam was pleased, I thought; the same however could not be said for the nuns at school. Each time I had the misfortune to pass one by in the corridor; I'd get a clip across the side of the head.

'Mary Ryan' they'd say while eyeing me with contempt, 'where do you think you're going in that skirt? The rule is four inches below the knee, not four inches above. You look like a trollop!'

Thanks be to God I thought, remembering; I never regretted leaving school because with the wages from work I could buy whatever clothes I needed and most importantly, I could buy clothes that fit.

There was extra excitement that year as we drew closer to September 1st. It was time for Barbra the 'baby' of the family to start school. I didn't envy her, but hoped it would be different for her than it had been for me, with the help of God, I thought, she'll be brainy like Maggie. The morning of the first of September soon arrived and our kitchen in Cratloe was like a scene from a mental home. Complete pandemonium would best describe it. The boys were cranky and squabbling with each other, unhappy to be out of bed so early. Barbra was having second thoughts about starting school at all, and was playing with the cereal in her bowl, quite obviously in no hurry to leave home.

The boys had thought it hilarious the night before to tell her all about the teachers in the school. There was Mr. O'Reilly, who would pull the hair out of your head if you so much as looked at him crooked, Miss Hanley who spent the day picking dandruff out of her unwashed hair; she wouldn't hit you; but if you got a question wrong you'd be standing in a corner facing the wall all day. 'Oh yeah,' James added 'and watch out for Shovels Barbra.' 'Who's Shovels?' Barbra had asked. 'Fr. Nolan,' James replied eagerly. 'That's what they call him, his hands are so big if you get a slap, it's like getting hit with a shovel.' The boys hadn't stopped 'til they had the living daylights frightened out of her.

Mam was at the kitchen counter making sandwiches for their school lunches, and shouting questions and orders as she worked. 'If ye don't give over the bickering and get on your coats, you'll be walking to school, 'cause at the rate ye're moving ye'll miss the bus. 'Yes Barbra, you have to go to school, how else are you going to read and write? Ah will ye hurry on and put your lunch boxes into ye're bags. Robert have you your shoes tied yet? You're as slow as molasses. Mary will you brush James' hair; it's like a crow's nest. Michael, straighten your tie. It's your last year in primary and you need to get a good report, right, have ye got everything?' she asked pausing to catch her breath and take one last look at them.

'Yeah Mam,' they answered together. 'OK off ye go and hurry!' Mam watched as they walked down the hill together, with Rogue the dog following closely at their heels. 'Michael,' she shouted after them, 'hold your sister's hand, and ye better mind her. If anything happens to her I'll kill ye.' 'OK Mam,' she heard them say as they reached the bend in the road and disappeared from view. Hail, rain or snow, for many years Rogue could be seen making his way down the road at three o'clock to meet them getting off the bus.

Mam was delighted that Barbra was starting school, not that she wanted to see the back of her, but it meant that with the boys and Barbra at school every day until three o'clock she could look for a job and found one working part time in the village shop. It was great for Mam. She finally had some money she could call her own and more importantly, depend on. It also did her the world of good to get out of the house. She loved chatting to all the customers and would arrive home every day with all the local gossip. It also helped that Paddy was gone away again and wouldn't be back 'til Christmas.

Chapter 8

CHITTY, CHITTY, BANG, BANG

The months flew by, Halloween had come and gone and autumn had turned to winter. It was dark each day by five o'clock, but in the city the streets were bright with the twinkling of Christmas lights. All the shop windows were transformed for the festive season. There were stalls selling Christmas trees and holly. There were 'Santa's' of all shapes and sizes collecting money for local charities, and on every street corner there were choirs singing Christmas carols. The shops were full to capacity with shoppers laden down with bags and rolls of wrapping paper, each one of them wondering if they had the time or the energy to face the next shop. Every now and again you'd see a couple doing a frantic headcount of their children and realising to their horror that they were missing one, only to find him or her, a few minutes later playing in the 'toy section' oblivious to the fact that they'd taken ten years off their parents' lives with the shock.

At home in Cratloe, we were also making preparations. Mam had baked her Christmas cake in November, placed it wrapped in grease proof paper in an old biscuit tin at the back of a high kitchen cupboard, hoping it was safely hidden from the boys. Most of her spare time was now spent sitting at the kitchen table, writing out lists of what she needed to buy. It was a stressful time of the year because there was never enough money to go around. Her biggest worry was being able to buy the 'Santa' presents, new outfits for the boys and Barbra to wear to Mass on Christmas Day and of course the turkey and ham. Once she had these covered she would relax a little and even begin to enjoy it. 'There's no more I can do,' she would say, 'with the help of God I'll catch up with the bills in the New Year.' I think to Mam, Christmas was like giving birth; when she saw the baby she forgot about the pain 'til the next one came along.

Barbra helped me to put the decorations on the tree, insisting that the ones she made at school be placed at the front for all to see. Michael, perched on a chair patiently tried to unravel the ball of fairy lights and couldn't understand why one faulty bulb would prevent the rest from working; while Robert and James discussed what they hoped Santa would bring.

Robert said that his whole class had written to Santa and he had asked for a set of drums, but Mam on hearing this shouted from the kitchen, 'you better ask Santa for something else Robert, he'll never manage to get those down the chimney.' There was no way Mam was going to listen to 'that racket' first thing Christmas morning. Michael didn't believe in Santa, but knew better than to say anything to the boys or Barbra. 'If you know what's good for you,' Mam had warned, 'you'll keep your mouth shut!'

By the twentieth of December, I didn't know who was more excited, my brothers and Barbra anticipating Santa's imminent arrival or Mam waiting for Maggie. She had called to say she'd be flying into Dublin Airport and asked if Mam would drive to Dublin Airport to collect her. 'Do you think you could take the day off work Mary?' Mam asked. 'Dublin Airport is over a hundred miles away and it would be great if you could come along and keep me company.' I called my boss immediately and after ten minutes of persuasion and pointing out to him that I hadn't had a day off in three weeks, he finally agreed to give me the time off, on the condition that I worked double shifts for the following week. I hung up the receiver and returned to the kitchen to tell Mam it was all arranged only to find her and Michael were having an argument.

'Mary,' Michael asked, 'will you tell Mam she'll have to borrow a car from someone; she would have to be crazy to drive that car,' he said pointing out the kitchen window to where the car was parked in the yard. 'It could blow up,' he added, appealing to my better judgement. 'The cheek of you Michael,' Mam barked. 'That's a perfectly good car, it's certainly good enough when you need a lift to work or to the céili on a Friday night.'

Mam was highly insulted, but she was right. Michael often asked her to drive him if the weather was too bad to walk or cycle, but she never noticed that all those times that he did, he would always ask her to stop and let him out about two hundred yards short of his destination, claiming that 'a bit of fresh air' would do him good. He tried to avoid telling her the truth and hurting her feelings. The truth was his life wouldn't be worth living if he was seen getting out of that car, it just didn't bear thinking about. The young waitresses at the hotel, or Brigid O'Connell from the farm over the hill, who he thought was a 'vision of loveliness', none of them would give him a second look if they saw him getting out of that car; all he would have to look forward to was bachelorhood!

Mam never liked to discuss what was wrong with the car if she did she would be forced to admit that the car was a symbol of her life in general, shite!

Instead she chose to focus on the positive points, praising the car for being economical to run or pointing out what a great little heater it had. If the car failed to start and the boys had to give it a push down the hill in the hope it would jump to life, she would blame the cold weather, stating that 'Even a new car would have problems starting after the frost we had last night.' If any of us disagreed we would always hear the same response, 'doesn't it get us from A to B?' Mam just didn't see it, but we knew that apart from all the other problems the car had, she must have been the only person in Ireland driving around in a car that had no front passenger seat.

I knew that I would have to use every ounce of diplomacy I had, to convince her that Michael was right, because I most definitely didn't want to tell her that Maggie would probably prefer to walk from Dublin than to be seen getting into a car that wouldn't look at all out of place in a scrapyard. So I sipped my tea, let Mam and Michael argue back and forth while I carefully chose the appropriate words. 'Mam, I think Michael is right. Mam will you stop shouting and just listen for a minute? What Michael is trying to say is that Maggie is going to be absolutely exhausted from all her travels when she lands in Dublin. I'm sure all she'll want is to get home to her bed as soon as possible. The last thing you'd want Mam is for the car to break down and end up stranded on the side of the road.' Mam didn't say a word for quite a while, and it was clear to me that as she sat with her head in her hands at the kitchen table she was playing out in her mind the scenario that could possibly unfold, should she decide to drive her car. She frowned as she must have realised that, as much as she was looking forward to seeing Maggie, she didn't relish the idea of being stuck listening to her at the side of the road. She'd never hear the end of it. 'Alright, alright,' she finally spoke, throwing her arms in the air in surrender; 'I'll borrow a car from someone!'

Chapter 9

Wide-Eyed and Legless

On the morning of the twenty second of December, Mam was up at the 'crack of dawn.' After ushering the boys and Barbra out the door to school she started to clean the sitting room and instructed me to clean Maggie's room. She then turned her attention to dinner and made a big pot of stew with creamy mashed potatoes which would be ready when the 'gang' arrived home. Michael would babysit while we made the trip to Dublin.

The boys and Barbra hot-footed in from school in their usual state of disarray: Michael and Robert were complaining that they were starving; James was holding a dripping wet school bag claiming Robert had pushed him, causing him to drop the bag into a pool of rainwater on the side of the road. Barbra was sulking because she wasn't allowed to accompany us on the journey to Dublin to collect Maggie. 'If you're very good for Michael, Barbra,' Mam said, 'you can stay up and watch television until we come home' and in the same breath 'James take your books out of that bag and dry them beside the fire.' 'Robert, I've a good mind to give you a dig, look at the state of his bag, Mary here, put these plates of stew on the table.' Mam was waving a ladle around as if at any moment, someone would get a slap of it. 'Mam', I said, watching the clock on the wall nervously, 'we have to go now or we'll never make it.' 'I know, I know,' she replied in a voice bordering on hysteria. 'Just give me a minute to think. Where's my handbag and the car keys? I'm sure I left them on the counter.' 'Mam, I have them,' I replied. 'Here, put on your coat.' 'Michael,' she was still shouting as she opened the car door, 'Michael are you listening to me? Don't forget to put coal on the fire, Robert you can wash the dishes, James, Barbra no fighting, and will ye for heaven's sake go in and shut that back door and don't be heating the neighbourhood. Mary have we got everything?' 'Yes Mam,' I said, weary before we even started. Considering we left home an hour later than previously planned and met all the five o'clock traffic in Limerick which was bumper to bumper, once we reached the city limits we made good progress, with dry roads and traffic that was miraculously light, we reached our destination with a few minutes to spare.

We eventually found a parking space while Mam complained bitterly that at any moment her bladder would explode.

'I shouldn't have had that second cup of tea,' she said as we rushed towards the terminal. 'Mary go over there and wait,' she said pointing to a doorway where a crowd had started to gather under a sign that read 'Arrivals.' 'I'll be back in a minute,' she said and rushed off to find a toilet.

She returned a few minutes later looking relieved, just in time to see Maggie strolling through the doorway as 'cool as a breeze.' Mam was smiling from ear to ear. 'Mary, take that rucksack and carry it for your sister, she must be exhausted.'

'No Mary I'm fine' Maggie said smiling at both of us 'It's light as a feather, there's nothing in it except a few bras and knickers.'

'What do you mean Maggie?' Mam asked looking around her mortified that anyone could have heard what Maggie said 'Where are your clothes? Were you mugged? 'Oh no Mam, nothing like that, I had to sell them to pay for my flight home.' Mam was looking at Maggie with absolute horror 'Maggie, what would you have done if you hadn't managed to sell them? 'Mam I could have gotten twice what I asked for them, jeans and sweatshirts are like gold dust in Russia, I even sold my pink lady shave razor to a man, can you believe it Mam? Russian women don't shave', anyway where's the car? she asked looking around her. As we made our way across the car park Mam was silent and obviously in deep thought. Maggie broke the silence 'Mam can we stop for food somewhere? I'm starving.' 'Yes of course Maggie,' Mam replied as she fumbled for the car keys in her bag. 'Great Mam, just make sure it's a pub, I'd murder a pint.' Mam was speechless, I don't know if it was because Maggie sold all her clothes to get home or that having a pint was 'top' on her list of priorities, but she reluctantly agreed to stop once we reached the half-way stage of our journey.

We arrived in Portlaoise and Maggie was staring out the window looking from left to right 'look there's a pub' she said and motioned to Mam to pull over. 'We'll surely get a sandwich to eat there,' she said leaping from the car. Mam found a seat at a table near the door. I could tell she wasn't one bit happy to be in a pub. But thankfully was keeping her feelings to herself and instead reminded Maggie 'we can't stay long Maggie, Michael is babysitting and we'll be lucky if he doesn't burn the house down.'

We decided to have toasted ham and cheese sandwiches. Mam would have a cup of tea with hers, Maggie a pint of lager and I'd have a coke. 'I'll get these Mam' I offered 'It's my treat.' 'Thank you very much Mary' Mam said 'that's very good of you'. 'Yeah, thanks Mary' Maggie said 'I've no money so I'll owe you one.' 'No problem Maggie it's your welcome home treat, I'll just go to the bar to order.' There were several men perched precariously on high stools at the bar when I approached. Most were silent and happy to stare into their pints of stout almost oblivious to anything going on around them. One man, intent on solving the country's problems, kept nudging the man sitting next to him, guaranteeing his undivided attention, while at the far end another man who looked a little past his 'sell by date', belted out his own rendition of the song 'It's A Long, Long Way From Clare to Here' much to the annoyance of the barman. 'Will you ever shut up Paddy? You're like a scratched record; you'd give a Disprin a headache!'

A few minutes later after placing my order with the weary barman I returned to the table where Mam and Maggie were in deep conversation. Placing Mam's tea and the drinks on the table I told them 'the sandwiches will be ready in five minutes, I'm just going to the ladies.' I omitted to tell either of them, that while ordering the drinks, I had asked the barman to 'quietly' pour a scotch whiskey into my glass of coke. It had been a long day and I felt I deserved one, but I didn't want Mam to know because she was already giving Maggie disapproving looks every time she took a mouthful of her pint. Little did I know that Maggie would guess what I had done and while I was at the 'ladies', she had decided to have a 'little taste of my coke' saying to Mam that she had almost forgotten what it tasted like, but after tasting it, began making faces and handed it to Mam insisting that she try it. 'Oh Mam' she said 'Mary should bring this back; it doesn't taste right at all.' When I returned from the ladies Maggie was laughing so much, she was almost choking on her sandwich, she had never been able to resist and opportunity to get me into 'trouble.' I was looking at Mam who was staring at me and if looks could 'kill', I'd be dead. 'Coke my arse Mary' she said 'I am so disappointed with you.' Mam barely spoke to me on the rest of our journey home and as if 'things' weren't bad enough, as we approached the house we were just in time to see Paddy falling out of a taxi 'legless drunk.'

'Oh, tis the season to be jolly,' I hummed to myself, before taking to my bed, leaving Mam and Maggie in the kitchen discussing some place called 'Red Square'.

Chapter 10

Wouldn't It Be Lovely

I woke to the shrill of my alarm clock, which was sitting on a small shelf at the opposite side of the room. I placed it there to ensure that I couldn't reach out, turn it off and fall back to sleep. As I pushed back the bedclothes, the cold hit me and I reached for my slippers, dressing gown and clock all at the same time. I slept in a small bedroom in the attic, which had a tiny skylight window which looked out on the forest and hills beyond. It was usually a view of many shades of green, but this morning everything was white. It had frozen hard during the night and the peaks of the distant hills were dusted with snow. I shivered again pulling the dressing gown tight around me and tip-toed down the narrow stairs trying to avoid waking Barbra, James and Mam who slept in the room below. I opened the door into the sitting room which was still warm from the fire the night before. The kitchen was freezing, but it will soon heat up I thought when I light the portable gas fire which stood beside the radiator that hadn't worked since the previous winter. The precious heating system that Mam had been so proud of when we first moved in had 'broken down' and although Mam had been reassured that it could be fixed, she just didn't have the money.

I had just made a pot of tea when Mam came into the kitchen. She looked tired and was struggling to wake up. 'Late night?' I said pouring her a cup of tea and placed some bread under the grill to toast. 'Three o'clock,' she yawned. 'Why didn't you stay in bed for another while Mam?' You must be tired after that long drive yesterday.' 'No, no,' she said reaching for a knife to butter her toast 'I have a lot to do today, I promised the boys and Barbra I'd bring them to town to see Santa and have our photograph taken. I have to do the grocery shopping and collect the turkey and ham from the butchers, God I hope the car will start after all that frost, that's all I need now and I didn't get a wink of sleep with that fella last night. I could hear him talking about his Seafaring adventures.' 'Who was he talking to Mam Maggie?' 'No Mary, Maggie wouldn't give him the time of day, he was talking to Rogue.' 'Rogue!' I exclaimed. 'Yes Mary, he's reduced to talking to the dog because, nobody else will listen to him. And I'll tell you something else Mary, I wouldn't be a bit surprised if he's missing a finger or two when he wakes up.' 'What do you mean Mam? I asked as I reached for another slice of toast.

'Well Mary, I think 'Rogue' got sick of listening to him too, 'cause I heard him growling and then he snapped and must have bitten him because, I heard him say "what did you do that for Rogue? I'll probably have to get a tetanus shot", then he fell over the armchair as he stumbled to his room, serves him right' she said handing her second piece of toast to 'Rogue' who was sprawled under the table. 'Good dog,' she said smiling as she patted his head!

I started off down the road hoping that one of the neighbours, who drove to Limerick each day for work, would stop and give me a lift. If not I'd hitch a lift when I reached the main road over a mile away. I explained to Mam before leaving, that there was no need for her to keep a dinner for me because I was working a double shift and wouldn't be home until late, and asked her to tell Maggie that I'd catch up with her then. Mam said 'Maggie was planning to go down to the hotel to let them know she was home and available for work. Michael had told her it was very busy with Christmas functions and office parties, and reckoned they needed all the help they could get.'

I walked as quickly as I could, hoping it would stop the frost from getting at my toes, keeping my hands in my pockets to prevent my fingers turning numb, only taking one hand out briefly to wave at Mr White, a farmer who was forking hay from a tractor trailer into a field for his cattle. 'Hardy weather Mary,' he said tipping his cap as I passed. 'Tis, Mr White,' I replied 'it's freezing.'

I reached the bus stop having failed to secure a lift, but I knew there would be no bus until about lunch time. I stuck my arm out with my 'blue with cold' thumb in the air and nearly jumped for joy when five minutes later a huge cement truck pulled up beside me and the passenger door swung open. 'Where are you off to miss?' the driver asked looking down at me. 'Town' I replied, 'hop in then'; he said 'that's where I'm heading.' 'Thanks very much,' I said, climbing up into the warm cab. I was at work twenty minutes later.

Chapter 11

Come Fly With Me

It was past midnight when I got home, fortunately, because I had worked a fourteen hour shift my boss paid for a taxi. I was tired, every muscle ached and I smelled of burgers, chips and grease. Maggie was in the kitchen ironing a work uniform for the hotel. 'Got your job back then Maggie?' I said.

'Oh yeah Mary, it's hard to get good staff', she answered smiling. 'I'm working St Stephens Night'

'Where's Mam Maggie?'

'She went to bed over an hour ago Mary.'

'I'm not surprised Maggie, she was really tired this morning.'

'Your must be wrecked yourself Mary, Mam said you're working every hour God sends, you must be raking in the money.'

'What do you mean Maggie?' I asked while reaching for the kettle. I decided to have a cup of tea before heading for the bathroom to have a shower. I dreaded facing the cold in the bathroom, stripping off in there deserved a medal for 'bravery.'

'I'm just saying you must have loads of money, it's not as if you go anywhere Mary or spend it on clothes.'

'That's my own business Maggie,' I snapped, noticing the way she was staring at my ripped jeans. I really wasn't in the mood for her smart comments or sarcasm.

'Oh God no, I didn't mean it that way Mary', she said apologetically, 'look sit down a minute and we'll have a cup of tea, I'll make it, you must be dead on your feet.'

I really didn't know what to make of Maggie, she didn't usually offer to make cups of tea for me, and I certainly didn't remember her wanting to 'chat' to me in the past. 'Maybe' I thought 'the trip to Russia had changed her, maybe, just maybe she actually missed me'. I pulled up a chair and sipped on the tea, while she began telling me about her exploits in Russia, the places she'd seen, the people she met. 'What an experience, it's true what they say Mary, travel is an education in itself, really broadens the mind, you should try it yourself Mary.'

'Maybe I will someday Maggie, who knows?'

'Oh I just know you'd love it, I'm going to America for the summer and I'd love if you came with me Mary.'

'What Maggie? America? June? With me?'

'Yes Mary, we'll have a great time, if we go in June we can stay until the end of September and come back home with loads of money and a tan.

I was really taken by surprise; Maggie wanted me to go with her to America and not one of her friends! Russia really had changed her. 'I really don't know Maggie; I'm not sure I'm ready for something like that, I mean I'd be quitting my full time job.'

'Are you for real Mary,' Maggie scoffed as she lit another cigarette, 'you're cooking burgers for God's sake, can't you find another job when you come back, or if you're that good, they'll give you back your job. Mary you can get a better job in America, I hear they make a fortune on tips; they don't call it the 'land of opportunity' for nothing.

'What about Mam Maggie, you know, with the two of us gone?'

'Mary will you stop worrying, Mam will be fine, Michael and Robert will watch out for her. Please say yes Mary.' 'I'll give it some thought Maggie' I said, not wanting to be put on the spot. 'I'm going to have a shower now and then go to bed; I've got work again in the morning.'

'Just don't take too much time thinking about it Mary, there's plenty of my friends who would jump at the chance.'

After I had a shower, I crept into the bedroom where James and Barbra were sleeping soundly in their bunk beds, with Mam beside them in a single. Mam woke though I barely made a sound, she was such a light sleeper, I often wondered if she slept at all. 'What time is it Mary?' she whispered. 'It's nearly two o clock Mam' 'have you work again in the morning Mary?'

'Yes Mam, but I'll be home by six, the place will be closing early for Christmas Eve, I'm going to bed Mam, I'm shattered. 'G'night Mary' she whispered as I began to climb the narrow wooden stairs. 'Mary' she called again, just as I reached the top, 'is that fella in yet?' 'What do you think Mam, he has money hasn't he?'

I set the alarm clock and fell into my bed, but no matter how much I tried, I couldn't sleep. I plumped up the pillow, I twisted one way and turned another, and then I lay on my back staring through the sky-light at a million stars. America, I thought to myself, maybe I should go, I certainly could afford it, I'd been saving since I started working so I had almost enough for the plane fare, and over the next few months I could save toward my spending money. I wouldn't need an awful lot, just enough to keep me going till I found a job and Maggie had said, there was plenty of work available there. Then I thought of 'Rogue' and how much I'd miss our walks together in the woods. I tried to imagine myself in a big city, I could barely cope with Limerick at the best of times, but it was very nice of Maggie to ask me, after all she had a dozen friends she could ask, she was so popular. Round and round I went in my head, till my brain was spinning and still couldn't decide.

I must have dozed off eventually, but when the alarm clock started ringing I was sure I had only been asleep five minutes. 'Oh God, how am I supposed to face work' I thought, close to tears, 'I'll burn every burger in the shop.'

Chapter 12

Tis The Season To Be Jolly

I managed to catch the last bus out of town that evening. It was packed with last-minute shoppers, screaming babies, and people like myself, exhausted from work and just wanting to get home. The frost that had numbed fingers and toes the day before had been replaced during the night by torrential rain and gale force winds. I stepped off the bus with shoulders hunched, hanging on to the hood of my rain coat, expecting to be drowned or blown away any minute. I thought of the long walk I had ahead of me and shuddered. I had just about adjusted my eyes to the 'pitch black' of the country road, when the headlights of a car coming behind me lit my path. Then I heard the horn and I smiled while saying a quiet thank you to God. There was only one car with a horn like that; it sounded more like a 'honking goose with sore throat.' I never thought I'd be so happy to see that car.

'Your limo awaits' Maggie said, smiling 'reckon you could do with a lift, you look like a drowned rat.'

'Thanks a million Maggie for thinking of me' I said wiping the rain from my face 'I'm soaked to the skin.'

'No problem Mary, I told Mam I was borrowing the 'limo' 'cause we couldn't have you walking up the road in this weather, but I needed the car anyway, to collect a few bottles. 'Look' she said pointing to a bottle of whiskey and bottle of wine that were rolling around on the floor. 'I thought you didn't have any money Maggie.'

'I don't Mary, but I thought we could have a few 'Irish Coffees' later and it wouldn't be Christmas, if we didn't have a glass of wine to 'wash down' the turkey, so I convinced the manager of the hotel to let me have them, and told him he can take the money out of my wages 'Stephen's Night, I knew he'd give them to me Mary, 'cause he fancies me, big time.' Maggie I thought to myself always came up smelling of roses.

When we arrived into the kitchen, Mam was in the middle of stuffing the turkey and the steam from the smoked ham, which was boiling on the cooker, was running down the kitchen walls. 'Mary' she said looking up from her work, 'if you want something to eat fix it yourself.'

'No, I'm not hungry Mam, I'll just get out of these clothes and then I'll give you a hand, what do you need me to do.' 'If you can give James and Barbra a bath, that would be great Mary, and Maggie, if you could get the good dinner set out of the china cabinet and dust it off, and Mary, tell Michael and Robert to stop their horsing around, I was cleaning that sitting room for an hour today and the way they're 'carrying on' it will look as if a bomb has hit it! I don't know why I bother, nobody notices whether I clean or not.' I could tell by Mam, that her stress levels were climbing by the minute and I knew why.

Paddy, hadn't come home at all the night before and she was most likely envisioning the state he would be in when he finally decided to 'grace us' with his presence. If there was one thing that Paddy excelled at, that was, ruining special occasions. We all secretly hoped that he would just stay away.

Mam always cooked a delicious Christmas dinner. For her, it was the highlight of the festive season, she very rarely spent any money on herself and apart from a gift we would 'pool' our savings or pocket money to buy, and the odd well-meant box of biscuits or chocolates from friends or relatives, she had very little to look forward to. As for Paddy, we knew he wouldn't arrive bearing gifts, 'cause all Mam got from him for a long as we could remember was black eyes and for us, another Christmas to remember for all the wrong reasons. Mam really wanted everything to be perfect that year especially because Aunt Maureen, her sister was coming to dinner. So, at nine o clock Christmas Eve she was still finding work to do. 'Yes, I'll sit down in a minute, I'm nearly finished now' she said. Maggie roared at her again from the sitting room. 'Mam, will you come in and sit down by the fire, you've enough done, the rest can wait till the morning, there's a great movie starting soon, it's called 'The Godfather' and Mary is going to make us a nice 'Irish Coffee' for the three of us, aren't you Mary?' 'Maggie, why do I have to make them? Is there something wrong with your legs Maggie? 'Cause I was standing on my feet all day and I can't even feel them.' 'Aw come on Mary, you know you make the best Irish Coffees, whenever I make them the cream sinks to the bottom.' 'Oh Maggie' I said 'you say the nicest things when you want something.'

A few minutes later and after more coaxing from me, Mam finally sat down. We were sipping our 'Irish Coffees' and toasting ourselves with the heat from the blazing fire; the boy's and Barbra all dressed in pyjamas and slippers were helping themselves to biscuits from a USA tin that sat on the coffee table. We were as happy as 'pigs in shit.' That is, until we heard a car pull up in the yard, and our hearts sank. Nobody said a word except for Maggie 'well, that was nice while it lasted' she said throwing her eyes up to heaven. Mam was the next one to speak 'Robert, James, Barbra, take one more biscuit and off to bed with ye, fast now' James and Barbra didn't have to be told twice and disappeared into their room.

We knew it would be about ten minutes before Paddy actually arrived in the door because he would always be at least that long arguing with the taxi driver over the fare. Robert decided to use this time to talk Mam into allowing him to stay up a little longer, 'Mam why do I have to go to bed and Michael is allowed to watch TV? It's not fair' he moaned. 'Robert just do as your told,' Mam yelled.

'Mam it's not fair just 'cause he's coming in drunk again, he always has to ruin everything.' 'Robert don't you dare 'back answer me.' Mam was getting more irate by the minute. But Robert wasn't giving in 'Mam, maybe he'll come in and go straight to bed.' I knew there was better chance that 'pigs would fly!' Just as Mam opened her mouth to yell at Robert again, the sitting room door flew open. 'Oh you're all looking very cosy with your Irish Coffees, ye must be very fond of yourselves all together.' Paddy always had a sneering arrogant manner when

he was drunk, almost as if he derived great pleasure from causing havoc. Mam was watching his every move. 'Why don't you just go to bed and let us watch the television in peace' she pleaded.
'Actually' he replied leaning on the back of the couch to steady himself 'I wouldn't mind an Irish Coffee myself.' 'There's no more whiskey' Maggie quickly lied 'we only bought a baby bottle.' There was no way Maggie was going to give him one drop of the whiskey she still had to work a night to pay for. 'Is that right?' He said staring at Maggie between the eyes and quite obviously not impressed.

He didn't even look in my direction; instead he turned his attention to Michael and Robert who were still sitting on the couch, Michael doing his best to ignore him and Robert wishing now that he had listened to Mam. 'What are the two of you doing up at this hour' he said nudging Michael in the back of his head with his fist.
'Will you stop Dad?' Michal asked 'we're trying to watch the movie.' 'Yeah just go to bed' Maggie added 'if you think you're getting any drink you're sadly mistaken.'
'Oh is that the way it is now' Paddy said sneering 'you lot are telling me!' With that, he drew back and gave Michael a fist to the side of the head. Robert leapt from the couch and stood by the door not knowing whether to stay or make a run for it. Mam was screaming and crying telling Paddy he was nothing but a 'gurrier.' Maggie was looking at me knowing that at any moment I might pick up the brass poker from the fire and beat him half to death with it. The thought had 'crossed' my mind but I didn't get the chance, Michael who a moment before was trying to 'rub' away the pain in his head, jumped to his feet and 'flattened' his father with one blow. Robert who was a lot bigger than Michael, ran to try and break it up, pulling at Michael, who was now on top of his father and like a person possessed, Robert gave up, and I thought for an instant he was going to walk away, but instead decided to take his brother's side and thumped Paddy as well!

Paddy was still in a heap on the floor when the movie ended and Mam turned off the television. She took the 'Santa gifts' from the wardrobe in Maggie's room where she had hidden them and placed them under the tree. We turned off the light and went to bed. As I pulled the blankets over my head I smiled to myself and thought 'what goes around comes round.' The wheel always turns.

I woke the next morning to Barbra shaking me and pushing the doll Santa had brought her into my face. 'Look Mary, look at what Santa had brought me' she squealed 'isn't she lovely?'

'She's beautiful Barbra,' I said. 'Santa must have known what a good girl you are to bring you a special doll like that.'

Climbing out of the bed and into my dressing gown and slippers, I watched Barbra looking at the doll in total adoration. As I descended the stairs with Barbra close on my heels, pictures of the night before flooded my brain. James was reversing a tractor-trailer in the bedroom below, too busy to even notice me.

'Mind you don't crash into that bed James' I said joking. 'I won't Mary' he said giving me a big smile, and went back to imitating the sounds a real tractor would make, in his imaginary world of farming.

After breakfast, Mam, having coaxed Robert, James and Barbra away from their toys with promises of sweets, left the house to go to Mass. Michael said he wasn't going 'cause he wasn't feeling well and Mam didn't insist. Maggie was still in bed and I hadn't been to Mass in years, since the priest told me, Rogue, my dog, wasn't welcome. So I promised Mam I'd wash the breakfast dishes and clean out the ashes from the fire the night before. Just as she was about to go out the door and at the same time trying to explain to Barbra why she couldn't bring her doll with her, she turned to me and asked 'Mary, do you think we should check on 'him' to make sure he's not dead in the bed?' 'Mam don't you know you can't kill a bad thing' I replied. 'Don't be worrying, I heard him snoring his head off when I passed the bedroom door.' 'Right O' she said relieved, 'we'll be back soon, I have to collect Aunt Maureen after Mass.'

It was nearly four o'clock when Mam called us to take our seats at the table that Maggie had set. There was a candle glowing softly at each end, red serviettes that she had creased into the shape of small fans and pride of place was Mam's best china, expensive remnants of days long since passed, and reminders of a previous life, where she, Maggie and I had wanted for nothing.

Aunt Maureen took her seat at the table quite oblivious to all that had happened the night before. Michael was quieter than usual, obviously concerned that there might be some kind of repercussion for lashing out at his father the night before. Robert and James were pulling Christmas crackers while Barbra was deciding whether to have 'Coke' or Orange with her dinner. Maggie began pouring wine, Aunt Maureen adamant that she only have half a glass. 'I don't want to be tipsy' she said. Mam was looking at me and I knew she was thinking exactly as I was. 'Maybe Paddy was dead in the bed' but just then we heard the handle of the bedroom door turn and Paddy stepped into the sitting room, all 'spruced up' in his best suit pants and a new sweater that Mam had bought him. He took his seat at the table and began carving the turkey. 'Happy Christmas Maureen,' he said placing an ample portion of turkey breast and stuffing on her plate.

'It's good to see you Maureen, you're looking well.' 'Oh thank you Patrick,' Aunt Maureen replied, blushing shyly at the compliment. 'You don't look too bad yourself.' It took all of us, every ounce of self-control we had not to collapse into fits of laughter; Aunt Maureen's sight had obviously deteriorated and she didn't see that Paddy's two eyes were the same colour as the Cranberry Sauce and his nose to say the least was off – centre. Nobody commented, we 'tucked' into our dinners and raised our glasses in a toast to the 'New Year.' Yes I thought, the New Year and America, Maggie was right Mam would be fine.

Chapter 13

Leaving On A Jet Plane

I finished up in my job in mid-June, having given my boss ample notice of my imminent departure. Though disappointed to see me leave, he gave me a glowing reference and assured me that should I decide to return, there would be a job waiting for me. 'You don't know how lucky you are' he said 'to have an American passport and not have to worry about Visa's or Green Cards. You'd be crazy Mary, not to go; people would give their right arm for an opportunity like that.' My boss wasn't alone in his opinion, some of my work mates were green with envy, so I found reassurance in the knowledge that they all agreed that America was indeed the place to be.

The week before our departure was hectic. Maggie who was 'beside' herself with excitement, was barely at home insisting that she had to meet up with all her friends 'to say goodbye' while I travelled to the American Embassy in Dublin by train to collect my passport. Then I went to town to buy a rucksack similar to the one Maggie had travelled to Russia with. I thought it was far more practical than a more traditional suitcase and certainly a lot easier to carry around. Last but not least, I went to the bank to get some 'travellers cheques', Mam had insisted saying it would be ludicrous to carry cash. Maggie agreed with her that I should get cheques but said that she herself would carry cash, her argument being that we didn't know how soon after landing in America we'd be able to find a bank. Mam wasn't convinced, 'couldn't you change some of your money to cheques Maggie? I don't like the idea of you walking around with all that cash, you could get mugged.' Maggie laughed, 'I won't Mam, will you stop worrying, didn't I make it to Russia and back?'

'I suppose you're right Maggie,' Mam said giving in, 'but another thing I'm not happy about is that you have only bought one-way tickets, are you sure you're both coming back?' 'Of course we are Mam' Maggie said at an attempt to reassure her, there's no need to buy return tickets until we know exactly when we're coming home.' 'And you're sure you and Mary will find work?' 'Yes I'm sure Mam' Maggie sighed, weary of Mam's interrogation. 'There must be hundreds of hotels and restaurants Mam, we have great references and you said yourself that 'they love the Irish', I can't wait to go.'

'At least I won't have to worry about you two having a place to stay, your Aunt Nelly is looking forward to seeing you both and said ye're welcome to stay as long as you want, she'll hardly recognise ye, it's nearly fourteen years since she last saw you.' Aunt Nelly was actually our Grandaunt, our deceased father's aunt. She was eighty four years old and lived alone in an apartment on Long Island, New York.

Chapter 14

Deep Inside The Forest

We flew in to Logan Airport in Boston. Maggie announced at the last minute prior to buying our tickets that she had called Lisa, a girl of Russian descent and fellow student she'd met while studying in Moscow. She told Lisa about our planned trip and asked if Lisa could 'put us up' for a few days that we'd love to meet up with her. So it was all arranged, Lisa lived in a place called Providence, Rhode Island, which was about an hour from the airport and she said she would pick us up. We would be spending our first week in America with her and her family before heading for Long Island to stay with Aunt Nelly and look for work.

Staring out the window of the plane in an effort to distract myself from the 'popping' sensation in my ears, while the plane gradually lost height and prepared to land, I was amazed at the amount of swimming pools I could see below us in almost every back garden. I thought to myself as the 'fasten your seat belt sign' flashed before me, that Maggie was right when she said America was the land of opportunity, if they can afford swimming pools, they must be earning a fortune. Another vivid memory I have was the heat that hit me straight in the face when the Air Hostess opened the plane door, allowing us to exit. It could only be compared to the opening of an oven door. The temperature was ninety degrees.

Lisa had told Maggie that she would meet us at the main door of the terminal. As we made our way through the crowds of people towards an 'exit' sign we could see in the distance, I couldn't help but look around me at the sheer scale of the building. 'Oh my God Maggie,' I said in awe 'this place is huge.' 'I know' Maggie replied, as excited as ever 'isn't it great!' Then all of a sudden she was waving her hands about wildly at a face she had seen in the crowd and desperately trying to run with the rucksack on her back, toward a girl who was standing about one hundred yards away. Maggie threw her arms around her and both of them were shouting over each other for what seemed like the longest time. Eventually they came to their senses and Maggie introduced me to Lisa 'this is my sister Mary.' Lisa gave me a warm smile, a hug and a kiss on the cheek. I was to realise later that all Americans greeted each other that way, unlike the Irish who were more reserved and just offered a 'handshake.'

'Welcome to America Mary,' she said sincerely, 'I hope you enjoy your stay.' She seemed like a really nice girl. 'The car is parked over there' she said pointing to thousands of cars of all shapes and sizes. As we made our way across the car-park Lisa explained that we were going to a place called 'Plymouth' for the weekend and that her boyfriend Jake, who was waiting in the car would be going too. There were more hugs, kisses and words of welcome from Jake who I was trying hard not to stare at, but just like the airport, the cars and the surrounding buildings, he was huge. Standing six foot six and almost as wide, Lisa explained that he was a professional football player for the 'New York Giants.' He was definitely 'living up' to the name I thought; there couldn't have been any shortage of food in his house growing up!

As we set off in the car after squeezing our rucksacks into the boot, Maggie and Lisa were chatting away to each other non-stop and 'filling' Jake in on all their exploits in Moscow, while I was happily gazing up at the cloudless sky and soaking up warmth of the sun through the open window. It felt like heaven on my skin.

As we arrived in 'Plymouth' about an hour later, Lisa explained that 'Plymouth was a place of great historical significance and thus attracted throngs of tourists from around the world.' 'This is where the ship the 'Mayflower' came ashore in 1620' she said. I remembered being taught about the 'Mayflower' in history class by Mrs Collins, one of the very few teachers who was nice to me.

Plymouth was a quaint little town. It had a small town feel to it with tiny replica wood cabins displaying how the first American settlers had lived. There were narrow streets lined with rows of small shops and cafes, teaming with people of every age, shape and colour. Lisa pulled the car over and parked in front of a small grocery store 'let's buy some food for the weekend' she suggested, and we stepped inside a small air conditioned store. Maggie offered to push the shopping trolley and we watched as Lisa randomly plucked items from shelves and fridges. Bacon, eggs, waffles, maple syrup, muffins, hot dogs, tomatoes which were the size of apples, a gallon of milk, a gallon of orange juice, chocolate chip cookies and a 'case' of beer. Most of these items would certainly never be on 'Mam's shopping list as they would have been considered to be luxury items, but to Lisa they seemed to be basic every day necessities. On and on she went placing one item after another into the trolley, Steaks, sweet potatoes, which I had never heard of before, aubergines and last but not least chocolate brownies. All I could do was stand there with my mouth watering. Maggie fished some money out of her pocket and gave it to Lisa while I helped Jake carry our 'hoard' to the car. It was enough to feed a small army!

We arrived at our destination a half hour later and I remember thinking to myself that I'd died and gone to heaven. Lisa's family holiday home was a little log cabin, which set nestled in the middle of a forest, right on the water's edge of a huge lake. It was, I thought, the stuff that picture post cards were made of, just breath taking. I grabbed a bag of groceries and rushed toward the door, eager to see inside. It was like stepping back in time and reminded me of a scene from an old 'cowboy' movie. Red chequered curtains framed the tiny windows. The fireplace was built of stone and had an abundant supply of chopped firewood on each side. The huge chimney breast separated the sitting room from the kitchen which had a six foot dresser on one side displaying the dishes, and on the other were several small shelves with rows of jars containing a variety of fruits and preserves. Taking centre stage was a large but simple wooden table with a vase of dried flowers at its centre. Climbing the narrow ladder like stairs we found two bedrooms with sloping ceilings and tiny windows offering views of the shimmering lake. 'Well Mary', Maggie asked as we began unpacking some clothes 'are you glad you came?' 'Definitely' I smiled 'all I expected to see in America Maggie was concrete jungles and traffic, this place is beautiful I won't want to leave, it's so peaceful.'

We spent three glorious days in Plymouth lazing around doing very little and eating too much barbequed food. I spent hours of each day swimming in the lake and even managed to surprise everyone by swimming two miles out and back from a small island that sat out in the middle of the lake. Maggie and I both tried our hand at water skiing from Jake and Lisa's small speed boat, but without much success, although we had great fun trying. It was a memorable few days and I would happily have stayed there for the rest of my life, unlike Maggie, who was once again yearning for the bright lights of the city. All too soon for me she got her wish and we were packed up and on the road again.

Chapter 15

New York: New York

As we drove along the highway, Maggie gave Jake a tape of 'Bagatelle' to play on the stereo and as we made our way to Providence we sang along to the song '*Summer in Dublin.*' Jake was really impressed with 'Bagatelle' saying their music had a 'cool beat' and that up until then he had only ever heard the old Irish ballads, which were played all day long in the Irish pubs on Paddy's Day. 'Bagatelle' he said were certainly a 'breath of fresh air.'

We arrived at Lisa's family home in the mid afternoon. It was what Americans would call 'A New England' town house, set in the historical part of the city, in an area that Lisa explained was known as the East Side and although it seemed to us to be a quiet secluded area with huge old trees and Victorian street lamps, Lisa assured us that the area became a hive of activity when students from all over the country moved in, to pursue their studies at the nearby 'Brown University.'

Inside, the house took on the look of a Georgian period residence. Large square rooms with high ornately designed corniced ceilings, several marble surround open fireplaces and walls with floor to ceiling shelves displaying thousands of books. In one room a grand piano took centre stage. I remember thinking that Lisa, who had no 'heirs and graces' about her, was obviously as Mam would put it 'from good stock.'

The next few days we spent familiarising ourselves with the area. We bought postcards to send to family and friends at home and strolled around at our leisure looking at the abundance of shops and restaurants Providence had to offer. Maggie was 'oohing' and 'aahing' at every shop window displaying clothes. But fortunately I was able to dissuade her from buying, by reminding her that we had to find work first. 'There'll be plenty of clothes shops in New York Maggie, you'll just have to wait,' I said. So we would console ourselves with

a trip to the nearest fast food restaurant and gorge ourselves on burgers and milkshakes. At night we'd venture out to do a tour of the many trendy bars and night clubs in the area. Initially we were shocked to be told that the legal drinking age in Rhode Island was twenty one. In fact Maggie was more than shocked; I actually thought she was going to have a 'panic attack!' Fortunately, each time the 'bouncers' stopped us, Lisa was able to persuade them to let us in, by telling them we were tourists from Ireland and were only in town for a few days.
Later we laughed as we told Lisa how surprised we were at the 'drink laws.' 'Lisa' I explained 'in Ireland you'll get served in a bar if, one, you can stand and two, you can reach the bar.' 'Oh my Lord' she replied 'that's awesome.'
The week in Providence came to an end all too soon and Maggie telephoned Aunt Nelly to remind her we would be arriving early that Friday evening. 'Old people need reminding' she said 'for all we know Aunt Nelly could be half senile.'
To save money, we decided to travel the three hour journey by bus to New York and then catch a train to Long Island. Lisa, once again offered her services and drove us to the bus stop, and after many goodbyes thanking Lisa for her wonderful hospitality and promises to 'keep in touch', we boarded the bus and arrived at 'Port Authority' in New York mid-afternoon. We were stiff from sitting in the cramped bus for such a long time and I was relieved when Maggie said we would have to walk to 'Penn Station' to catch our train, an opportunity, I thought, to stretch our legs. As we stepped out of the relative coolness of 'Port Authority' onto the New York street my eyes were drawn to a large electronic billboard displaying the afternoon temperature. It was ninety six degrees and the humidity caused us to sweat profusely. As we made our way through the sweltering streets, weighed down by the rucksacks which felt like they were fused on our backs. The sheer scale of the buildings, the noise, the traffic and the seemingly unending 'throngs' of people was, I found, totally overwhelming; Maggie on the other hand was disappointed that we didn't have time to go window shopping or see the 'sights' like Time Square

or The Statue of Liberty. 'Thank God' I thought to myself, I couldn't wait to get out of there. At one point while making my way through the crowds I slowed to adjust the shoulder strap on the rucksack, only to get a slap of a handbag a lady was carrying, across the side of my head, while at the same time she was yelling at me 'you're walking too damn slow honey, get a move on' and then she just hurried on about her business. I looked at Maggie in shock; she took one look at the expression on my face and almost fell to her knees laughing. 'Well Mary' she said barely able to speak 'what do you think of the Big Apple?'

We were so relieved when we finally reached Penn Station; any reprieve from the blazing sun was appreciated, a building of gigantic proportions with just as many people inside as were outside on the street.

There was just no escaping the crowds, but I was happy just to be able to lift the rucksacks off each other's shoulders and lay them on the ground, giving ourselves a well-deserved rest. Sadly that respite was too short and sweet, because no sooner had Maggie left me in charge of our luggage to go off in search of a ticket desk, to purchase our train tickets, I saw this policeman – who looked as if he had eaten too many doughnuts in his day, come marching toward me, wiping the sweat from his brow with one hand, and swinging a baton in the other. 'Move along Ma'am' he ordered. 'But' I said in protest staring up at the large silver police badge which was pinned to his shirt 'I'm not in anyone's way, I'm just waiting for my sister.' 'You can't stand there Ma'am, you got to keep movin,' he said towering over me 'if you don't keep movin' Ma'am you'll get mugged.' When Maggie returned about twenty minutes later waving two train tickets in the air, she found me on the verge of collapse. Carrying one of the rucksacks on each shoulder and struggling to put one foot in front of the other. 'Maggie' I said gasping for breath 'get me out of this crazy place!'

Chapter 16

California Girls

The train came to a halt in 'Kings Park' Long Island around five thirty, and I was relieved to see, that it was a place not much bigger than a small village in Ireland. A real suburban area with more houses than shops with ample space and green park areas to be seen. Maggie's vivid memory of Kings Park really amazed me. She was little more than five years old when she left America fourteen years before but when I asked her should we ask somebody for directions to Aunt Nelly's address, she replied 'no need Mary, I know the way.' I followed her, much too tired to argue, but managed to smile as I watched several squirrels blissfully hopping around beneath the trees and others clinging to tree trunks. 'This is more my pace of life' I thought and before I knew it, we were knocking at Aunt Nelly's door.

Aunt Nelly was short in stature, a lady with short wavy steel grey hair. She greeted us with a welcoming smile then scrutinised us from head to toe through big bluish-grey eyes which looked out over, black rimmed spectacles that balanced precariously on the end of her nose. 'You girls sure have grown up,' she said as she ushered us inside.

Aunt Nelly had spent most of her working life employed as a nurse's aide in the nearby hospital. Looking a lot younger than her eighty four years would have suggested. She was very capable and proud of the fact that she was still managing to remain independent. Her compact one bedroom apartment was immaculate, even it was a little outdated and reflected more of a sixties style. Aunt Nelly's apartment was the ground floor part of a two family home and she had lived there most of her life. She seemed genuinely pleased to see us and insisted that we should have her bedroom for the duration of our stay, and that she would take the sleep sofa in the sitting room. I urged her to stay in her room, feeling guilty that she was going to such lengths to accommodate us, but she wouldn't listen to another word. 'That's final' she insisted, waving her pointed forefinger at both of us. Aunt Nelly was a woman Mam would have described as 'a tough old bird.'

It had been a long day and I sat down on Aunt Nelly's bed, slipped off my shoes and rubbed by tired and swollen feet. Maggie, realising I was exhausted, suggested we postpone any grocery shopping until the next morning insisting 'you'll be fine Mary after a good night's sleep' and volunteered to walk to the pizzeria we had seen on the corner of the street. She decided she would order some food and pick up a few cans of beer on the way back in the off licence across the street. Reaching for her handbag, she called to Aunt Nelly who was sitting in an armchair in the sitting room watching the evening news. 'Aunt Nelly, what kind of beer would you like with your pizza?' The expression on Maggie's face made me laugh when she heard Aunt Nelly's response. 'A bottle of beer Maggie, I'm eighty four years old and I didn't get to this age by drinking liquor. I've never been in a Saloon an' drinking is only for 'bums!'
The next morning we were feeling rejuvenated. Having slept well, despite the fact that we had shared Aunt Nelly' single bed. After showering, we set off to buy necessities at the local supermarket and of course the compulsory six pack of beer for Maggie. I didn't want any beer. It had nothing to do with Aunt Nelly's obvious hatred of drink, it was simply because I had never taken to the taste of beer or lager, and anytime I had tried it, I had immediately regretted it, suffering pounding headaches for hours. No, I was a whiskey drinker when socialising, but with temperatures in the nineties and humidity which caused you to perspire constantly, Scotch was a real 'no-no.' I was quite content drinking ice cold glasses of orange juice, a luxury we could never afford at home. We strolled back home laden down with our purchases, we paid particular attention to any signs displayed in shop windows advertising job vacancies. Aunt Nelly had told us that it might be worth our while buying the local paper and checking out the classified section, but, that it wouldn't be in the stores till the following

day. We unpacked the groceries. Maggie carefully placing the six pack of beer at the back of the fridge behind a large head of iceberg lettuce, feeling 'safe' in the knowledge that Aunt Nelly wouldn't see it. I agreed with Maggie when she said 'there was no more we could do in regards to finding work till we read the newspaper and that we should make the most of whatever free time we had left.' So it was decided. We would spend the afternoon at the beach and 'work' on our tan.

'Sunken Meadows' beach Aunt Nelly told us was at least a mile away, but this didn't deter us. Why would it? When we were used to walking that distance and more every day at home in Cratloe.

Car horns blew and drivers stared out their car windows at us as we made our way along the wide open road that led to the beach. I don't know if this was because we were walking such a distance to the beach and it would have been quite obvious that we were, because we carried our towels rolled up under our arms, or if it was that they were amused at the sight of two young girls, one blonde and one redhead, breathlessly puffing and perspiring profusely with every step. At the very least, they saw us as strange, walking was an activity that seemed alien to most Americans, they drove everywhere!

Maggie however, decided to take a more positive view of the intermittent honking, flicking back her shoulder length blonde hair and adjusting her sunglasses, she strutted on, nose in the air and said 'those drivers, Mary, more than likely fancy us.' I personally found this a little hard to believe especially where I was concerned. We were both about fifteen pounds overweight, more noticeable on me, as I was two inches shorter than Maggie's five foot eight inches height. Maggie was better able to carry the extra pounds, whereas I just looked freckled and frumpy as I plodded on after her.

When we finally reached our destination, we were amazed at the over flowing buses, arriving by the minute to deliver hundreds of excited day-trippers from New York City, happy to escape the smog and unyielding humidity for a few hours. Maggie and I were parched with the thirst and hurriedly bought a large iced soda from one of the many vendors on the endless boardwalk. As we sipped our sodas our eyes scanned over the thousands of bodies lying on the beach, searching for a small patch of golden sand on which to lay our towels. 'There' Maggie said suddenly, pointing to a small patch about a hundred yards away. 'Quick Mary, before someone else takes it, time to get our tan.' With that she took off across the burning sand, dodging countless bodies on her way to stake her claim. We laid out our slightly thread bare towels and began splashing on suntan oil that promised a 'tropical bronze tan.'

We were like two milk bottles and we both had a good laugh after looking around us, realising that it wasn't just that we were paler than everyone else, as far as the eye could see we were actually the only white people on the beach, so we stuck out like a sore thumb! That day is a day I will never forget and we both learned a very tough lesson, which was, that white skin is better than skin the colour of lobster! We lay on that beach for hours, four hours to be exact, turning this way and that, following the sun to capture as many rays as we possibly could. On two separate occasions, concerned people approached us, urging us to get out of the sun. 'Excuse me Ma'am' one woman said looking out from under the peak of a baseball cap. 'My husband and I can't help notice how red you ladies are getting; I know it's none of our business, but that sun is awful hot.' Maggie thanked the lady for her concern but insisted that we were fine, 'after all' she said 'we're only a little pink.' An hour later another lady passed by eating a hot dog 'oh my word' she said speaking with her mouth full. 'You ladies are gonna suffer tonight, if you two don't cover up, you both is gonna be like fried chicken!'
I agreed with Maggie, that there seemed to be little change in our skin, apart from the fact that there seemed to be more and more freckles 'popping' out on mine by the minute. But seeing the lady enjoying her hotdog made me realise just how hungry I was. Reminding Maggie of the long walk home, she finally agreed that we should go home and cook dinner and admitted we probably had enough sun for one day.

As it turned out, it was enough sun to last me a lifetime. I have never lain out in the sun since, and to this day if somebody suggest that look a little pale, my response is 'of course I'm pale, I was born white!' It was safe to say we did our penance for any sins that day and the next and the next. It only became apparent later on that evening when we undressed to take a cold shower. I had noticed the two white rectangular shapes around Maggie's eyes when she removed her sunglasses upon entering the house, but didn't quite know how to break the news to her and decided she might be better to discover it by herself. Maggie didn't usually take criticism very well. Sure enough, a half hour later, the screams coming from the bathroom could be heard all around the apartment. 'Look at my face, oh my God, I won't be able to go out for a week, nobody is going to want to give me a job looking like this!'

After making polite conversation with Aunt Nelly for an hour and drinking almost a gallon of water, we retired to the bedroom. Maggie was pacing up and down with the rigidity of a corpse and I was shivering and shaking uncontrollably. I knew there was no way I could share the single bed with Maggie, the thought of someone even brushing off my skin was too much to bear, so I peeled the sheet from the bed, placed it on the timber floor boards and prayed for a miracle.

Maggie was raving and adamant that we should sue the suntan oil company and then in the same breath decided she should have a beer, obviously believing it would make her feel better. I watched her, listening with her ear to the door, for any sound of life coming from the sitting room. She didn't want Aunt Nelly to know she was drinking. After a few minutes believing the coast was clear, Maggie tip-toed past Aunt Nelly on the sofa and made her way toward the kitchen and the refrigerator in the dark. Just as she thought her mission was accomplished she heard Aunt Nelly calling from the sitting room. 'Maggie, turn on the light or you won't be able to see the beer.' Aunt Nelly was not the senile old lady Maggie had predicted.

Chapter 17

Patricia The Stripper

Needless to say, neither of us slept very well that night and woke the following morning feeling sick, sore and sorry. I couldn't bear the thought of squeezing into my jeans, so I opted for one of the three loose fitting cotton sun dresses which I had brought with me and rooted it out of my rucksack. I slid my swollen blistered feet into a pair of flip-flops. Maggie sat on the edge of the bed looking very forlorn and I had to sympathise with her, as bad as I looked, Maggie who had even paler skin than me looked worse. Her shoulders and shins had huge blisters on them resembling jelly fish. She pulled a cotton night dress on over her underwear swearing as she did that she wasn't setting foot out doors for the day.

I volunteered to go to the convenience store and buy some doughnuts and the local newspaper. 'There's some change in my purse' Maggie gurgled through a mouthful of toothpaste. I opened her purse and she was right, there was more than enough change, I counted out four dollars in quarters, dimes and nickels and told Aunt Nelly who was pottering about in the kitchen that I'd be back shortly. It was only as I walked to the store and moaned as the morning sun beat down on my tormented skin that the penny dropped. I visualised myself looking into Maggie's purse as I had done a few minutes before. And yes, there had been change but no notes. 'That's strange' I told myself. But then decided Maggie must be keeping her notes in a safe place after all. Maggie, I knew had spent less than a hundred and fifty dollars on food and drink to date, I had cashed some of my travellers cheques to cover the bus and train tickets from Rhode Island to New York. 'Yes' I consoled myself, Maggie had told me before we left Ireland that she had the same amount of money as me, so with that in mind I found reassurance in the knowledge that we should have about two hundred dollars each and with the help of God and the local newspaper we'd be able to start work by the end of the week.

I made my way back to the house and after a breakfast of French toast and maple syrup. Maggie and I spent the rest of the day scouring the situations vacant section. Alas, there were only two jobs listed for the Kings Park area, one for a confectioner in the local bakery just around the corner and the second was for cleaning staff at the nearby mental hospital. I thought the latter was worth a shot but Maggie was adamant. 'No way Mary' she said stubbornly, 'hadn't we enough of dealing with lunatics at home?' We decided to widen our search to include all the neighbouring towns and although there were quite a number of jobs on offer, there was little in the line of hotel or restaurant work. Just as I was beginning to feel a little despondent Maggie spotted one. 'Now Mary, here we go, this one sounds as if it's right up our alley.' She said very optimistically and began to read the 'ad' aloud.

Several vacancies exist in our trendy bar/night club, bartenders, waitresses, dancers and doormen. Applicants must have a good appearance, be friendly and outgoing. Top wages and tips guaranteed. Please apply in person to the manager of the 'Foxy Lady Club', Smithfield, Long Island.

'Oh Mary that sounds just perfect' Maggie continued with renewed enthusiasm 'with our experience we should have to problem at all, I told you we'd make a fortune on tips. We'll catch a bus there first thing in the morning after the banks open.' 'Why Maggie has the bank to be open,' I asked her believing that securing a job should be our priority. It was better I thought to be making money than spending it.

Maggie looked at me as if I had two heads 'to cash one of your travellers cheques Mary, what else?'

'But Maggie, I thought we had decided to spend your cash first, remember what Mam said about carrying around as little cash as possible?'

'Yes Mary,' Maggie replied, a little annoyed now that I was questioning her judgement, 'I know what we decided and I know what Mam said.'

'Well that's it then' I said 'we'll stick to our plan and save my travellers cheques until your money runs out.' I thought I was hearing things when Maggie, while reaching for her cigarettes said 'it already has!' I really could have swung for her at that point. I knew then that the reason she asked me to go to America all those months before was because she knew that I'd do the sensible thing and save while she continued to socialise with her friends right up until the time we left.

But I knew that arguing wouldn't improve our predicament and I certainly didn't want to worry Aunt Nelly who was blissfully watching her soaps on the television, quite oblivious to the whole situation. So I just said to Maggie in as calm a voice as I could possibly muster 'you better pray Maggie that we get that job tomorrow.'

We set off early the next morning after a breakfast of toasted muffins with grape jelly which I managed to eat despite my lack of appetite. I was anxious about the day ahead and prayed that it would have a happy outcome.

Maggie explained to Aunt Nelly that we expected to be gone for most of the day and not to worry about cooking dinner. 'We will organise that,' she told her, when we get back.' We caught a bus to Smithfield after first going to the bank to cash the travellers cheque and I tried to put the concern about our finances to the back of my mind and concentrate on the task at hand – finding work.

Walking at a brisk pace and asking directions from people we met along the way, we arrived at the 'Foxy Lady' nightclub about twenty minutes later and our hearts sank. We looked at the signs and billboards outside the building in disbelief. 'Topless waitresses, lap dancing, private dance booths 24/7 stared back at us. We turned on our heels trying to get as far away from the place as quickly as possible, afraid that anyone watching would think that we worked there. And we kept walking until we came to a small park where we sat on a bench to rest. 'Now what do we do Maggie?' I asked hoping that she being the genius in the family would have some words of wisdom to offer. She said nothing for a few minutes, just puffed away on her cigarette and stared into space. 'What about that shopping mall we passed on our way? There must be loads of shops and cafes in there' she finally suggested. 'Yeah, ok' I replied 'let's try there; our luck is bound to change.' It didn't. We tried every restaurant, burger joint, pizzeria and ice cream parlour at the mall and with every rejection felt worse and worse. The word 'no' took many forms. 'I'm sorry ladies we have all the staff we need' or 'we won't be hiring again till the Fall,' or 'business is quiet, we're not hiring.' Feeling totally defeated we made our way back toward the bus stop with not one word spoken between us.

America was not at all what Maggie had predicted and seeing her confidence levels so depleted after our failed search didn't help and my mind began to wonder.

I had a vision of us being homeless and destitute like the poor lady I had seen in 'New York', dressed in black refuse sacks and pushing a shopping trolley which was filled with her meagre possessions. My heart was pounding in my chest as panic began to take hold and once again I prayed for divine intervention. A few minutes later as we rounded a corner, I believed my prayers had been answered. Hanging from a flag pole was the Star Spangled Banner, and underneath it in big, bold letters was a sign which read 'United States of America Army Recruitment Office. I opened the door and walked inside before Maggie had a chance to react. Sitting upright in his stiff uniform behind a large wooden desk, wearing a big welcoming smile was the recruitment officer. 'So ladies' he said 'sizing us up from head to flip-flops, 'you have decided you want to serve your country?' 'Don't look at me' Maggie replied 'it's my sister Mary who wants to enlist, Mary are you sure you know what you're doing?' she muttered as we watched the officer shuffling the paper work on his desk. 'No, I am not sure Maggie, the only thing I am sure about is that we're running out of money and I don't want to starve, if you have any suggestions Maggie, I'm all ears!' 'Aah, Mary is it?' the officer interrupted our bickering 'what makes you think you've got what it takes? he asked looking at me with raised eyebrows. 'Well' I replied struggling to find my voice 'my father was a soldier; he served in the Second World War under General McArthur.' All of a sudden the officer dropped the papers he was fidgeting with and was now giving me his undivided attention. 'My father was also the youngest Sergeant to serve in the Pacific. He was just seventeen and his father before him, my Grandfather won the overall boxing championships for a few consecutive years.' 'My, my' the officer seemed genuinely in awe 'with a history like that Mary, I've no doubt your army material, it's in your blood' he said and began reading through the application forms. The procedure was, he explained, to fill out the form and within seven days I would be called to sit an aptitude test. After completing the forms he shook hands with both of us and told me he was looking forward to our next meeting. He seemed bemused by our accent, 'the Irish brogue' he called it, and said we were very brave to come to America on our own. At least, I thought to myself he didn't call me an 'Eejit!' We left the office and ran to the bus stop only to discover that we'd missed the bus.

We sat and waited for the next bus which wasn't due for an hour. I was deep in thought and resigned to the fact that we could do no more, but growing more anxious that we would be getting home to Aunt Nelly's a lot later than we earlier anticipated. Maggie was looking at me as if I had two heads and she finally spoke 'Mary are you sure you know what you're doing, joining the army I mean?'I replied trying not to sound annoyed 'it doesn't look like I have a lot of options; it's either the army or the mental home. And the way things are going I won't get a job there either, the way I'm feeling at the moment I'll be ending up there as a patient!'
Maggie didn't respond and was quieter than I'd ever known her to be, all the way home on the bus and was even more dumbfounded when we turned a corner onto the street where Aunt Nelly lived laden down with the bags of groceries we'd bought earlier to see there was a police patrol car parked in the driveway of Aunt Nelly's house. My heart skipped a beat thinking something awful had happened. We dropped the bags

of groceries on the lawn and ran into the house to find Aunt Nelly in the kitchen talking to the police officer. 'Thank God she's alive,' I thought. 'What's happened Aunt Nelly? I asked concerned and wasn't at all prepared for Aunt Nelly's response. 'Where in God's name have you both been till this hour?' she said obviously very distressed. 'I thought something awful had happened, Maggie, have you been dragging your sister into Saloons again?'
Maggie looked at Aunt Nelly in disbelief, 'no Aunt Nelly I haven't' she said, mortified in front of the policeman, 'we told you we were going out to look for work, for heavens' sake Aunt Nelly it's only six o'clock!'

Chapter 18

On The Road Again

I don't know if it was the fact that Maggie realised at that moment, that even if we managed to secure work in Kings Park she wasn't going to have any freedom with Aunt Nelly or if it was the thoughts of calling Mam to tell her that I'd enlisted in the army and that I wouldn't be home for about two years, that made her reach the decision that Long Island New York was not the place for us. And two days later, once again we were on a bus heading for Providence, Rhode Island and my 'army' life was put on hold.

Maggie had called Lisa and explained that to say the least things were not at all going to plan. Lisa suggested that we return to Providence saying that if the newspapers were anything to go by, there was plenty of work to be had. She also added that some student friends of hers, who had left Providence for the summer, would be willing to sub-let their apartment to Maggie and I for the incredibly low price of fifty dollars. It was, she said, a three bedroom apartment with one other student called 'Oswald' who Lisa said was very rarely there. Maggie was really excited about having our own apartment and if she was in anyway worried about the fact, that after paying train fares, bus fares and rent, we were left with a measly fifty dollars, she didn't show it. All I could do was hope that her positive attitude paid off.

Lisa collected us from the bus station and drove us directly to our new home, a ground floor apartment which was one of two in what would have originally been a large family home. It was quite impressive from the outside, with steps leading to a covered porch and a front door which was flanked on either side by large bay windows. The inside was spacious with lots of natural light and high ceilings, but the apartment in general had seen better days, paint was peeling off the walls and ceilings. There was a family of cockroaches residing in the bathroom and each room was desperately in need of a thorough cleaning.

The furnishings were pretty sparse and well worn. There were no curtains or blinds to offer any privacy. There was a double mattress leaning haphazardly against the wall in one bedroom and what was the base of the bed in the other. I suggested to Maggie that we put the bed together and share as we had done in Kings Park. But Maggie thought this was ridiculous and said 'Mary, aren't we paying for two bedrooms, we might as well use them?' So I didn't argue. The sitting room was nice.
It had a large three seater sofa, an armchair, a coffee table whose top bore the stains of many tin cans and cigarette burns, and to our surprise sitting on the two large speakers in the corner was a record player. The kitchen was bright and sunny with primrose coloured kitchen presses, but it was difficult to ignore the charcoal like burnt-on grease on the stove top.
We hurriedly unpacked our clothes, then dressed the mattress and base in sheets loaned to us by Lisa. Thankfully with the temperature nearing the nineties there was no need for blankets. But we both agreed that once we managed to find work we would make buying sleeping bags a priority. Our next port of call was the supermarket which was a twenty minute walk away. We wanted to buy some cleaning products and much needed food, while desperately trying to make our last fifty dollars stretch as far as possible. Maggie placed a carton of cream in the shopping basket I was carrying. 'Put that back Maggie' I said knowing that the cream was sadly a luxury we couldn't afford. 'Mary' she said holding the cream as if her life depended on it 'we have a bottle of whiskey and if we have any visitors you can make Irish Coffees.' It was true, we did have a large bottle of Irish whiskey, it was a gift we had given to Aunt Nelly upon our arrival to Kings Park, not knowing she was a tee-totaller and despised drink. She had insisted we take it with us when we left. After much deliberation I agreed to pay for the cream on the condition that Maggie place two of her four cans of beer back on the supermarket shelf.
The remainder of the afternoon we spent scrubbing and polishing every inch of the apartment and we were both quite pleased with the results. It smelled fresh and even if it was quite

bare, it was, we agreed very presentable. It had been a long day and although we were tired from all the travelling and hot and sticky from the humidity and our hard work, we were happy and feeling optimistic. We each had a cold shower and changed into T-shirts and shorts, feeling fresh but relaxed we lounged on the sofa and sifted through the 'situations vacant' section of the newspaper we had bought earlier. There were many vacancies and I began to feel like our luck had finally changed. That feeling however didn't last very long, after ten minutes sitting on the sofa we both leapt to our feet at the same time, and I'm sure that if anyone was looking in the window, they would have sworn we were doing some kind of tribal dance. We were leaping around the room slapping our arms and legs. The sofa was infested with fleas!

I barely slept at all that night. I felt like my skin was crawling and kept jumping off my mattress on the floor to turn on the light and check the sheets and myself for fleas. Making my way bleary eyed the next morning, to the sun soaked kitchen I tried to keep as far away from the sofa as was possible. I realised there was absolutely nothing we could do about the fleas for the foreseeable future, the sofa wasn't ours to throw away and we didn't have enough money left to buy insecticide. Until we started to earn some money we would have to avoid the sofa like the plague and hope that the fleas didn't spread to the rest of the apartment.

Maggie woke just as I was filling bowls of Cheerios, 'morning Mary,' she said still looking behind her at the sofa as she entered the kitchen, afraid that the fleas might have seen her crossing the sitting room. In between spoonful's of cereal she kept scrutinising her arms and legs in case the fleas decided to launch another attack. 'Mary, we just have to find work today,' she said stating the obvious. 'So it's important Mary that we make an extra effort to look our best, you should wear your good shoes, they're certainly more presentable than flip-flop sandals. We need to make a good impression Mary, so make sure to put on some make-up and a little eye shadow.' I wasn't relishing the idea of wearing high heels on our search for work,

I could barely walk in them at the best of times, but I decided not to say anything, because if we failed to find work by the end of the day, I didn't want Maggie blaming it on my choice of shoes.

An hour later Maggie stepped out of her bedroom and anyone would be forgiven for thinking she was going to a wedding. She stood five foot eleven in her heels, she wore a blue floral dress, the same colour as her eyes and her make-up was applied to perfection, even the scarring on her shins from the blisters the week before were barely visible through the tan nylon stockings. 'Right Mary, ready to go?' she said 'first stop the Biltmore Hotel.' She picked up her handbag and handed me the newspaper which had all the vacancies outlined in red. 'Let's hit the road Mary,' she said enthusiastically and we set off at a brisk pace for the city.

Chapter 19

It's A Long, Long, Way From Clare To Here

Three hours later with ninety two degree rays of sunshine cutting into our skin like laser beams, the scene was altogether different. We looked like uneaten ice cream cones melting on the sidewalk. Our make-up had all but run off our faces and I was sure if my feet got any hotter they would explode into flames. The only respite we found from the heat was when we stepped inside a restaurant or hotel to ask for work and the air conditioning would cool us for a brief few minutes. Once again, as we had on Long Island, we faced one rejection after the next and to add insult to injury some people even laughed when we told them we had references. I knew Maggie was close to slapping the face of a manager in a Greek restaurant, when he practically threw her reference back in her face and sneering said 'who do you think you are kiddin', there are no hotels in Ireland, just houses with straw roofs and donkeys.'

I almost had to pull Maggie by the arm out of the restaurant, before she did or said something she'd regret. Outside we searched once again through the newspaper for any jobs we might have missed. Both of our hands black with ink. 'Here's one Mary' Maggie said, desperately trying to muster some cheer in her voice, knowing that I was near to breaking point. 'Full time counter assistant wanted for deli', she read aloud and before I could respond she stopped a woman in the street; 'Excuse me,' she said 'could you please tell me where Lincoln Avenue is?' 'It's about ten minutes that way on the other side of the highway,' the woman replied, pointing with her out stretched arm in the direction we were to take, then hurried on her way. By that stage we were moving at a snail's pace and every step was agonising in our high heels. We finally reached our destination which took twice the time the woman had anticipated and Maggie suggested that I go in alone. She hadn't quite recovered from the man's rebuke in the previous place. I struggled to fix a smile on my face as I opened the door and went inside, only to be told quite bluntly that the vacancy had been filled.

'Well, that's it Maggie' I said returning to sit beside her on a low wall. I thought of the full time job I'd left behind in Limerick. I thought of Cratloe Woods and the happy times I spent there with my dog 'Rogue' and I thought of the long walk we now had to face back to the apartment, which in flat shoes would take a half an hour.

I cringed and my stomach rumbled as I thought all we had to look forward to was left over pizza. 'Let's try that restaurant over there' Maggie said pointing to a building on the opposite side of the street. 'Maggie' I almost cried 'I can't get a job in a bloody sandwich bar, do you really think they are going to hire me in there, it looks really posh.' 'It's their loss Mary if they don't', Maggie said in a desperate attempt to boost my confidence. 'Come on,' she said 'it's worth a try, if they say no we'll call it a day and head back home.' 'To what Maggie,' I almost screamed 'cold pizza and fleas?' 'Oh don't remind me Mary,' Maggie said giving a little shudder as she crossed the road.

Chapter 20

Working 9-5

The building that housed the 'Little Sicily' restaurant consisted of two floors. The restaurant which was on the first had floor to ceiling windows over-looking the street. Underneath on the ground floor rear was a service door leading to the kitchens and to the fore was a drive through car port which delivered customers directly to the valet parkers' desk. At the main entrance, the glass double doored foyer had a wide carpeted stairs with mirrored walls leading to the dining area above. When we reached the top of the stairs we paused for a moment to check our appearance in the large gilt framed mirror. Taking a deep breath we stepped inside. Its decor was fresh and modern, but large tropical plants strategically placed around the room gave it a relaxed garden like feel. At the far end of the room we could see a small serving area with a large salad bar and to the right of this, tucked away neatly in a corner was a cocktail bar and seating area for customers to enjoy a drink while waiting on a table to dine. A tall slim young lady with long dark hair approached us with a smile 'hello' she said 'I'm Cindy, your hostess, would you like a table for two?'

'No', Maggie replied, probably wishing that she was there to dine because the smells that were wafting toward us were divine and my mouth was watering. 'We're looking for work' Maggie said then quickly added 'we have references to show we're experienced.' The lady who called herself Cindy was playing with one of several heavy gold chains that hung from her all to delicate neck, and after eyeing us up and down with a perplexed expression which showed she was bemused by our accents, she turned toward the bar and called out to a man she had been speaking to when we entered. 'Enzo' she said in a much louder and less sweet voice than she had greeted us with; 'These ladies don't want no food, they're lookin' for work.' The man got down from his barstool and began to approach us. He was a low-sized man about five foot four in height,

appeared to be in his early forties, he had dark hair which was beginning to turn grey at the edges and slightly receding on top. He was neatly dressed in a black suit with white shirt and a grey and white striped tie. 'Where you from girls?' he asked.
'We're from Ireland,' Maggie and I both answered together.
'Ah Ireland, I heard it's a really beautiful country' he said, and before we got a chance to agree he asked 'what kind of work are you looking for?'
I decided to let Maggie do the talking. 'Anything at all' she replied, bar work, waitressing, kitchen work.' 'Oh' he said impressed 'so you girls can cook?' 'No, we can't', Maggie replied 'but we can wash dishes!' There were a few sniggers from the far corner of the room where a group of waiters had stopped whatever they had been doing, also curious about the strange accents. 'I dunno girls,' Enzo replied, looking more at Maggie than at me. 'I have a bartender and enough waiters.' My heart began to sink again. 'The only job on offer at the moment is for a valet parker.' 'A what?' Maggie asked, never having heard the term before. 'You know' Enzo explained 'parking cars for all the customers.' I was waiting for Maggie to jump at the opportunity; this was our chance I thought and I didn't want to miss it. We had five dollars left to our name. I couldn't help myself and blurted 'Maggie is a great driver; she drives my mother's car all the time.' Enzo looked at me then put his hand into his pocket and produced a set of car keys which he dangled in front of Maggie 'I'll tell you what I'll do girls' he said 'see that car parked in the lot across the street' he pointed.
'Ah yes,' Maggie responded nervously 'the black Jaguar that looks all shiny and new?'
'That's the one' Enzo replied, proud to call the very expensive car his own. 'If you can drive that car to the other end of the lot and park it, you've got yourself a job, and I'll give you a job' he said looking at me 'clearing tables?'
I don't know if it was the fact that I was staring at Maggie, willing her to do it, or if it was the fact that the waiters were now taking bets on whether she'd crash the car or not, which

seemed to diminish any reluctance on her part and before Enzo had a chance to renege or listen to the advice the waiters were giving him, she reached out, grabbed the keys and said 'No prob' then disappeared out the door and down the stairs. I was almost afraid to look out the window to watch Maggie. But the waiters were watching every move she made and between them were relaying a running commentary to Enzo who had surprisingly returned to sit at the bar, seemingly quite unfazed by the risks involved.

I prayed as I watch Maggie start the car, then watched with my heart in my mouth as the car lurched forward. One of the waiters yelled to Enzo, 'Say goodbye to your car Enzo.'

Then another waiter said as he covered his eyes, 'she's gonna hit the dumpster, oh man, you must be crazy to let a 'broad' drive a beautiful car like that.'

On and on they went, but they were all wrong, I was so proud of Maggie when she reversed the car neatly into place.

She had a real spring in her step when she returned to the restaurant, despite the high heels, and was grinning from ear to ear when Enzo said, 'meet Cindy, first thing in the morning she'll take both of you to the tuxedo store to be fitted for your uniforms, you can both start work the following day.'

Our first day at work in Little Sicily was a Saturday and we were told by Cindy that we would receive our first pay check the following Friday, but our boss Enzo assured us there would be money made each day on tips, especially for Maggie working as a valet parker. Her wages would be two dollars an hour, the going rate. I, Enzo explained would be on a higher rate of pay at three dollars, fifty cents an hour and although I wouldn't be entitled to any tips from customers, the waiters were obliged to give me a percentage of theirs in return for me assisting them with their tables. They were to pay me my share at the end of each shift. We were to work split-shifts, eleven in the morning until three o'clock each afternoon to cover the lunch trade. Then return at five o'clock each evening until close, which they said was normally about midnight. The hours would be long we knew, but we didn't care, we would be earning money at last and no longer had to worry about becoming destitute.

Maggie complained about our uniforms and I had to admit they weren't very flattering. Made of brown polyester they clung to our bodies in the sweltering heat and Maggie was convinced they made her already ample breasts look even bigger. So each day she would apply a little more colour to her face in the hope it would draw attention of on-lookers away from her chest.

Every morning Maggie dreaded the walk to work, not the distance of over a mile, but each day meant having to pass the 'Providence Journal' newspaper building, at a time when all the employees, most of which were men, sat outside on benches enjoying their mid-morning coffee break. We would hurry past with our heads down trying to ignore the wolf-whistles and comments which varied from sexual innuendos to pleasantries like 'here come the Irish girls.' I could only assume at the time that it was my auburn hair and freckles that gave the game away.

Then there were the men who brazenly asked 'where are you girls workin?' We never responded to any of them, we just kept walking but by the third day Maggie had, had enough. Once again there was a chorus of 'where are you workin?' and Maggie replied in the haughtiest voice 'actually we are air hostesses' she said to my surprise, then stuck her nose in the air as she passed them. She gave a little laugh when she saw the expression of surprise on my face. 'Shut your mouth Mary before you catch a fly,' she said 'I was hardly going to tell them I park cars for a living.'

Chapter 21

If You Want My Body

It was also on our third day of work that Maggie introduced me to Kieran. Maggie had mentioned him a few times in the course of our days' work and had actually met him within a few hours of her first day. She said he would stop by several times a day to use the public phone in the foyer of the restaurant and each time he did, he would stop for a few minutes to talk to her at her desk, where she waited for customers to pull in. He introduced himself as Kieran Hennessy and told her his family were of Irish descent, something Maggie would have known immediately with a name like 'Hennessy.' He told her it was great to meet a real Irish girl who was, as he put it 'straight off the boat.'

At the end of our third night at work Maggie had finished before me and was sitting at the bar counting her tips. I went to the ladies to freshen up and stuff, two left over slices of garlic bread in my mouth. I was starving as I hadn't eaten all day. We were not entitled to any free meals when we worked and the food in the restaurant was way too expensive for our budget. Maggie had fared out better than me in that regard because each day one of the cooks in the restaurant called 'Angelina's', across the street would hand her out delicious plates of pasta, free of charge.

On my return from the ladies room, I couldn't help but notice a man who was speaking to our boss Enzo. He was tall, standing about six foot two, of medium to strong build. His brown hair was neatly cut and combed back off his forehead. He was immaculately dressed and it didn't take a genius to know that the clothes he wore were expensive. It seemed to me that he must be a close friend of our boss or at least a man that Enzo held in high esteem, because he seemed really pleased to see him and was telling him 'to order whatever he wanted, free of charge.' 'Your money is no good here' he kept saying. The other thing that struck me immediately was that all the time while Enzo was speaking to him, the man had his eyes fixed on Maggie, who was sitting facing the bar with her back turned to him.

I pulled up a stool beside Maggie and ordered a drink from Bobby the bartender, only to be told that our drinks had been paid for by Kieran Hennessy. 'Oh Maggie,' I asked 'is that the man you've been telling me about?' 'That's him,' Maggie said wearily, rolling her eyes up to heaven.

'Don't you like him Maggie?'

'It's not that I don't like him Mary, it's just that he never shuts up talking about Ireland and the Irish. In fact I wouldn't be surprised if he told me he had a shrine in his house devoted to Irish martyrs. When I'm sitting at the desk downstairs, I feel like I'm back at school in Mrs Collins history class. In the last three days he's told me about Kevin Barry, Padraig Pearse and Bobby Sands. He'll be telling me next Mary that he's going on hunger strike!'

'He's obviously not short of money Maggie, his clothes are very expensive with designer labels, has he told you what he does for a living.'

'Yeah Mary, he says he's in real estate, you know, buying and selling houses.'

'Oh right, I'll tell you something Maggie, he's besotted with you.'

'Do you think so Mary, what makes you say that?' Maggie asked as she gave him a quick glance over her shoulder.

'Maggie, he hasn't taken his eyes off you since he came in.'

'I don't care Mary, sure he's ancient, he must be nearly thirty.'

'So Maggie, your saying that if he was younger you'd fancy him?'

'Yeah, I suppose Mary, he is kind of good looking.'

'Yeah Maggie, and don't forget our dad was ten years older than Mam.

Maggie was just about to respond when I saw Kieran walking toward us. 'He's coming over,' I whispered.

'Hey Maggie' he said with a cheeky grin, 'you gonna introduce me to your kid sister?' 'Mary, this is Kieran' Maggie said 'Kieran

Hennessy.' 'Pleased to meet you Kieran' I said and reached out my hand to shake his 'and thanks Kieran for the drink, Maggie was telling me you're very proud of your Irish roots.' 'Sure am Mary and I can prove it, you wanna see?' Before I had a chance to respond Kieran had removed his jacket, loosened his shirt and showed us a small green shamrock which was tattooed on his shoulder with the words 'Proud to be Irish.'

'I was young and dumb when I got that on,' he said. 'Why' Maggie asked 'do you regret it Kieran?' 'Sure do Maggie.' 'Why Kieran, are you worried it will take from your good looks?' Maggie asked laughing.

'Na', Kieran replied smiling at Maggie's sense of humour 'it's just if I get arrested I can't lie about who I am.'

Kieran looked from Maggie to me and watched our shocked expressions, then he burst out laughing 'I had you girls that time, yeah I really had you going, fooled you Maggie, didn't I?' Maggie stepped off the barstool to reach for her handbag 'we better get going Mary, it's getting late' she said.

'I was about to call a drink for myself' Kieran said sounding disappointed to hear that we were leaving 'can't you have one more drink?' he asked Maggie. 'I don't think so' Maggie replied. 'It is late and we have a long walk ahead of us.' It was Kieran's turn to be shocked 'what do you mean, walk home? You girls can't walk home it's after midnight, are you crazy? Where you living?' 'We're living on the East Side Kieran, not that it's any of your business' Maggie said 'and we are quite capable of looking after ourselves, thank you very much, we're not stupid you know.' Kieran was grinning again 'Mary' he said almost as if Maggie wasn't there 'you're sister's got a real mouth on her, and for someone who's going to college, she's pretty dumb too.' Maggie was furious. She never took kindly to being told what to do and she certainly wasn't accustomed to being called 'dumb.' 'Who do you think you are? She snapped 'speaking to me like that.' 'I'm Kieran Hennessy' Kieran replied calmly 'and I'd like to see that you girls get home safe, so if you won't have another drink, let's go. I'll give you a ride home. That is on one condition.' 'What's that' Maggie asked and looked as if she wasn't too sure whether she wanted to hear his reply, but decided we'd better hear it before getting into his car. 'I'll give you and your sister a ride home' Kieran said 'as long as you promise Maggie, not to take advantage of me, keep your hands to yourself ok.' 'Kieran' Maggie replied 'I might be fed-up but I'm not hard-up.' Once again Kieran was roaring with laughter, he seemed to really enjoy Maggie's fast, witty sense of humour. There was a real 'Irishness' to Kieran's sense of humour, he enjoyed winding people up and I felt Maggie had really met her match.

Instead of returning to the apartment on our break between shifts, we spent our first few days familiarising ourselves with the area. Lincoln Avenue mainly consisted of small family run businesses and many restaurants which all served Italian food. The neighbourhood was also known as 'Colonial Hill' and almost everyone who lived there were Italians who had been born and raised there. Everybody seemed to know each other or were related in some way, which explained why people were so curious about Maggie and I. They would stare at us or huddle together whispering when we passed by. Maggie and I weren't particularly surprised by this, Colonial Hill was very much like a little village and certainly we knew that if somebody moved into Cratloe, it was the 'news' of the day, even the dog on the street would know about it. So, we paid little attention to the stares and just carried on about our business.

We treated ourselves to lunch in Angelina's restaurant. The food was delicious and very affordable. It was there I discovered eggplant ptarmigan, one of my favourite Italian dishes to this day. We also found the neighbourhood bar conveniently situated about one hundred feet away from Little Sicily and right next door to the convenience store on the corner. It was a small bar and not at all glamorous, but it had a great juke box. Each night when we finished work we would have one or two drinks there while listening to our favourite music, before making our way home.

We settled into our new routine very quickly and life was good. Our boss Enzo, seemed pleased with our performance at work. The waiters were friendly and courteous towards us, even if they were very chauvinistic and they were constantly competing against each other to see who would make the most tips. Maggie and I weren't exactly making a fortune, not even close to what Maggie had anticipated before leaving Ireland. But, we were making enough on tips to cover our day to day expenses and we were counting down the days to our first pay check.

Chapter 22

Endless Love

Kieran continued to use the coin phone in the foyer each day, and each time spent several minutes talking to Maggie and asking her a hundred and one questions about Ireland. So I wasn't a bit surprised when a few days later after I first met him Maggie announced that he asked her out on a date. 'Are you going to go Maggie?' 'I dunno Mary, what do you think?' 'It's not up to me Maggie, but I know he really likes you, do you like him?' Maggie didn't answer that question but instead said 'I suppose there's no harm in going on one date, I could suggest going to see a movie, you know keep it casual, that way if it doesn't work out it's no big deal.'

The following day Maggie agreed to go out with Kieran and stuck to her plan of 'keeping it casual.' She suggested they go to see the latest new release starring Brooke Shields called 'Endless Love!' Maggie bought a new red blouse for the occasion and although she was behaving as if she couldn't care less about the date, she didn't fool me. And I knew that she was secretly looking forward to it because by the time Kieran arrived to collect her, she had checked and rechecked her image in the bathroom mirror a dozen times.

I was in bed when Maggie came home that night. She knocked on my bedroom door 'are you awake Mary? Can I come in?' 'How did it go?' I asked dying to hear her response. 'Yeah, fine Mary, the movie was alright, we went for a meal afterward and he insisted on paying for everything.' 'And' I said in anticipation. 'He was really nice Mary, he kept asking me if I was ok.' 'So Maggie, why do you sound as if there's something wrong?' 'I just think it's a bit weird, that's all, I mean, I was getting a bit nervous when we pulled up outside, I really enjoyed the night, but I didn't know how he was expecting it to end and there was no way I was inviting him in after one date. He walked me to the door and I stopped, hoping he'd get the hint that I was going inside alone.' 'And what happened

Maggie? Will you hurry up and tell me?' 'Well' Maggie said beginning to blush and a little embarrassed 'I was waiting for this romantic kiss but instead he shook my hand and thanked me for a lovely evening! Don't you think that's weird Mary?'
'No I don't Maggie, he sounds like a real gentleman to me, even if he is a little old fashioned, wouldn't you have felt worse Maggie if he insisted on coming in or even mauled you on the front porch?'
'You're right Mary, I hadn't looked at it like that, I suppose I'm just really worried that he's regretting asking me out.'
'I very much doubt that Maggie' I said struggling to keep my eyes open 'now go to bed.'

Chapter 23

Money, Money, Money

The next day was Friday and we both woke with a 'spring' in our step, happy that our long awaited 'pay day' had arrived. We had made a list and had a plan as to how the money would best be spent. We weren't too knowledgeable about the American tax system but, Maggie was confident we should clear two hundred and fifty dollars between us. We had after all worked almost sixty hours. Sleeping bags, groceries, insecticide, the list was endless. Maggie also suggested having a phone installed. That way, we could phone Mam and she could phone us. I agreed that it was a good idea and Maggie said she would ask Enzo for a few hours off early the following week to make the necessary arrangements with the phone company. Finally, we agreed that we would treat ourselves to something to wear, to reward ourselves for all our hard work. It would be great to have something new to wear; it didn't have to be something expensive, just new. When we left Ireland, to travel light we only packed a very basic wardrobe, we were so tired of wearing the same clothes we had started swopping. I'd wear Maggie's and in turn she would wear mine just to look different. Yes, we had it all planned, when we finished our lunch shift we would go to the bank on Colonial Hill, where we'd opened accounts a few days before, cash our cheques and spend the afternoon shopping. 'Oh Mary, one more thing,' Maggie said as we arrived at Little Sicily to begin our shift. 'What's that Maggie?' I asked. 'I want to buy some house plants so the apartment will look nice when I invite Kieran over.

I left Maggie at her desk in the car port and went upstairs to begin my usual routine of polishing the glassware, rolling the silverware in linen napkins and setting tables. I wasn't quite sure what time we'd be given our pay checks and just hoped we would have them by the end of our lunch shift, either way I wasn't about to ask, I didn't want to appear desperate. Maggie didn't care and was probably at the end of the line when

God was handing out patience! The minute Enzo pulled into the carport in his car, she asked him for hers. 'Don't worry Maggie' he said reassuring her 'all the cheques are upstairs, ready to be handed out to everyone.' Maggie had become a little sceptical about Enzo, because most of the waiters had told her he was a real 'cheapskate' saying he would even yell at them over the intercom system to 'shut the door' if they left a refrigerator door open for longer than he deemed necessary, claiming they were wasting electricity, so she followed him up the stairs, knowing she wouldn't relax until she had the cheque in her hand.

But true to his word, he collected a neatly stacked bundle of envelopes from behind the bar, sifted through them and handed one to Maggie and one to me. 'Thank you girls for all the hard work,' he said giving us each a warm smile. Maggie thanked him and returned to her position by the front door. I shoved my cheque into my handbag and decided I'd open it after I'd finished stocking the salad bar.

Two minutes later Maggie was back in the restaurant and looked like she had just seen a ghost 'Mary look at this' she said waving her cheque in my face 'there must be some mistake' she said struggling to maintain a calm voice 'I only got paid one hundred and three dollars.' I took the cheque from Maggie and realised very quickly that Maggie had only looked at the amount in numbers, not only had she failed to look at this correctly but she had also omitted to read the printed figure. 'Maggie,' I said 'look again,' not really wanting to break the news to her, 'you only got ten dollars thirty cents.' 'What?' She said in utter disbelief, 'how much did you get Mary?' She said still staring at the figures in front of her. I pulled the envelope from my handbag, ripped it open and found a cheque for thirty dollars!

'There's no way he's getting away with this Mary' Maggie said shaking with temper. 'He must think he's dealing with 'Eejit's, but we're no 'Eejit's.' I was quite chuffed that Maggie no longer put me in the 'Eejit's category, but I only got to savour that feeling for a moment because Maggie had almost pranced to the bar area where Enzo was sitting. 'Excuse me Enzo', she said calmly 'may I ask you something?' 'Certainly Maggie,' he said in his usual charming manner, how can I help you?' 'Enzo, can you tell me how much it costs you to run your beautiful Jaguar on gas for a week?' Maggie asked equally as charming. Enzo, always willing to discuss his most prized possession replied 'I guess about thirty bucks a week Maggie, why do you ask?' He said smiling 'are you thinking of buying one?' I knew in looking at Maggie that she was near to slapping him in the face, but instead she replied, on the verge of hysteria. 'Why do I ask? Why do I ask?' She repeated. 'You're telling me Enzo, that you spend thirty dollars a week on gas and you expect me to live on ten dollars thirty cents?' She almost spat the words at him, but Enzo didn't seem at all upset.

'You must realise Maggie,' he said hardly batting an eyelid, 'that the uniform you're wearing has to be paid for; they cost over a hundred dollars.' With that he stepped off his stool and went down the stairs to the kitchen.

Bobby the barman, who could not help but overhear the entire conversation seemed genuinely sympathetic to our plight and couldn't understand why Enzo wouldn't make the same arrangements for us as he did with all the other staff, who paid five dollars a week toward their uniforms.

'I know why,' Maggie said still seething with temper, 'he knows he can get away with it, 'cause he knows that we really need the work!'

Maggie and I were disgusted with Enzo's attitude but we felt there was nothing we could do about it. He had us over a barrel and we knew it, without our jobs we had nothing. It was so disheartening to be treated so badly, we had worked a long hard week, almost twice the hours that were expected of the other staff and we had been looking forward to our shopping spree. So, after what seemed like the longest day at work we decided to drown our sorrows in the 'By Way' pub.

I was at the bar ordering drinks and Maggie was putting coins in the juke box when Kieran walked in with another man whom he introduced to us as his friend Rocco Delmonte. Kieran explained that he and Rocco shared an apartment together, which was just around the corner. 'You know Maggie,' Kieran said 'you and Mary should call around in between your shifts, you know ye could chill out, save yourselves the long walk, you know Rocco, these girls walk to work from the East Side at least twice every day, ain't that somethin' Rocco?' 'Yeah, that's a pretty long walk and the heat don't help,' Rocco replied. 'It sure is Rocco and they're working long hours too, you wouldn't catch any of the girls round here workin' like that, easily known they're Irish, Maggie you and your kid sister can call anytime, the back door is always open. If you wanna take a shower, watch TV, whatever, you're welcome, aren't they Rocco?' 'Yeah sure thing Kieran' Rocco replied getting up to call another drink. 'We might just take you up on that offer Kieran,' Maggie said 'it's really nice of you to offer.'

I watched as Rocco carried the drinks to the table and thought what an odd pair they made. Kieran was twenty eight, tall, well-built and his appearance was always neat. Rocco on the other hand was I would have guessed at least sixty, about five foot two in height and was dressed in a long baggy tee shirt and faded jeans. Kieran didn't smoke and Rocco seemed to light one cigarette after another. Their personalities were totally different also.

Kieran was warm and welcoming and he always seemed interested in what we had to say, Rocco was distant, not much of a conversationalist and my initial impression was that he was only being civil toward us for Kieran's sake.

'You putting some songs on the juke box Maggie?' Kieran asked fishing a handful of coins from his pocket. 'Put them on yourself Kieran, I'm not your maid' Maggie replied sarcastically. 'Your sister is in a bad mood Mary, what's up?' I didn't get a chance to reply 'cause once again Maggie snapped at Kieran 'you'd be in a bad mood too,' she said 'if you were working for nothin'.' 'What are you talking about Maggie?' Kieran asked surprised at her outburst. Maggie took a deep breath and another mouthful of beer and then proceeded to explain to Kieran about our paycheques. 'That's no good is it Rocco?' Kieran said after listening to everything she had to say. 'Na, that ain't right Kieran,' he said shakin' his head.

We left the 'By Way' pub after our second drink. Kieran drove us home and this time Maggie invited him in. I think she felt guilty for snapping at him. 'Mary will make us an Irish Coffee Kieran' she said volunteering my services. I didn't mind though, I felt it was the least I could do in return for the ride home. 'I wanna see you makin' those,' Kieran said following me into the kitchen. 'The whiskey is up there Kieran,' I said pointing to one of the wall cupboards. 'I'll get the cream.' 'Ah Jameson Irish Whiskey' he said 'I drank this before Mary, it's really good.' I explained to Kieran that we in Ireland pronounced it 'Jameson.' 'Oh, ok kid' he said repeating what I'd said. I opened the refrigerator to remove the cream and I knew that Kieran noticed that apart from the cream, an almost empty jar of grape jelly and a dribble of milk it was bare. He turned to Maggie who had just returned from removing her make-up in the bathroom. 'Maggie you got no food here, you girls watchin' your figures or somthin?' 'Yes I know that Kieran,' Maggie replied. 'We were supposed to go grocery shopping today.' 'You girls want some money for food?' Kieran asked reaching for his wallet.

'Kieran, don't think we don't appreciate the offer,' Maggie replied 'cause we do, but no thank you, we have enough to get groceries in the morning.' 'There's no problem Maggie' Kieran offered again 'you can pay me back when you have it.' 'Thanks again Kieran' Maggie said and I knew the discussion was over. I finished making the 'coffees' by slowly pouring the cream over the back of a spoon, as Kieran looked on in amazement. 'Hey, that's really something Mary,' he said watching the half inch of cream floating effortlessly on top of the coffee.

'I've seen them been made in the Irish pubs in South Boston Mary, but nothin' like this' he said holding up his glass. 'They used whipped cream kid, out of a tin.' Maggie and I laughed at the idea of an Irish Coffee looking like an ice-cream sundae. 'Yeah,' Maggie said after taking a sip from hers 'Mary makes the best.' I took to my bed half an hour later, leaving Kieran and Maggie sitting chatting to each other in the sitting room. I was weary from the disappointment we had faced at work, but managed to put it to the back of my mind and soon fell into a deep sleep.

Chapter 24

Suspicious Minds

I woke up the following morning to another glorious clear blue sky and I felt fresh having slept so well. Maggie however was looking the worse for wear, but despite this was in great spirits, and was humming Diana Ross and Lionel Ritchie's song 'Endless Love.' 'What are you so happy about Maggie?' I asked as I poured us each a glass of orange juice. 'You're grinning like a Cheshire cat.'

'Oh God, Mary I really enjoyed last night, it was almost dawn when Kieran left. We talked and talked about everything and anything. He told me all about his family; he has three brothers and one sister. His mother works in a bank but sadly his Dad who was a lawyer, passed away some years ago when Kieran was in his teens.' Oh God,' I said 'that must have been really tough.' 'Yeah Mary, he was quite emotional speaking about his father. He also said that being the eldest he felt somehow responsible, that it was up to him to watch out for his brothers and sister. Actually he told me a very funny story about his brother coming home from school one day, saying some older boys had slapped him around, Kieran said he went to the school the next day and lay in wait for the biggest of the boys, vowing to teach him a lesson.' 'What happened Maggie?' 'Kieran said his plan back-fired Mary, and the boys beat the crap out of him!' I laughed imagining Kieran telling the story. 'So is his family from Colonial Hill Maggie?' 'No Mary, he told me he moved to Colonial Hill when he was nineteen to be close to his Grandfather, who was living in a retirement home, you know that tall building Mary, at the end of the street?' 'Yes I know it Maggie' I said and thought Kieran obviously had a lot of responsibility at a very young age. 'Kieran seems to have a lot of good qualities Maggie. Spending time with their Grandfather would be the last thing most young guys would want.' 'Yeah I know Mary, I'm really beginning to like him a lot and I think he likes me too,' she said once again smiling from ear to ear. 'Not only did I get a kiss when he was leaving, he also told me that his boss wants to meet us, so he must have been saying nice things about us.' 'When are we to meet his boss Maggie?' I asked. 'Kieran said he'd collect us after work tonight Mary and we're to meet up with his boss in the 'By Way' for drinks.'

It was no news to me that Kieran was crazy about Maggie, but hearing that we were to meet his boss only confirmed it. 'You better bring your 'glad rags' with you to work so Maggie' I said 'if you want to make a good impression'.

That night, for once, I was finished before Maggie and was sitting at the bar waiting for the waiters to pay me my share of the tips. I watched as the last of the customers got up from their table to leave, knowing that once Maggie had delivered their car to them at the door, she would be finished too. Five minutes later she rushed through the restaurant past me, grabbing a bag from the cloakroom which contained her change of clothes. 'Just typical,' she complained 'the one night I wanted to be finished early.' She disappeared, not waiting for me to comment, into the ladies.

Kieran arrived a few minutes later as promised. Enzo, our boss was the first to see him. 'Kieran' he said holding his arms out to greet him, 'How are you doing my friend, so good to see you again so soon, what are you havin?' 'No thanks Enzo' I heard Kieran say 'I'm just here to collect Maggie and her kid sister Mary, how are they doing by the way?' 'Fine Kieran, just fine, always here on time, not afraid of the hours and all my customers seem to like them, Yep Kieran, those two Irish girls are workin' out real good.' 'I'm glad you feel that way Enzo, 'cause you know they seem like really good girls to me.' Kieran took a step closer to Enzo, as if to whisper in his ear. Just at the same time Bobby the barman turned off the music system which played background music for the diners. The place was silent apart from Kieran's barely audible voice 'just say it with money Enzo, you got it?' Enzo seemed almost to lose his balance as he took a step backward from Kieran. 'Su, sure thing Kieran' he stammered. 'Hey Mary' Kieran called to me, turning away from Enzo 'where's that sister of yours, she gonna be powdering her face all night?'

When we entered the 'By Way pub Rocco, Kieran's friend was sitting at the bar talking to Lynn the bar lady who seemed pleased to see us. 'Long day again girls?' she asked. 'Yeah Lynn, just finished thank God,' I replied. 'I guess you'll be havin your usual Mary' Lynn said reaching for some glasses. 'Yes please Lynn, a Scotch on the rocks with a splash of soda, a Bud for Maggie and whatever Kieran and Rocco are havin'. 'I got these, kid,' Rocco said as he watched me remove some dollars from my jeans.

'No Rocco,' I insisted you got the last round last night, it's my twist, here you go Lynn' I said handing her the money' and make sure you take one for yourself'. 'Thanks doll' Lynn said smiling. 'You go sit an' rest Mary,' Rocco said 'I'll bring the drinks over.' 'Hey Kieran,' Rocco shouted 'we got to bring these girls out more often.' 'Why's that Rocco?' Kieran asked. 'Cause Mary just paid for our drinks and I can't remember the last time a lady bought us a drink.' Kieran smiled and seemed pleased that Rocco was being a little friendlier and more jovial toward us than on our first meeting.

Maggie returned to join us at the table after playing our usual requests on the juke box and when the door opened a moment later Kim Karnes was belting out Kieran's choice 'She's got Betty Davis Eyes', a large man with a strong muscular build walked in. He was dressed in shirt and pants, the shirt which was open at the neck allowed him to show off his display of heavy gold chains. He also wore a heavy double breasted leather jacket which looked a little unusual considering the humidity driven warm evening temperatures. He glanced around the bar, nodded to Kieran then pushed open the door behind him to allow two more men to enter. The third man was similarly dressed to the first and had wavy black hair which was tamed with generous helpings of Brylcream. It was the second man however who caught my attention the most, although smaller in stature, about five foot nine or ten; he had an air of importance about him that even I couldn't fail to recognise. Approaching our table he removed a navy blue sports jacket and handed it to the first man who carefully folded it and placed it on the back of a near-by chair. Underneath was a crisply starched white shirt with a pale grey silk tie, his hair, which was black and neatly combed back off his face, had tiny slivers of silver going through it. He was, I thought, a man in his early forties. And one would be forgiven for thinking he was a banker or commercial businessman, who wouldn't have looked out of place in a luxury hotel or private club house. He smelled of two things, expensive cologne and money!

Both Kieran and Rocco stood up to greet him and solemnly shook hands. 'Gerard' Kieran said towering over the man 'these are the two Irish girls I've been telling you about. Maggie, Mary, this is my boss Gerard Molyneaux.' 'Pleased to meet you Gerard' we both said shook his hand.

'I've heard a lot about you girls' he said pulling up a chair to sit down. Rocco beckoned to Laurie behind the bar to fill a drink for Gerard and I gathered he wasn't a newcomer to the place because she seemed to know what his drink of choice was. The two men who had entered with Gerard Molyneaux did not join our company, but sat close to the door at another table.

Gerard Molyneaux seemed eager to talk to us and Maggie and I were relieved to find him so friendly. It was obvious that he was interested in knowing all about us, with the amount of questions he asked, but I couldn't help but notice how intense the expression in his eyes was as he stared into ours and calmly waited for answers to his every question. 'Are you tellin' me?' he asked 'that out of the whole of America you decided to look for work on Colonial Hill.' 'No, of course not,' Maggie laughed and began to tell him of our trials and tribulations, how we stayed with Aunt Nelly, but in failing to find work on Long Island, had come to Rhode Island. 'And you know nobody here?' Gerard said. 'Nope,' Maggie replied 'apart from Lisa, a student I met in Moscow. Lisa lives over on the East Side.' 'Oh so, you're telling me you've been to Russia too?' Gerard said a little sarcastically. 'Why' Maggie replied a little annoyed, knowing he didn't believe her 'do you want to see my passport?' she asked and immediately produced it from her handbag. 'Look' she said handing it to him. As Gerard Molyneaux flicked through the pages of Maggie's passport, I looked at Kieran who had been unusually quiet since his boss had begun speaking. But he was smiling now, knowing Maggie was telling the truth about her time in Russia because she had already told him about it. Gerard returned the passport to Maggie without commenting and called to Lynn behind the bar to fill another round of drinks. 'I dunno Rocco,' he said after a few minutes silence. 'What's that?' Rocco said as he handed Lynn a fifty dollar bill to pay for the drinks.

'I don't know what you find strange about it,' Maggie interrupted sounding totally exasperated 'maybe' she continued 'the Italians are afraid to cut the apron strings and leave their mothers but we're not, the Irish have been travelling all over the world in search of work for hundreds of years, it wasn't the Italians who built America you know it was 'the Irish!' I looked again at Kieran who was now grinning from ear to ear.

'What makes you think I'm Italian kid?' Gerard Molyneaux asked Maggie.

'Well, aren't you?' Maggie replied. 'I'm half Italian and half French, my mother was Italian, my father was French, Molyneaux, bet you can't spell it' he said all of a sudden turning his attention to me. 'Oh God help me' I thought, I had been quite happy to, as usual, allow Maggie to do the talking knowing that if anyone would make a good impression on Kieran's boss she would, and now I was going to ruin all her efforts by making a complete 'Eejit' of myself. I stopped for a moment to think and noticed that even Gerard's friends by the door were staring and waiting in anticipation for my response. His name was pronounced 'Molino', but I thought because he was so confident I'd get it wrong, it couldn't be that easy. There had to be a catch. At that moment I must have received some divine inspiration and for a split second I was back in my classroom at school, studying French, and 'o' in French was spelt 'eaux', It was worth a try, 'M.O.L.Y.N.' I began slowly, watching Gerard Molyneaux who was now staring at me in disbelief, 'E.A.U.X' I finished.

I don't think Gerard Molyneaux would have been as surprised if he was told he won the State Lottery, he jumped to his feet, grabbed me and began swinging me around the bar. 'I don't believe this,' he was yelling, 'Mary you are the first person I've met in my whole life that got it right, you've got to be a real smart kid.' I looked at Maggie who was equally surprised at me, 'how did you know that Mary?' she asked. 'Easy Maggie' I lied and breathed a sigh of relief. Gerard Molyneaux still had his arm around me when he said 'I dunno Kieran, you were right when you said they were too dumb to be undercover cops, but they're not that stupid and I like them, yeah I really like these Irish girls.'

Maggie was not about to let it go, that someone had suggested she was dumb but before she had a chance to open her mouth, Kieran said a hasty goodbye to his boss, spun her on her heels and ushered her out the door, ignoring her protests. 'Hope to see you again Mary,' Gerard said as I hurried after them.

Kieran held the car door open for Maggie and was ignoring her pleas for an explanation. 'Dumb!' she said 'who does that guy think he is anyway.' I climbed into the back seat and realising how tired I was I just wanted to go to bed. Maggie continued to give Kieran an earful as he drove the car toward the city centre. 'What exactly did you mean?' she asked 'when you told your boss we were dumb.'

'I didn't mean anything, how about we get some food?' he suggested, quite obviously trying to change the subject. 'You two must be starving after working all day, these guys serve the best steak sandwiches' he said pointing to a Mobile diner parked in the square. 'Haven Brothers Diner,' I read aloud. 'Yep' Kieran replied 'they've been here for years, I'll be back in five minutes' he said and left to order food. Maggie was sulking in the front seat, 'he has some nerve calling us dumb, what do you think Mary, aren't you annoyed?' 'I'm too tired to be annoyed Maggie,' I said 'and I'm so hungry I'd eat a scabby child!'

Kieran arrived back to the car a few minute later laden down with food. 'Wait, till you taste these girls, they're real good,' he said handing each of us a parcel. I couldn't wait until we got home to eat and I peeled back the foil wrapper and took a huge bite. 'Good, kid?' Kieran asked lookin' at me through the rear view mirror. I nodded, unable to answer him with my mouth full. 'You still didn't answer my question' Maggie said as she stirred her kidney beans around a Styrofoam cup, while making it quite clear that she wouldn't or couldn't be bought with a steak sandwich. 'All I said to Molyneaux was that you girls couldn't be cops,' Kieran said while trying to drive and eat at the same time. 'What made him think we're cops?' Maggie asked, surprised 'cause if you ask me, he's the one who's dumb if he thinks we'd be killin' ourselves working in Little Sicily if we were cops.' 'Maggie, can you forget about it, he just thought it was strange, that's all. You and Mary appearin' out of the blue and gettin' work in an Italian neighbourhood. Any Irish in this city are usually in the cops or the fire department, but I told Gerard there was no way you girls were cops 'cause you were too dumb, I didn't mean nothing by it, I meant you were too young.' 'I'll have you know Kieran, that I'm highly intelligent and don't ever try to suggest otherwise' Maggie said and took a bite of her sandwich, unable to resist the temptation any longer. 'Anyway Kieran' Maggie said before taking another mouthful 'what has Gerard Molyneaux got against policemen?' 'Ah, nothin' really Maggie,' Kieran replied as he parked the car outside our apartment. 'They don't see eye to eye, the cops are always giving him parking tickets.' 'Oh right' Maggie said, a bit calmer and happy that she'd managed to get an explanation. 'I'm going to bed' I said, opening the car door 'thanks for the food Kieran you were right, it's delicious.' 'You're welcome kid, see you tomorrow.' Maggie and Kieran were still talking in the car when I turned off the bedroom light.

Chapter 25

Halleluia, Halleluia

Maggie and I left for work the following morning after a breakfast of pancakes and maple syrup. I was full and felt good knowing that they would sustain me well into the day. Maggie was looking a little under the weather and her mood that morning confirmed it. She was cranky and complained bitterly about having so little money. 'I suppose Maggie, you can't blame Kieran or Gerard Molyneaux for thinking we were stupid,' I said as we briskly walked along the tree lined streets of the East Side. 'What are you talking about Mary?' 'Let's face it Maggie' I said half sorry that I'd mentioned it 'most people would say we were crazy if they knew we had come all the way to America on the chance of finding work, with no return ticket, if we didn't.' 'Yes, but we did find work Mary and with a bit of luck we won't have to walk home today after the lunch shift. I told Kieran we'd take him up on his offer and call around to his place for a while, my legs could really do with a break from all this walking.' 'Well you can imagine how mine feel so Maggie, at least you get to sit all day at the desk; you should be in my shoes.'

We arrived at work to find our boss Enzo waiting for us. 'Good morning girls' he said cheerily 'can I have a word with you both when you're ready?' 'Yeah, sure' Maggie replied 'are you going upstairs Enzo?' 'I sure am girls, another day another dollar, you know how it is?' 'We just have to punch our time cards and we'll be right up Enzo.' 'No problem, you girls take all the time you need.' We watched Enzo go in the front door of the restaurant and Maggie looked at me. 'What do you think he wants us for Mary?' She asked, and then answered herself 'he better not think I'm doing any more hours this week after what he did to us.' It was only then that I remembered the night before in the restaurant and the conversation I'd overhead between our boss and Kieran. I had completely forgotten about it and hadn't even mentioned it to Maggie. I suddenly had a sinking feeling in my stomach and was sure we were about to be fired. One look at Maggie and I knew she was thinking the same but was just putting on a brave face.

We reluctantly approached the bar to where Enzo was sitting in his usual place, watching the monitor of the close circuit television, which allowed him a full view of the kitchens below and all the staff. As we got closer, I was sure I was going to throw my pancake breakfast up on top of him.

'Girls' he said smiling 'I was looking at my accounts for the wages last week and I've realised that my book-keeper made a terrible error. I can't apologise enough and I want to put things right immediately. I'm even going to pay you girls what you're owed in cash, so you don't have to wait for the cheque to clear. 'Bobby, hand me those envelopes that are in the cash drawer please' Bobby the bartender handed Enzo the envelopes. 'Now Mary this is yours and this is yours Maggie, and I even put an extra twenty bucks in each so there's no hard feelings, ok girls?' 'That's fine, thank you very much Enzo' I said speaking for both of us 'cause Maggie was struck dumb. 'No, no, no, Enzo' said giving us a warm smile 'thank you, you girls are my best workers and anything I can do for you, all you got to do is ask, you hear me?' 'Oh we will Enzo' Maggie replied feeling a lot more confident than she'd been a few minutes before and was trying desperately to mask her surprise. 'Actually Enzo' she said 'there is one more thing.' 'Please Maggie' I thought 'don't start complaining, we haven't even opened the envelopes yet.' 'What's that Maggie?' Enzo asked with what looked like to me to be a very false smile. 'I was wondering if I could borrow your car tomorrow, just for an hour. You see, I've arranged to meet the man from the telephone company to connect our telephone and it would really save a lot of time and energy if I had a car.' 'You wanna borrow my Jaguar?' Enzo said as he swallowed hard and glanced out the window to where his 'pride and joy' was parked across the street. He hesitated for a moment and loosened his tie as if it would help him to breathe easier. 'No problem Maggie, sure you can, I just told you, anything at all.' I don't know what shocked me more, Maggie being brazen enough to ask for his car or our boss, agreeing to give it! Bobby the barman was obviously just as shocked 'cause his mouth dropped open so wide, he was in danger of catching flies!

Maggie and I almost ran to the ladies room after our boss went downstairs to yell at the kitchen porter. We tore open the envelopes to find a hundred and twenty dollars in Maggie's and a hundred and sixty in mine. 'Oh this is fantastic Mary' Maggie said staring at the notes in her hand, 'we'll be able to go shopping after lunch and buy everything we need, I take back everything I said about Enzo.' 'I actually think Maggie; it's Kieran we should be thanking.' 'Kieran Mary!' What on earth are you talking about? What's it got to do with him?' I explained to Maggie about the conversation I overheard the night before. 'Really Mary?' 'He actually said 'say it with money?' 'Oh yeah Maggie, I heard him as clear as day.'

'God that's strange Mary, what do you make of it? 'I don't know Maggie, Enzo always seems so pleased to see Kieran, I mean he practically kisses his arse.' 'Yeah, you're right Mary, I noticed that as well. Maybe Kieran is, you know, one of those silent partners; maybe he has shares in the restaurant.' 'Could be Maggie, even the way he insists on buying Kieran drinks, I've never seen him offer to do that for anyone else Maggie.' 'God no Mary' Maggie suddenly laughed 'he's as tight as a frogs arse!'

When our lunch shift ended we strolled around the corner to Kieran's and Rocco's building after stopping first at the convenience store on the corner to buy doughnuts. The building Kieran and Rocco lived in was the second house on the left hand side of a narrow street just off Lincoln Avenue. It was called Nimnuc St. Kieran's red Chrysler sedan was parked outside; you couldn't miss it because the registration plate had the initials K.H. stamped on it. The building was that of a typical tenement house built, I would have imagined around the turn of the century to house the working class people of the area. A simple rectangular design, it was featureless and not a building you would look twice at. Kieran had told us that his street Nimnuc was called after a tribe of Native American Indians.

Kieran answered the door to us with a big welcoming smile 'come on in' he said 'make yourselves at home girls, Rocco is in the kitchen, he's been cooking all morning, ain't that right Rocco?' He shouted over the sound of the television in the direction of a doorway at the far end of the living room. Rocco appeared in the doorway wearing an apron which almost touched his ankles due to his short stature, and he was sampling what appeared to be tomato sauce from a large wooden spoon. 'It's all good Kieran' he said licking his lips 'this is real good, you girls ever had homemade Italian Sausage?' 'No Rocco,' we answered 'but it smells delicious.' 'You gotta have some,' Kieran said. 'Rocco makes the best,' and then Kieran changed the subject. 'Hey Maggie, what do you think of me an' Rocco's bachelor pad?' That's my room there,' he said pointing at an open door off the living room. 'Yeah it's nice,' Maggie said, 'love the sofa, I always wanted one of those corner suites. You keep your bedroom really tidy Kieran,' I said noticing that everything in his room was in its rightful place. 'Sure do Mary, can't say the same for Rocco though, his bedroom is off the kitchen, but don't look in there, it's a mess.

Rocco's a real slob.' 'Yeah Kieran, you'll make someone a great wife someday,' Rocco joked from the kitchen.

I didn't usually feel comfortable visiting other people's homes. I was really shy and always worried that I'd break something or make a mess, but Kieran's warm welcome made me instantly feel at home. He couldn't do enough for us. 'You girls want somethin' to drink? There's juice 'n' coffee in the kitchen.' Rocco also made an effort 'the bathroom is out there if you wanna take a shower or somethin' he called from his place at the stove.' 'No, we're fine, honest Rocco,' Maggie replied. 'Maybe before we go back to work, God, it's great not havin' to walk home isn't it Mary?' 'I know,' I said sitting on the sofa rubbing my tired feet. 'Hey Mary,' Kieran said 'put your feet up on the sofa' and began moving the daily newspaper out of the way. 'I dunno, how in the hell you keep standin'.' 'What about me Kieran?' Maggie asked, noticing his lack of concern for her feet. 'Na, you're ok' he said winking at me 'you're sittin' on your ass all day!'

Maggie thought about sulking but decided she had to see the funny side and knew in her heart what Kieran said was the truth, her job was a doddle compared to mine.

'Mary and I are thinking about doing some shopping. Enzo, our boss had a change of heart and paid us each twenty dollars over and above what he owed us Kieran' Maggie said watching the expression on Kieran's face and curious to see if he would admit having some hand in Enzo's sudden 'about turn.' But he didn't. 'Hey, that's good news girls, did ya hear that Rocco? These ladies are loaded.' 'You should go to 'Ann and Hope' Rocco suggested; 'that's a pretty good store, they got everything there.' 'How far is that from here Rocco?' Maggie asked. 'Ah, I dunno, fifteen, twenty minutes I guess? 'Ok' Maggie said 'that's not so bad, we could get the bus there and at least we won't have to carry the groceries all the way home, we have enough money now to take a taxi.' 'Forget about it,' Kieran said 'you don't gotta take a bus, take my car.' 'What Kieran?' Your car! Maggie stammered 'are you serious?' 'Sure I am Maggie, just don't get lost, cause me 'n' Rocco gotta be somewhere in a couple of hours.' 'No of course we won't Kieran I promise we'll be back in an hour. How do we get there?' Maggie asked still amazed at Kieran's generosity. 'I'll write down the directions for you Maggie,' Kieran volunteered 'no point askin' Rocco, he gets lost drivin' around Colonial Hill!'

It was such a perfect day. Maggie did very well driving on the high way for the first time and when we walked in the door of Ann 'n' Hope Department Store we were spoilt for choice and felt like millionaires with our hard earned dollars. We bought ample supplies of much needed groceries; two sleeping bags which we decided were more practical than individual bed clothes. Maggie got her wish and bought two small houseplants. 'They'll look nice on the kitchen and sitting room window sill,' she said fingering the delicate foliage of the Boston ferns. We pushed our trolley to the clothing department where I bought a turquoise coloured strapless sundress which had a sixties style full skirt and a boned bodice, which I fell in love with the first moment I saw it.

Maggie bought jeans, underwear and two lipsticks because she couldn't decide which one she liked best. Last, but not least, was a large tin of insecticide for the sitting room sofa. Maggie had told me that on Kieran's first visit to the apartment, he couldn't understand why she wouldn't sit beside him on the sofa and he had obviously reached the conclusion that she was too shy. 'Come on over and sit beside me Maggie' he had coaxed 'I won't bite you.' 'No' Maggie had said, but the fleas will!' Kieran, much to our amusement, was still bearing the scars of the attack and scratching three days later!

We were delighted with our purchases and even managed to get back to Kieran and Rocco's fifteen minutes ahead of schedule. Kieran and Rocco were coming out of the back door when Maggie drove the car into the yard. Kieran was making long easy strides across the yard. Rocco with the shortest of legs was almost running to keep up. 'Look at that Rocco,' Kieran smiled 'back in one piece, and on time, we gotta go girls, the back door is open, help yourselves to some food, we'll catch you later.' Maggie handed Kieran the car keys and he gave her a kiss on the cheek. 'Don't work too hard,' he said out of the window as he reversed the car out of the yard.

Chapter 26

Rock With You

As each day passed, although we lived on the East Side of Providence we began to feel more and more at home on Colonial Hill. We got to know our way around and everywhere we went people recognised us. Whether we were strolling along Lincoln Avenue or buying something from one of the many small shops, people were much friendlier than when we first arrived. People waved to us and smiled and sometimes we would hear people say 'there's the Irish girls.' It gave our spirits a lift to be made feel so welcome. Kieran was becoming more and more a part of our lives every day. He was either at our apartment with Maggie or we were at his. We came and went as if it was our own. The back door as Kieran had promised was always unlocked and we would let ourselves in, regardless of whether Kieran or Rocco were there or not, but we never took the situation for granted and made sure each time we were there to clean up before we left. Maggie to my surprise despite her hatred of cleaning turned into quite a domestic 'goddess,' which I knew was done in the hope of impressing Kieran but she'd never admit that. Instead she would emphasise the fact that if it were not for the kindness of Kieran and Rocco, we would have to walk at least an extra two miles each day.

Kieran seemed happy to spend every spare minute he had with Maggie and at times I felt like I was in the way and thought that Kieran must surely want more time with her alone. But, if he ever did feel like that he never said anything and always made me feel welcome. He did however suggest that he and Maggie would have to find me a 'nice boy.' Something I hadn't even considered or had little interest in doing. But despite my protests they set me up on a 'blind' date with Brian, Kieran's youngest brother. Brian and I went out a couple of times but I think Brian was like me, only agreeing to it because he didn't want to offend Kieran, the brother he obviously idolised. So, after a few dates we went our separate ways but remained on good terms. Kieran was always suggesting new places for us to try and if he had gotten his way, we wouldn't have paid for anything. 'What kind of man let's a woman pay?' he would ask. But Maggie and I always insisted, if it was our turn to buy a round of drinks or a meal. Kieran always seemed surprised by this but I think he also respected us because of it. 'You girls don't have to pay,' he would say looking almost embarrassed if Maggie or I slipped the cash to the waiter or bar tender when he wasn't looking.

'We always pay our way Kieran, it's only fair,' Maggie would say a little annoyed 'we've been through this before, we're paying and that's that'. Kieran would eventually surrender, knowing this was one argument he wasn't going to win. 'Rocco bet you wish some of the women you met were like these girls,' Kieran said one evening after the usual dispute. 'Don't think I ever met any girls like these Kieran.' 'I know' Kieran laughed, 'if you got a dollar for every fur coat or car you bought for a woman, I guess you'd be a millionaire.' 'No kiddin' Kieran and every friggin one of them dumped me when they got what they wanted.' Fur coats and cars I thought, a woman in Ireland would think she met prince charming if her boyfriend remembered to get her a 'Valentine's Day' card. Maggie obviously read my mind. 'You know Rocco' she said, 'the women in Ireland would really love you.' 'You think so Maggie?' Rocco responded quite seriously, as if he was almost considering taking a trip. 'I hear' Kieran said changing the subject, 'the Jacksons' are in concert in The Civic Centre this weekend.' 'I know' Maggie said 'but I heard the tickets are completely sold out. They'd probably be very expensive anyway.' 'I dunno' Kieran said 'I could check it out, why? Do you girls like those guys?' 'Oh they're fantastic,' we both replied. 'Their music is great' Maggie said. 'I love the way they dance Kieran' I added. 'I'll see what I can do so,' Kieran said 'I know a guy who works there, and he owes me a favour, maybe he can rustle up a couple of tickets.' Maggie and I were really excited. 'Imagine' we said, 'being able to tell people at home we'd seen the 'Jackson Five.'

That Saturday we managed to get the night off from work with absolutely no objections from Enzo, our boss. Despite the fact that it was going to be a very busy night at the restaurant, with every table double booked. 'No problem girls,' Enzo had said to our surprise 'enjoy the concert.' Kieran insisted on driving us to the concert venue even though it was only a few minutes' walk from his apartment. 'Me an' Rocco will meet you in the By Way' when you're done ok Maggie' Kieran said parking the car outside the civic centre in a 'no parking zone.' 'Yeah, fine Kieran' Maggie said opening the car door. 'Don't you know about parkin here Kieran' Rocco said 'the place is you know, crawlin' with cops.' 'Yeah, yeah' Kieran replied 'I'll only be a minute 'what are they gonna do, gimme a parking ticket?' he smiled. Maggie and I were really excited and looking forward to the evening ahead.

We had never been to a concert before and we looked around in amazement at the thousands of people who were being ushered into line by security staff, waiting impatiently for their turn to go inside. 'Give me the tickets' Maggie said beckoning to Kieran. 'Right girls' Kieran said ignoring her request 'come with me.' 'See you later Rocco' we said turning to wave. 'Ok, see youse,' Rocco replied almost bluntly and sounding a little annoyed. It was difficult to say whether it was Kieran's illegal parking or the fact that we would be meeting up later that was the cause of his annoyance. But I was convinced it was the latter. At the very least, I believed Rocco was glad to see the back of us for a short while and have Kieran's company all to himself, that was, I thought, perfectly understandable. Rocco had been used to having Kieran around, twenty four seven, but this had all changed when Kieran met Maggie. Rocco was seeing less and less of Kieran, and Kieran unlike before, didn't always include Rocco in his plans. I had a sneaky suspicion that Rocco was not at all adapting well to the change. 'Don't we have to get in line Kieran?' Maggie asked as he walked us up the steps past the throngs of people, to the main entrance. 'No way' Kieran replied 'friends of mine don't stand in line. Wait here a minute, I gotta talk to this guy'. Kieran walked over to a man in uniform who was holding a walkie-talkie and looked like he might be the person in charge of security. Kieran spoke to the man briefly, who smiled back at him nodding in agreement with whatever he was saying. 'Right' Kieran said returning to the place where we were standing 'told you I'd sort it' he said sounding quite proud of himself. 'One more thing Maggie' he said 'you gotta take off that gold cross and chain, the ring too, you too Mary.' 'What Kieran?' Maggie shouted horrified, believing that Kieran had somehow secured a deal with the security man in exchange for our few precious pieces of jewellery. Holding on to the small Celtic cross that hung from her neck she screamed at him. 'What have you done? We're not giving you our jewellery.' 'Stop goofin' around Maggie' Kieran said impatiently, 'if you don't want to take off the jewellery you won't be getting in.' 'Well, if that's the case Kieran we don't want to go in' Maggie said almost on the verge of tears. 'It's not worth it if it means we have to sell our jewellery, my mother gave me this ring for my birthday, isn't that right Mary?' All of a sudden Kieran was looking more shocked than we were and now even more irate than Maggie. 'You've got to be friggin kiddin' me' he said and began to wave his hands in the air in a manner we had grown accustomed to seeing the Italians in the neighbourhood doing it if they were unhappy about something.

Kieran was looking toward the heavens as he spoke, is if hoping for some kind of divine inspiration. 'God' he asked 'what am I going to do with these girls?' He took a deep breath in an effort to calm himself, still holding one hand to his forehead and frowning as if suffering the symptoms of a massive headache; the other hand was still waving about wildly above his head. He finally calmed himself enough to speak. 'You girls think I've sold your jewellery, what kind of looser do you think I am?' Kieran looked from Maggie to me and the anger in his face which was so plain to see a few seconds before had now been replaced by a deep look of hurt in his eyes. 'I don't want your jewellery,' he continued 'nobody gets in there wearin' jewellery 'cause people have been mugged in those places before, while watching a concert. One woman even had her finger cut clean off for her ring!' 'Oh my God Kieran,' I said wincing at the thought of the woman's pain, but also cringing at the fact that we'd doubted Kieran.

We knew Kieran, although it felt much longer, a brief few weeks and in that time he had never given us any reason to doubt him. He owed us nothing, but was always kind and helpful. He was always respectful toward us and I knew by the way he looked at and listened to Maggie that he really loved her, even if she did drive him crazy at times with her brazen attitude. I got the impression Kieran wasn't used to being spoken to the way Maggie did and I could relate to the fact that she had that effect on him at times because I was often close to killing her myself!

Mam always said Maggie was as brazen as 'brass' and that she had been that way since she could walk and talk. She said she always knew that Maggie had great confidence in herself form the day she took Maggie to Mass for the first time in Limerick, shortly after her return from America. Struggling to carry me in her arms, hold Maggie by the hand and find an empty pew in the large over crowded church, she stopped in the aisle to genuflect before the altar just as the priest began Mass. She made the mistake of letting go Maggie's hand for a second and to her horror, Maggie ran up the aisle, on to the altar and turned to face the congregation. In a voice as loud as she could muster for a five year old she said 'hello! My name is Maggie Ryan and I'm form Kings Park, Long Island, New York!'

Standing outside the Civic Centre I was struggling to hide my sense of shame for not trusting Kieran and stared at the pavement beneath me. Maggie, not one to admit being wrong and slow to apologise decided that the best form of defence was attack. 'Well why didn't you say that in the first place Kieran, you feckin' 'Eejit'', she said giving him her jewellery and a peck on the cheek. I looked into Kieran's eyes as I handed him my birthstone ring and I think he sensed how bad I was feeling. Suddenly he was smiling 'ok girls' he said. 'Let's get you two inside', while signalling to Rocco in the car to give him two minutes. He walked us over to the man he had been speaking to a short time before. 'This is my girlfriend Maggie and her kid sister Mary, you make sure an' take care of them, you hear?' 'Will do Kieran' the man said 'you can trust me Kieran, I'll look after them, you betcha.' The man was looking at Kieran as if he was honoured to be put in a position of trust. 'Ok girls,' Kieran said 'you have a good time and I'll see youse later.' He turned toward the direction of the car only to see one of Providence's mounted police slapping a ticket on the windscreen. 'Friggin cops' he said 'you'd think they'd give a nice guy like me a break.' 'Well, what do you expect parking in a 'no parking area?' Maggie asked. 'Who do you think you are Kieran, Michael Jackson?' Kieran hadn't time to respond because Rocco was frantically waving at him with his short little arms from the car window to hurry on. As he stared up at the sixteen hand police horse who was looking in the open window at him!

The security man ushered us through the crowd at the door and occasionally moved people out of our way allowing a clear path. The stadium was massive but was filling up fast with excited fans. The man guided us to our seats which were only a few feet from the stage, allowing us a perfect view of everything. Before leaving us he said 'when the show starts ladies, I'll be standing right up there' and pointed to an exit door. 'If you need anything, just come get me.' 'Ok' we both said and thanked him. We sat down in our seats feeling quite special.

The Jacksons concert was spectacular and Maggie and I couldn't help but be in awe of their energy on stage. They sang and danced non-stop for two hours and we couldn't have enjoyed it more. We were looking forward to meeting up with Kieran to tell him all about it and I hoped that the earlier misunderstanding about the jewellery had been forgotten, but didn't know at that time, that the incident involving the jewellery was to be just the first misunderstanding of the day.

We were still singing to ourselves and moving to the music when we walked into the 'By Way.' Kieran, true to his word was sitting with Rocco waiting for us. 'You two obviously had a good time,' he said smiling at Maggie's dance moves. 'Oh yeah' Maggie replied 'we're still on a high, we had great craic, didn't we Mary?' 'Yes' I agreed 'great craic altogether Kieran.' Maggie had been making her way to the juke box to see if it had any of the Jacksons hits on it but was stopped dead in her tracks when Kieran leapt to his feet and lunged toward her roaring 'What do you friggin mean you had great crack?' 'What Kieran?' Maggie asked and was as shocked as I was. 'What's got you in such a bad mood? If you're still moaning about a parking ticket, don't think you can just take it out on us.' 'Bad mood Maggie!' Kieran said looking at her in disbelief 'you just told me you and your kid sister had great crack.' 'Well, if that's what's bugging you Kieran, you shouldn't have got us into the concert. What's wrong with you anyway? Can't you stand the fact that we had a good time without you?' Kieran turned to Rocco in such a rage I thought he would burst a blood vessel. Throwing his arms up in the air he said 'Rocco, I just don't friggin believe this.' He gave Maggie a look of disgust before turning and heading off in the direction of the toilet, but not before punching the wall with his fist first.

'If you think you can treat me like this Kieran Hennessy,' Maggie shouted after him 'you've got another thing comin', nobody treats me like that; what in the name of God is wrong with him?' She asked Rocco as I turned to the bar to call a drink and wondering if I should call a double for myself. 'He's just real pissed Maggie' Rocco said as calmly as if he were discussing the weather. 'Pissed' Maggie replied 'why?' How much has he had to drink, I've only ever seen him have two or three?' 'Na Maggie, he's pissed about the drugs, Kieran hates drugs, he even gets pissed at me for smokin' a joint.' 'What's drugs got to do with it Rocco?' Maggie asked even more confused. 'Are you stoned now Rocco?' 'You shouldn't have told him about doin' crack Maggie that was a real dumb move, that's serious shit!' All of a sudden the pieces of the puzzle began falling into place. 'Wait a minute' Maggie said and realising what had happened, began to laugh. 'Mary' she said hardly able to speak 'Kieran thinks we're on drugs!'

A few minutes later Kieran emerged from the toilets to find Maggie and I rocking back and forth in our seats, holding on to our sides with tears rolling down our faces, even Rocco was laughing.

Maggie couldn't even speak and looking at the sheer distain on Kieran's face made her even worse. 'Dunno what you're laughin' at Rocco,' Kieran said between gritted teeth, 'I thought these girls were good Irish Catholics, but you're so stoned all the time Rocco, for all I know you're probably takin' crack too. Maggie was complaining she was going to 'pee in her pants' she was laughing so much. 'Don't know what you find so funny Maggie,' Kieran said reaching for his jacket and obviously about to leave. 'You know what happens to crack heads?' He asked as a last ditch attempt to make her see sense. 'Kieran,' I said, 'Kieran listen to me.' 'An' you Mary' he said lookin' at me with pity, you're just a kid!' 'Kieran shut up and listen,' I said trying to keep a straight face. 'In Ireland when we say we had great craic, it means we had great fun.' It was Kieran's turn to be embarrassed but after the reality of the situation sank in, he too saw the funny side of it. 'An' by the way Rocco,' I said 'while we're on the subject of misunderstandings, when we say we're pissed it means we're drunk and when we're annoyed we're pissed off.' Kieran thought that was hilarious. 'Maggie,' he said by way of apology for his outburst, 'are you still pissed off with me?'

Chapter 27

These Shoes Were Made For Walking

The following night was an extremely busy one at the restaurant and I was literally run off my feet. Maggie was not supposed to leave her desk at the front door but every now and then she would come running up the front or the back stairs depending on which area of the restaurant our boss was in. Usually it was to ask me how much I expected to make in tips, or share some snippet of local gossip with me. This night however she arrived with a big smile on her face and a shoe box under each arm. 'Look what I just bought Mary' she said placing the boxes on the counter in the service area. She removed the lid of each box to reveal two very expensive looking pairs of shoes. 'Aren't they lovely Mary? I can't wait to show Kieran.' 'Where did you get those Maggie?' I asked 'they look really expensive.' 'See that elderly man sitting at the table by the window?' 'The one with the young girl who's pregnant?' I asked. 'Yeah that's him Mary, he's a shoe salesman, and he said he'd give them to me for cost price. I got both pairs for fifty dollars! Can you believe it? They must cost twice that much in a shop,' Maggie said rubbing the soft crocodile skin between her fingers. 'I've got to get back to work Maggie,' I said 'and you'd better get out of here before Enzo sees you.' 'Yeah, I'm going now Mary, I'll leave these here with you till I'm finished. What time do you think you'll be done Mary?' 'I'm hoping in an hour Maggie,' I said wearily 'my feet are killing me.'

Sadly, Maggie's excitement about her new shoes was to be short lived. Kieran arrived into the restaurant to meet us, just as my last table, the elderly man and young girl were getting up to leave. Maggie wearing one pair proudly showed them to Kieran 'I bought them from that nice old man over there,' she said pointing to the elderly man who was now helping the expectant mother on with her coat. 'Aren't they great Kieran?' The change of expression on Kieran's face could best have been described as a metamorphosis. He went from smiling to seething with temper in about ten seconds flat. 'How in the hell do you know him?' he asked Maggie in a voice that was more of a growl in the now almost silent room. 'I don't know him,' Maggie replied 'he just came up to me at the desk with his daughter and told me that he had some shoes for sale that he thought would look really good on me, and he gave them to me at a knock down price. Which I think was very nice of him, what's your problem anyway Kieran?' 'My problem, what's my problem?' Kieran was in danger of lapsing into the rage we'd witnessed the night before.

'That guy is scum Maggie, that's my problem. He's a fuckin pervert and that girl you think is his daughter, she's his girlfriend. Now do you get it?' It was the first time Kieran had used what we considered to be bad language in front of us, he usually stuck to the more acceptable swear word of 'friggin' rather that 'fuckin' and Maggie wasn't about to let it go. 'How was I supposed to know he's a 'weirdo' Kieran, I'm not psychic you know and by the way' she said 'don't you dare use that kind of language in front of me again! Now, I have to go and get his car from the lot, I'll be back in a minute.' 'You'd better change out of those shoes first Maggie' Kieran said. 'What Kieran? What do you mean?' 'Here' Kieran said 'handing her the box which contained the second pair of shoes 'give them back to him.' 'Don't you think you're over-reacting just a little bit Kieran?' Maggie asked almost pleading. 'No I don't Maggie, not for nothin', I don't want you havin' nothing to do with that scum, and tell him I said he's to give you back your money.' 'But Kieran' Maggie whined. 'But nothin', just do it. If you don't I will and so help me I'll give him a friggin slap, if you want shoes I'll buy them for you.'

That night after Maggie reluctantly returned the shoes; she returned to the restaurant but refused to have a drink there or anywhere else, so Kieran drove us home. Maggie didn't speak one word to him on the way and you could cut the atmosphere with a knife when Kieran pulled the car up outside the apartment. Maggie got out of the car, slammed the door behind her and never even said 'goodnight.' 'I guess that means no Irish coffee for me tonight Mary' Kieran said forcing a smile as he watched Maggie go up the front step and in the door. 'I'm only trying to look out for you and your sister Mary, that guy is bad news.' 'I know Kieran, I'm sure Maggie will have forgotten all about it in the morning,' I said, not all too convinced myself. 'We'll see you tomorrow Kieran, thanks for bringing us home.' 'Yeah, no problem Mary' he said. 'An' don't go forgettin' to lock that front door.' 'I won't Kieran, goodnight.' Kieran turned the car, waved, and sped off down the road.

'Is Kieran gone Mary?' 'Yeah he is Maggie; I told him we'd see him tomorrow.' 'I don't know if I want to see him tomorrow Mary' Maggie said in a voice that suggested she couldn't care less. 'Mary, I'm sick of him telling me what I can or can't do and I really loved those shoes, who does he think he is anyway?' 'I know you're annoyed Maggie; about the shoes I mean, but what if Kieran's right about that man? I mean you must have been as shocked as I was when Kieran said that the young girl was his girlfriend.

Maggie, she only looked about seventeen and he was sixty five if he was a day, it just gives me the creeps!' 'I know' Maggie admitted 'he's just a dirty old man' and then she laughed. 'If he was in Ireland he'd be happy to be able to drink a pint at this local and get on his knees to say the rosary, God Mary, Kieran has an awful temper hasn't he?' 'Yeah, he has Maggie; but not in a way that I'd be afraid of him. Why? Are you afraid of him Maggie?' 'No, not at all Mary, he's just a lot of hot air.' 'Well,' I said finishing the two day old doughnut I found in the refrigerator 'he wouldn't be Irish Maggie, if he didn't have a temper.' 'That's true Mary,' Maggie yawned getting up from the table 'I'm off to bed Mary, night.' 'Me to Maggie' I said yawning for the umpteenth time 'I'm so tired I could sleep standing.' Just as Maggie turned the handle on the bedroom door she turned 'did he say anything about me when I left Mary?' 'Yeah, he said he didn't think he'd be getting any Irish coffee tonight.' 'Huh' Maggie replied, 'Irish coffee, he's lucky he didn't' get a slap.' But she was smiling; Maggie loved Kieran's sense of humour.

The following morning Maggie woke in a very cranky mood and was still mourning the loss of her designer shoes. 'If he thinks I'm calling him today, he has another thing coming,' she said as she literally slapped the butter onto two muffins she had toasted. 'Yep, I'm going to let him stew for a while,' she continued before taking a bite. Maggie called Kieran every morning while I was having a shower, to discuss the day ahead and any plans they might have and also, I knew to reassure herself that he was home alone. I also was well aware of the fact that apart from calling Mam every other week to update her on any news and enquire about our brothers and Barbra, Kieran was the only reason Maggie had insisted on us getting a telephone. It wasn't as if we had an endless circle of friends, because apart from Lisa, Kieran, Rocco and Gerard, there was no one we knew well enough to call.

Chapter 28

HELLO

The first morning Maggie admitted to calling Kieran to check on him I was surprised. 'Why Maggie' I asked 'do you really feel like he needs checkin' up on?' 'It's not so much Kieran, Mary. It's that woman who lives next door to him that I don't trust.' 'Doris?' I asked. 'Yeah her, every time I pass by, no matter what time of day, she's perched on the front step of her house fixing her make-up. I've said 'hello' at least a dozen times and she never responds. But when Kieran appears she's all smiles and pleasantries. I'd bet any money she fancies him, what do you think Mary?'

I had to admit that Maggie had a point. Doris wasn't at all friendly like most of the other people we'd come to know in the neighbourhood. I had noticed how she and her family would stare rudely at us and even sneer when we passed by her house on our way to and from Kieran's. 'Even if she does fancy him Maggie,' I said after giving it some thought, 'it doesn't mean that he fancies her'. I hoped this would offer Maggie some form of consolation 'and' I continued 'he certainly wouldn't be spending all the time he does with you.' 'I dunno Mary', Maggie said in between sips of her tea and obviously still not convinced. 'She has a nice figure and Kieran says she's just divorced' Maggie replied. Believing she was making a mountain out of a molehill, 'what Kieran said was that she was divorced and struggling to rear a six year old girl on her own, almost as if he felt sorry for her.' 'What's he feelin' sorry for her for Mary? If she got her ass off the front step and found a job she wouldn't have to struggle.' 'Yes, you're right there Maggie, she seems more interested in looking good, than looking for work!' Doris' appearance was always immaculate when she sat outside catching the rays of sunshine that fell between the buildings on the narrow street. To look at, she was as we had come to know since starting work on Colonial Hill, very typical of how Italian women looked. She was slim in build, she had dark brown 'big' hair which was typical of the 'eighties', which she obviously teased and back-combed for even greater effect. I wasn't at all convinced though, that she was a follower of fashion or if it was a family tradition because her mother, who was in her sixties wore her hair in the same style, the only difference being she was 'Marilyn Monroe' blonde.

Doris always dressed in figure hugging clothes and anytime she waved at Kieran there wasn't a single chip to be seen on her all too brightly varnished nails.

'You know Mary,' Maggie said interrupting my thoughts as she stood up from the kitchen table 'I'm not going to give her another thought, I may be a little over-weight but I'm determined to lose that and to be quite honest I'd rather be over-weight than to have her nose!' Although I was surprised at Maggie's outburst of bitchiness, I had to smile and admit that no amount of make-up would disguise Doris's nose!

Maggie remained true to her word and never called Kieran that morning, nor did she make the customary visit to his apartment after our early shift ended. Instead she coaxed me into going shopping with her for shoes. We eventually found a pair that she liked despite the fact that they were nowhere near as expensive looking as the pair she had on her feet briefly the night before, she seemed to my relief, happy with her choice. I didn't need the added exercise after running around the restaurant all morning and my swollen feet were really beginning to suffer in the afternoon heat. After trying a half a dozen shops for the right pair, 'yes Mary' she said at last 'I'll get these, I really like them, I think I'll wear them to work tonight.' 'Just as well Maggie, you don't have to walk or stand too often at work,' I said. 'I know Mary, they are pretty high' she said looking admiringly at the four inch stiletto heel 'I'll be fine if I just take my time.' 'Ok Maggie, can we go home now, I can't wait to take a cold shower and if I don't rest my feet for a while I won't be able to walk tonight.'

Chapter 29

You're So Vain

Kieran showed up as usual that night, just a few minutes before the end of our shift. If he was annoyed at Maggie's lack of contact with him that day he never said and he was in a jovial mood and wearing a big smile. 'How do I look girls?' He said adjusting the collar of what appeared to be a new sports jacket. 'Where are you going?' Maggie asked ignoring his question. 'I thought I'd take you girls to a new joint down town, only open a few days, it's supposed to be real classy. It's called 'The Play Pen', Rocco is waitin' for us in the car, so you girl's better get a move on.' I knew Maggie was excited about trying someplace new, but she wasn't about to tell Kieran that, after all she was supposed to be still annoyed at him and his behaviour the night before. 'You could at least have given me a bit more notice Kieran,' she complained 'you're all dressed up in your Sunday best and I've just finished work. Look at the state of me?'

I couldn't help but smile at Maggie's over exaggerated view of her appearance, even though her make-up needed re-touching. With her big blue eyes, high cheek bones and full lips even without make-up, she would still look great. I, on the other hand was a completely different story all together. My short cropped wavy auburn hair, frizzy from the steam in the kitchen, was a disaster. There was neither shape nor meaning to it and any make-up I applied at the beginning of my shift had long since evaporated into thin air. I longed for a shower and was certain I was not night club material and would have been quite happy to go home to bed. But Kieran wasn't taking no for an answer 'come on girls! I just wanna check the place out, have one or two drinks and I'll have you home before you know it. I don't want you loosin' out on your beauty sleep Maggie.' That remark got Maggie's attention 'what exactly do you mean by that Kieran?' She snapped. 'Only kiddin', Maggie' Kieran said throwing his arms up in the air in surrender. Maggie glared at him 'are we going or not, if we are you better keep your smart remarks to yourself, you're no film star Kieran!' Kieran said no more but was smiling away to himself as we made our way to the car where Rocco was waiting.

He opened the passenger door for Maggie and just as she stepped into the car he said 'hey Maggie, are they new shoes you're wearin', they look real good.' Maggie didn't even respond, but she had a face on her that would stop a clock!

Kieran was right about 'The Play Pen.' Part of a newly built development near the river, there was a valet parker and two bouncers at the door. They greeted Kieran and held the door open for us to enter. The interior was dimly lit like most night clubs but it had a very modern finish. There was a bar which must have been thirty foot long with shiny chrome and leather bar stools. Around the dance floor there were red and black leather sofas and armchairs and no matter which direction you looked you could see yourself in the mirrored walls. The bar staff looked just as smart wearing white shirts, black waist coats and small red bow-ties. 'Not bad, eh Rocco' Kieran said. 'Yeah Kieran, nice joint, yeah I could get to like a place like this,' he said running his hand along the back of a sofa and noticing the quality. 'What do you think girls?' 'It's nice Kieran,' I replied politely, but truthfully it could have been the Ritz but I was too tired to appreciate it. 'How 'bout you Maggie, impressed?' Kieran asked. 'Yeah, it's ok, not as nice as the night clubs at home,' she lied 'and there's no jukebox!' Maggie was not going to give Kieran an inch!

Kieran went to the bar to order drinks and I followed him. 'What's up with you kid?' he asked 'you ok?' 'Yeah, I'm ok Kieran, I was just wondering if you could ask the barman if he has any milk, I'm really thirsty and I don't feel like drinking'. The truth was I knew if I drank, the Scotch would go straight to my head. I was really tired and I hadn't eaten since breakfast. 'Ok Mary, one large glass of milk coming up.' 'You got milk?' Kieran asked the barman who was placing the rest of the order on a small round tray. 'Ah, milk sir?' the barman asked, not sure if he had heard Kieran correctly. 'Yeah milk,' Kieran repeated 'for my friend here'. 'Certainly sir,' the barman said 'I'm sure we have some in the kitchen' and he scurried off to find it, returning a few minutes later with a tall ice cold glass full. 'What took so long?' Kieran asked the barman as he handed the milk to me 'did you have to milk the cow?' he laughed.

When we reached the table with the drinks, Maggie was sitting alone. 'Where'd Rocco go?' Kieran asked. 'Gone to the men's room' Maggie replied. 'Yeah, think I'd better go too before I sit down,' Kieran said and disappeared around the corner. Maggie and I just sat there taking in our surroundings. Rocco returned from the men's room but then decided he needed cigarettes and went off in search of a machine. 'What in the name of God is keeping Kieran so long,' Maggie complained 'he must have gotten lost?'

I was watching a group of people who had just walked in and were coming toward us. There were three of them. A very glamorous looking older lady who must have been in her late sixties, linking her arm was an equally glamorous younger lady about half her age and a man who I thought must be the younger woman's husband. Both ladies wore cocktail dresses and the man wore a navy blazer over white pants. He looked as if he had just stepped off a yacht. 'He's probably talking to someone Maggie,' I said as I watched the group place their drinks on the table next to ours. The man seated the ladies in a very gentlemanly fashion, holding each chair until they were seated comfortably. Then he turned toward our table, picked up one of the armchairs and walked back to his table with it. 'Excuse me,' Maggie said calling after him 'that seat is taken.' The man heard Maggie but chose to ignore her and sat down to join his female company. I thought how ignorant, 'you can dress them up, but you can't take them nowhere', a favourite saying of Mams came to mind.

Just then Kieran and Rocco returned together, Rocco unwrapping his box of cigarettes while Kieran was patting himself on the face and neck. 'This place is somthin' else' he said smelling his hands. They even have a vending machine in the men's room for aftershave.' 'What did you do Kieran?' Maggie asked 'use the whole bottle!' 'Why, do I smell good Maggie?' He asked. But before she could answer Kieran looked at me, I was trying to balance myself on the arm of Maggie's chair. 'Mary, what are you doin?' Where's your chair gone?' Maggie answered for me, 'that man over there came and took one of our chairs, didn't even ask, I tried to explain that the seat was taken but he didn't listen to me.' 'Did he now?' Kieran said frowning 'a real wise ass huh Rocco?' 'Looks like it to me Kieran' Rocco responded in his usual raspy voice. 'Well he's gonna listen to me,' Kieran said and went straight over to where the man was sitting. We could just about hear what Kieran was saying over the sound of the music playing in the background. 'Hey bud' he said as he towered over the group at the table and stared hard at the man who had obviously guessed what Kieran was about to say, but pretended not to hear. 'Hey bud,' Kieran repeated a little louder 'you deaf or somthin'?' You took my friends seat, ain't you got no manners?' The man looked up at Kieran, 'would you mind? We are trying to have a conversation, would you please go away?' 'You took my friend's seat and no, I won't go away until you move your sorry ass and give it back,' Kieran said.

Once again the man dismissed Kieran, this time with a wave of a hand as if to rid himself of a nuisance fly who was buzzing around. 'Go away,' he repeated.

Kieran's relative calmness was I could see, beginning to wear thin, so in an effort to diffuse the situation I walked over to Kieran, 'look Kieran, there's a free chair over there', I said pointing to the far side of the room. 'I can see it Mary, so why did that asshole take ours?' 'I'll go and get it Kieran,' I offered. 'Mary, you ain't getting nothin', go over to your sister.' 'If you know what's good for you,' he turned to the man 'you'll move your ass.' All three at the table were suddenly on their feet. 'How dare you threaten my son,' the older woman shouted, craning her neck backwards to look up at Kieran and at the same time prodding him in the chest with her forefinger. 'Sit down lady,' Kieran said 'before you get a heart attack or somethin'.' This started the younger woman screaming profanities at Kieran and the man lunged at him swinging his fist. Kieran saw the blow coming and swatted the man's fist out of his way. While at the same time with his right hand he slapped the man on the side of the head, turning him upside down on the floor. 'God' I thought 'I wouldn't like to get a dig from Kieran' if he can flatten someone with just a slap!

I watched as the two bouncers, who had saluted us on our way in, sprint the length of the bar with a third man closely on their heels and arrived at the table just in time to see the elderly lady pick up her drink and throw it in Kieran's face. 'Stop, stop' the man with the bouncers was shouting and I assumed he must have been the owner. 'Get them out of here,' he ordered the bouncers in a voice that was bordering on hysteria. The two women were now bombarding the bouncers with abuse while the man was trying to find his feet. 'What do you mean?' The younger woman screamed 'he hit my husband,' she said glaring at Kieran 'and you want us to leave?' The owner wasn't about to listen to anymore. 'Get out, get out of my club' he screeched 'get some towels for Mr Hennessy fast,' he called to the bartender. 'Mr Hennessy, I am so sorry. Oh my God, look at your clothes' he said grabbing the towel from the bartender and reaching upwards began to dry the drink from Kieran's face and hair. Rocco, who hadn't even moved from where he was sitting seemed totally un-fazed by the whole situation and just stared at the man who was now being linked by his mother and wife toward the door under the watchful eye of the bouncers.

'A bottle of champagne for Mr Hennessy's party' the owner once again called to the bartender as he continued to pat dry Kieran's clothes. Maggie who had a few minutes before being watching the scenario with disgust started to roar laughing

'You think this is funny Maggie?' Kieran said seriously as he examined his stained clothing. 'I do yeah,' she said laughing even harder 'that was an awful waste of money Kieran', she managed to say. 'Mary, what is she talking about?' Kieran asked annoyed that Maggie found the whole situation amusing.

'I think she means the aftershave Kieran,' I replied. 'Yeah,' Maggie said 'that was an awful waste of 'Brut!' The penny dropped and Kieran burst out laughing too. Soon all four of us were sitting down again and Maggie and I felt very 'posh' sipping champagne!

The next morning after breakfast of pancakes which were soaked in butter and maple syrup, I stood up from the table to have a shower and get myself prepared for another day of work. 'Mary' Maggie asked me as she ate her last mouthful 'do you think it's strange that people seem to go out of their way to please Kieran?' I mean, take the owner of the 'club' last night. He was in such a panic; I mean it was almost as if he was afraid.' 'He probably was Maggie, that is, afraid of losing a good customer like Kieran, he is only open a few days and he probably could use another twenty customers like Kieran. I've seen him buying rounds for people Maggie, he's certainly not afraid to spend his money and he's never short either.' Maggie was giving my explanation serious consideration, which went hand in hand with a second cup of tea and another cigarette. 'Maybe you're right Mary, it's just wherever we go people seem to know him and go out of their way to please him.' 'You did say that Kieran comes from a very respectable family Maggie.' 'Oh he does Mary, as I said his father was a lawyer and his mother used to work in a bank, I presume she's retired now.' 'His family are probably well known so Maggie,' I said thinking that in Ireland with credentials like that, you would be held in high esteem in any community. I began to wash the breakfast dishes and stared through the window at another beautiful clear blue sky. Maggie wasn't totally convinced. 'That's another thing Mary, I also think it's weird that Kieran never talks about work and he doesn't exactly kill himself either, he hardly ever works during the day and I've never heard of real estate agents working at night and that's the only time he's ever mentioned 'taking care of business!'

Even I had to admit that Kieran and Rocco seemed to work odd hours and Kieran spent most days working out at the Y.M.C.A. or in and out of a building just across the street

form Little Sicily which he explained was the neighbourhood men's club, where he would go 'shoot pool' or play cards. 'I don't know Maggie, who knows? Maybe his family are filthy rich and you've nabbed yourself a millionaire.
Maybe he doesn't need to kill himself working. Which reminds me Maggie, we're not in that category and if we don't get a move on, we're going to be late for work!

Chapter 30

Ebony And Ivory

As each day passed Maggie's feelings for Kieran grew steadily stronger. Any doubts she had initially, disappeared. So I wasn't at all surprised when one evening as we were about to finish work she asked if I would mind if she stayed over at Kieran's. She had been seeing him for almost two months and there wasn't a day that they didn't spend time together, and watching the way that they looked at each other I knew for quite some time that it was inevitable.

'Of course I don't mind Maggie.' 'Will you be ok on your own Mary? I mean, will you be nervous?' 'I'll be fine Maggie, Sure' who'd run away with me, I'll just get a taxi home after work', I reassured her. 'Ok, thanks Mary. Don't forget to lock up before you go to bed.'

Maggie arrived at work the following day in great spirits. 'Watch the smile on your face' I said joking 'you look like the cat that got the cream.' 'If you must know Mary, yes, we had a lovely time.' 'I guess playing those love songs over and over again paid off Maggie.' 'They sure did Mary.' Maggie had bought two 'singles' to listen to and anytime Kieran visited she would play them over and over. One was 'Slow Hand' by the Pointer Sisters and the second was 'Endless Love' a duet sung by Diana Ross and Lionel Ritchie.' To this day anytime I hear those songs on the radio, it brings me right back to Colonial Hill and I think of Kieran and Maggie and the good times we shared together all those years ago.

We met Kieran in the 'By Way' that night, but decided after a fast drink to get an early night. Kieran, as usual, drove us home but not before making what had become a customary stop at the Haven Brothers Diner for our usual midnight feast. When we got home I went straight to the kitchen to make tea, leaving Kieran and Maggie in the sitting room un-wrapping the food. 'This sure smells good,' I heard Kieran say 'come an' get it Mary, before it gets cold.' He didn't have to call me twice;

as usual I was weak with the hunger and couldn't wait to eat. I poured the boiling water into the teapot and carried it to the sitting room with three mugs, then sat sown to join them. I was really enjoying my steak sandwich, savouring every bite. 'Oh this is the life' I said aloud and took another bite just as the sitting room door opened and Oswald the tenant that we shared with, walked in on his way to his bedroom.
'Good night' he said shyly.' 'G'night Oswald,' Maggie muttered through a mouthful of steak. Kieran jumped to his feet, knocking his food, which had been resting on his lap, to the floor, just as Oswald closed his bedroom door behind him. 'Who the hell is that?' Kieran yelled. 'Oh, that's Oswald' Maggie and I answered nonchalantly. 'What the fuck is he doin' in your apartment?' Kieran said pacing the floor. 'Don't swear Kieran,' Maggie said in a reprimanding voice 'Oswald lives here. Kieran look at the mess you've made on the floor.' 'He friggin lives here?' Kieran yelled as if he hadn't heard right. 'Kieran will you keep your voice down or he'll hear you?' Maggie said. 'How do you know him?' Kieran shouted, right outside Oswald's door and looked as if at any moment he'd rip the door off its hinges and tear poor Oswald out of his bed and kill him. 'We don't know him at all Kieran.' I intervened believing that maybe he was a little jealous at the idea of Maggie sharing an apartment with another man and hoped by explaining to Kieran that we didn't even know the man that he would be reassured that he had nothing to worry about. 'He was already living here Kieran,' I continued 'when we moved in'. 'Jesus H. Christ, tell me these girls are kiddin' me' Kieran said looking up to heaven and hoping for divine intervention of some kind. But when he got no response from the powers that be, he looked at Maggie, who was peeling the steak sandwich off the floor and 'tut tutting' under her breath. Then he looked at me, but I thought I'd explained the situation so I said nothing, so then he looked at Maggie again 'you've got to be kiddin' me. You mean to tell me that you two are livin' with a 'nigger' you don't even know!' I thought Kieran was about to explode. 'There is no need to call him names like

that,' Maggie said 'it's not very nice.' 'Oh, so you're talkin' about being nice Maggie?' Kieran said in a sarcastic tone. 'Not for nothin' Maggie, it wasn't very nice of you, leavin' your kid sister here alone last night with a complete stranger who just happens to be black and for all you two dummies know, could be a serial fuckin killer!' Kieran was frantic and Maggie's temper was beginning to rise so at one more attempt to diffuse the situation I said 'Kieran, will you calm down. Maggie is right, there's no need to call him names. He seems like a nice guy and anyway he's hardly ever here.' 'Mary I'm not sayin' he's not a nice guy, maybe he's ok, but you two dummies didn't know that when you moved in.' Kieran wasn't getting any bit calmer. 'I've gotta get outta here,' he said once again waving his arms about haplessly, 'enough already, I gotta go' Kieran slammed the door behind him and was gone. All we could hear was the screeching of his car wheels as he drove away.

I listened to Maggie's rants about Kieran well into the early hours of the morning. How she wasn't going to tolerate him telling her who she could or could not speak to and if the walls could talk they would say she was deadly serious. But I knew having witnessed many a battle between them that after each 'new storm' would come the calm and before long Kieran and Maggie would be back together like peanut butter on bread. And if anything, with each dispute they seemed to fall deeper in love, while I was falling also, that is, falling down from the lack of sleep!

True to form Kieran didn't stay angry with us for long and I woke the next morning after what felt like a few minutes sleep to hear him persistently tapping on Maggie's bedroom window with his car key and hearing Maggie unimpressed at being woken so early on a rare morning off from work, telling him to 'get lost.' I got out of the bed to let him in the door, knowing that he was most definitely wasting his time with Maggie. 'Your sister always this pleasant in the morning Mary?' he asked with a big grin, while producing a box of doughnuts from behind his back and handing them to me. 'You better take these Mary, I don't want to end up wearing them' he laughed and turned in the direction of Maggie's room. 'Rather you than me' I thought as I heard him knock on the bedroom door. 'Rise and shine, the day is fine,' I heard him say as I closed the bathroom door behind me.

When I entered the kitchen a short while later having taken a shower, Maggie was slumped at the kitchen table holding a cup of tea in one hand and a cigarette in the other. I didn't comment on the fact that she had chosen to make tea for herself and none for me. 'Some things were better left unsaid' I told myself, especially when dealing with Maggie first thing in the morning. But Kieran was not in the least bit deterred by the scowl on Maggie's face, if anything it amused him and only fuelled his desire to wind her up!

'God I feel good' he said flexing his arms to display his more than ample sized biceps, then smoothing back his still wet hair with his hands, 'ten laps of the 'Y' pool this morning Maggie, yes I feel real good, you'd wanna think about quitting' those cigarettes Maggie, if you wanna look as good as me.' I had to admire Kieran's bravery, anyone who knew Maggie, knew to give her a wide berth for at least a half an hour after she woke up; even Rogue the dog knew that!

'Don't you think I look good Maggie?' he persisted, lifting the end of his sleeveless vest to display his flat stomach.

Maggie stubbed the cigarette into the ashtray with slow and deliberate moves, then raising her head to look at Kieran through coal black eyes, remnants of the previous days mascara she said 'you are the nearest thing to perfection I have ever seen. Yes Kieran, you are indeed a real vision of loveliness!'

Kieran's knees buckled at Maggie's sarcasm and he almost fell on top of the kitchen table he was laughing so much. Even I couldn't help myself and before long Maggie was smiling and ready to face the day. After gaining enough composure to speak Kieran said 'hey Maggie, get dressed, after we give Mary a ride to work there's someplace I wanna show you.' Maggie protested having planned a lazy day at home. 'Kieran, I've got loads to do' she said 'I've got to iron my clothes.' Kieran wasn't taking no for an answer. 'Maggie, you can iron your clothes later, don't bust my balls now, I wanna show you somethin'. Maggie, curious to know what the big surprise was finally relented and an hour later I got out of the car at Little Sicily to begin another split shift. 'See you later Mary,' Maggie said smiling 'have fun.' I watched as Kieran turned the car, waved good bye and sped away.

It was at quarter to three that afternoon when Rudi, the head chef called me down to the kitchen saying he needed my help. I knew it was quarter to three because for the previous hour I had been counting down the minutes to the end of my first shift and looking forward to my three glorious hours off. I was feeling more tired than usual due to lack of sleep and couldn't wait to be finished. Rudi knew I worked split shifts because, out of all the staff I was only one who did. So I was surprised on entering the kitchen when he shoved a big bowl of freshly made garlic butter across the counter followed by a large box of freshly baked bread rolls. 'Here, can you butter those?' He said in a tone that suggested it was more of an order than a request. I know it would take almost an hour to do the bread, so I gave him the benefit of the doubt and assumed he had forgotten about my split shifts. 'But I'm supposed to be off now Rudi, 'cause I'm back on at six.' 'And,' he snarled 'what's that got to do with me. Do you need the work or don't you?' I picked up the knife and began to butter the rolls, knowing well that I wasn't going to win this argument. Rudi was a small little weasel of a man who often seemed to call the shots in the restaurant.

I had often heard him shouting at Enzo my boss, and according to the waiters and bar staff, should, they said, be avoided at all costs, as he seemed to take great pleasure from insulting and humiliating the staff at any given opportunity.

I was about a half an hour into my task when Maggie came bursting into the kitchen in great spirits. 'Why are you still here,' she asked 'are you up for promotion Mary? You must be, working this late.' Maggie didn't wait for my response, 'great news Mary, Kieran has another apartment about fifteen minutes from here in a place called 'Cranston' and guess what

Mary? He wants us to move in! Oh wait till you see it Mary, you'll love it. It's only got one bedroom but that doesn't matter, the sofa looks really comfortable and the nights I'm staying with Kieran you'll be able to sleep in the bed, and oh yeah, his brother lives downstairs so Kieran says he'd feel a whole lot better knowing you're safe. He told me he wouldn't take any rent, but I told him we wouldn't be moving in unless we were to pay our way.' Maggie was so excited she was almost out of breath. Not just about the apartment but she said it was surely a sign that he was serious about their relationship. 'What do you think Mary?' She asked as if I didn't know the decision had already been made. Once again I didn't get a chance to respond but this time it was not Maggie who interrupted me, but Rudi, who unknown to Maggie was listening to everything she said from the far side of the kitchen where he stood cooking at the stove. 'You're hardly serious about Kieran Hennessy,' he said with a sneer. Maggie had to take a few steps closer to me and peer through a steel shelf with pots piled high to see where the voice was coming from. 'What do you mean by that Rudi?' She asked surprised. Rudi left his position at the stove and strutted across the kitchen until he was within a few feet of Maggie. 'You think he gives a shit about you, you're just his latest piece of fun, and if you can believe what he's telling the whole neighbourhood about you, then he's definitely havin' fun!'

I couldn't but see pure evil in Rudi's eyes as he watched the tears roll down Maggie's face. I was fuming and felt like pulling his chef's hat over his eyes and shoving his head in the pot of tomato and basil sauce that was sitting on a hot plate beside me. But I knew I couldn't, I'd get fired, so instead I stuck a knife in the bread with such force, Rudi, took a few steps back. 'Don't listen to him Maggie,' I said taking her by the arm and out the kitchen door away from any further remarks. 'And you,' I turned to Rudi before slamming the door 'you can shove that butter up in your arse for all I care, butter the bread yourself, you little shit.'

Maggie wasn't a person who was easily upset, even when all hell broke out at home she refused to let it distract her from her studies and when it came to boyfriends, although she had no shortage of admirers, very few qualified in Maggie's eyes as 'worth the effort.' If she did date anyone, and for whatever reason, it didn't work out she would just shrug her shoulders and say 'oh well, it's his loss.' She never let any man get her down. Seeing her that day standing outside the restaurant, lip trembling and failing to hold back the tears, confirmed to me how much she had fallen for Kieran.

'I can't believe Kieran has been speaking about me like that,' she spluttered, while blowing her nose in a serviette I'd grabbed form the kitchen. 'Maggie, listen, don't let Rudi upset you like that. I bet you Kieran never said any such thing. Why would he practically ask you to move in with him if he wasn't serious?' 'I don't know Mary' she bawled 'why would Rudi say it if it wasn't true?' 'Ah probably because he's a vindictive little shit who hates women. Let's face it Maggie, we have yet to meet someone who has a good word to say about him. So come on, dry your eyes and don't give it another thought. I know, let's treat ourselves to some lunch in Angelina's and we can have a drink in the 'By Way' before we go back to work.' 'I'm not hungry Mary,' Maggie snapped, her tears finally stopped and the only thing welling up in her now was her temper. 'I'm going 'round to see Kieran and tell him he can keep his bloody apartment Mary.' 'Maggie, will you calm down, Kieran is nuts about you.' 'What makes you so sure Mary? We only know him a few months and I'm not even sure he is an estate agent!' I had to agree with Maggie in relation to Kieran's work. He never kept to a routine as most people who worked in mundane nine to five jobs did. And he certainly rarely seemed pressed for time because most days I could see him from the restaurant window talking at his leisure for lengthy periods to the older men in the neighbourhood. Maybe the property market and his real estate business was going through a rough patch I thought, but once again I found myself questioning that explanation, because Kieran, although he led relatively simple lifestyle, his clothes always bore expensive designer labels and he loved the great food that was served in the up market restaurants that were in abundance in Lincoln Avenue, and money was, it seemed, never in short supply.

'Look Maggie,' I said 'all I know is that Kieran is mad about you.' 'How do you know that Mary? You'd swear the way you're talkin' you were an expert on relationships.' I knew Maggie was referring to the lack of boyfriends in my life, but chose to ignore her 'bitchiness' because I knew I was simply suffering the brunt of Rudi's ignorance.

'Maggie, I know I'm no expert' I said 'but I do have a pair of eyes and I see how Kieran looks at you. For God's sake Maggie, his face lights up when he sees you. Can't you see that? And God knows he spends every spare minute he has with you.' 'Yeah, you could be right Mary' Maggie said at last. As I watched her apply a light coat of pink lipstick to her lips and brushed a faint shadow of blusher in a sweeping motion across her cheek bones. Looking in the small compact mirror and then at me she asked, taking a deep breath 'do I look alright?' 'You look as fresh as a daisy Maggie, now come on we'll have a drink' I said, relieved that her mood at last sounded more upbeat. 'I'll meet you in the By Way in a few minutes' she said snapping her handbag closed. 'Where are you going now Maggie?' I asked even though I was sure I already knew the answer. 'Kieran's place' she called back to me over her shoulder, before turning the corner and disappearing out of sight. Maggie, I knew was going to demand an explanation from Kieran at the very least in regards to Rudi's comments. She found it very difficult to trust men and I couldn't blame her. After years spent watching Paddy, her only father figure, tell countless lies to Mam, she had every reason to be the way she was. I was relieved though to be going to the By Way pub rather than going to Kieran's place with Maggie because I suspected that if their previous altercations were anything to go by, Maggie and Kieran were about to have the mother of all arguments and I, for once, would not be caught in the middle.

When I stepped into the By Way my eyes took a moment to adjust to the dimly lit bar but for my skin, it was a welcome respite from the blazing heat of the sun outside. The bar was empty except for two young men playing a gaming machine in the corner, and Lynn, who was behind the bar and helping herself to a large slice of pizza. 'Hey Mary, howya doin' she smiled.

'You hungry Mary? Here, have some. You boys want some pizza?' 'No thanks Lynn' they replied still engrossed in the gaming machine screen in front of them. 'Mary, you gonna have a drink?' Lynn asked as she pushed the large pizza box toward me. 'Help yourself Mary.' 'Thanks Lynn, I'm starving actually, and it smells delicious and can I just have a large glass of orange juice Lynn?'

'Sure kid, no Scotch today?' she asked as she scooped lumps of ice into a tall glass. 'Maybe later Lynn, I'm back to work in an hour.' 'Where's that sister of yours today Mary?' 'Oh she'll be here shortly Lynn' I said trying to speak with my mouth full, she's called round to Kieran's for a while.' 'No kiddin Mary, those two are getting pretty serious. Kieran really likes your sister.' 'What makes you say that Lynn?' I asked curiously, but relieved to know that I wasn't alone in my understanding of Kieran. 'Aw, get outta here Mary, a blind man could see it, any night he's here with Rocco all he does is talk about her. It's Maggie this and Maggie that, he's watchin' the clock there on the wall like he's countin' the minutes till she's done workin'. Sometimes I think Rocco gets pissed with him though.' 'What do you mean Lynn?' I asked. 'You know Mary, with Kieran spendin' so much time with you girls. Rocco was used to havin' Kieran all to himself, an' not for nothin' Mary, my bet is, Rocco will have to get used to your sister bein' round.' I had liked Lynn since we first met. She was a straight talker, no beating around the bush, she called a spade, a spade and I suspected with her strong build that she'd take no prisoners in a bar room brawl.

I was about to ask her another question when the door swung open and Maggie walked in. She removed her sunglasses and placed them on the bar. 'Are you ok?' I asked noticing the pensive frown on her face. 'Yeah fine' she said bluntly, in a voice that suggested she was anything but fine. 'Can I get a light beer Lynn?' she asked. 'Sure thing honey, comin' right up,' Lynn replied and like all good bartenders, sensing a little tension in the air, she placed the drink in front of Maggie, then removed herself to the other end of the bar, giving Maggie and I a chance to talk.

Maggie took several mouthfuls of beer from her glass and just sat staring at her reflection in a large gilt framed mirror which hung behind the bar. Stained with years of smoke, it had definitely seen better days.

'Are you going to tell me what happened,' I asked impatiently aware that time was against us and we wouldn't have very much opportunity to talk at work.

'I just don't know what to think,' she said finally. 'Did you tell him what Rudi said Maggie?' 'Of course I did Mary.' 'And' I said, thinking it would be much easier to get blood out of a stone than getting answers from Maggie 'what did he say then.' 'He didn't even bat an eyelid Mary and just said that I couldn't know him very well if I thought he would say things like that about me.' 'You see Maggie, I told you that.'

'But Mary, he could see how upset I was and he was as cool as a breeze. In fact he seemed more concerned that he was going to be late for an appointment with Gerard Molyneaux across town. Then he tells me as he's rushing to the car that he won't be back until tomorrow. But, that he would be around to move all our stuff to his apartment.' 'And' I said once again, sensing some apprehension. 'Mary, I just won't be taken for granted and he's assuming that we are moving in.' 'Maggie' I said 'I don't think we are in a position to play hard ball, you know. I mean we have to be out of our place in a week anyway.' 'Yes Mary, I'm well aware of that' Maggie said. 'We'd better get going Mary it's almost six.' We said our goodbyes to Lynn and strolled the hundred yards to the restaurant just in time to see Rudi drive away in his black corvette sports car. 'That guy' Maggie said 'is so full of himself, he thinks he shits ice cream!'

'Kieran blew the horn in his car outside the apartment the following morning to signal his arrival. 'You girls ready to roll.' I heard him ask Maggie when she opened the door to greet him. 'Yeah we'll be right out Kieran' she replied. 'You need any help Maggie' he called out the car window. 'No we're fine, just give us a minute.' Kieran couldn't help but laugh as he watched us make our way down the path, carrying our meagre possessions. A rucksack on each of our backs, Maggie with a cigarette in one hand and her Boston ferns in the other and myself barely visible behind two sleeping bags hanging on for dear life to a bottle of Jameson.

As we reached the suburbs about fifteen minutes later, Kieran slowed the car down to a snail's pace, almost kerb crawling along the predominantly residential streets and began to give us a guided tour of what was to be our new neighbourhood. 'There's the bus stop, you can catch a bus there every twenty minutes and it will bring you to the city centre.'

On the opposite side of the street he pointed to a drugs store 'they open late every night' he told us as he turned the car right onto 'Maple Street'. As he parked the car about two blocks down he said 'how good is that? You guys have a convenience store just a few doors away. Have you got all that Maggie, I don't want you gettin' lost.' 'If I didn't get lost in Russia Kieran, I doubt I'll get lost here, so don't be smart,' Maggie replied. When we entered the three family home Kieran knocked on the door of the first floor apartment then walked in 'hey Danny' he said.

'Come meet my Irish girls.' Danny, Kieran's brother came toward the door. You couldn't deny they were brothers, both similar in height; about six foot two with the same colouring, Danny maybe a little blonder and ever so slightly lighter in frame. Kieran introduced us 'say hello girls to my kid brother. The good lookin' one in the family' he joked. After exchanging pleasantries with Danny for a few moments we climbed the front stairs to the third floor apartment which was in the eaves of the house. 'My brother bought this place a few years ago' Kieran said as we climbed. 'It was a total wreck and he managed to do all the work himself.' You could tell Kieran was really proud of his younger brother. Reaching the top of the stairs Kieran turned the handle on the unlocked door and showed us in.

I was immediately pleasantly surprised and for a moment my memories brought me back to Lisa's family holiday home in Plymouth, as Kieran's apartment resembled it in many ways. With its sloping attic ceilings and highly polished timber floors it almost had a cottage feel to it and the simple floral wallpaper added to the country 'look.' 'It's really nice Kieran' I said as I looked around. Even the furniture was a surprise, not at all what you would be expecting to find in a suburban home. The kitchen table was an antique, early American shaker style. And as I ran my fingers along its top I thought of all the people who must have sat around it through the years on the almost delicate ladder backed chairs. Simply furnished apart from the stove and refrigerator the only focal point was a large old dresser on the far wall. The bedroom was just as impressive with a beautiful pine bed with tapered bedposts taking centre stage, dressed in a simple cotton analgise quilt. Apart from the small bedside tables, there was a beautiful chest with a bevelled swinging mirror on top. I must have literally been standing there with my mouth open which didn't go unnoticed by Kieran. 'You like my place Mary?' 'Oh Kieran, it's beautiful, real cosy like an Irish cottage, you really have great taste.'

Kieran was beaming from ear to ear at the compliment. 'Wait till I show you this,' he said excitedly and ran his fingers down each of drawers on the chest until they came to rest on what appeared to be the frame. Pressing gently on the timber, out popped a secret drawer. 'God Kieran' Maggie said surprised 'you'd never know that was there.' 'It's where I keep my secret stash,' he replied in almost a whisper. 'Oh right' Maggie replied rolling her eyes up to heaven. 'Look Mary,' Maggie said when we entered the sitting room; we've even got a TV'. My mind was still on the furniture.

'It must have cost you a small fortune Kieran' I said as I continued to admire it. 'Yeah, it should have Mary, but this guy I know who deals in antiques owed me, so I told him I'd accept payment in furniture, 'luck of the Irish' eh Mary.'

Maggie placed one of her houseplants on the small kitchen window sill and was shuffling it back and forth trying to find what she thought was the right position. 'Maggie,' Kieran said as he watched her 'let's hit the mall and do some shoppin'. You wanna come Mary?' 'No, I'm fine here Kieran, you two go and I can unpack our things.' Maggie didn't have to be asked twice and after a momentary glance in the dressing table mirror to see if she looked alright, she grabbed her handbag and sunglasses from the kitchen table. 'Let's go so Kieran' she said impatiently and disappeared out the door. 'See you later kid, should be back in a couple of hours' Kieran said and then shouted after Maggie down the stairs 'wait up, here take my keys Maggie, you drive, I wanna see if your good enough to make a get-away driver.'

I hurried to unpack everything, allocating two drawers in the small chest for myself and another two for Maggie. We didn't really need a wardrobe, but I chose to hang the few dresses we had on a rail in a small closet Kieran had pointed to in the living room. Then I divided our groceries, placing the dry goods in the old kitchen dresser and the rest in the refrigerator, at the same time making a mental note of what I would need to buy in the corner shop later. Happy that everything was in its place, I ran a bath of warm water and while waiting for it to fill I organised our meagre collection of toiletries on a small corner shelf. I felt quite spoilt. As I relaxed in the bubble filled tub and thought what a 'God send' Kieran had been. We could never have afforded an apartment like this. He had helped us out so much in the months since we had met him and our day to day life had become so much easier.

Maggie still got into a 'huff' if he yelled at us, but I knew that he only yelled out of concern for us and that he had our best interests at heart. Yes, I thought as I watched the skin on my fingers take on the texture of prunes, I really could get used to this.

Kieran and Maggie returned a few hours later. Maggie with her sunglasses perched precariously on her head and carrying a large pizza and two strawberry milkshakes, 'thought you might be hungry' she said smiling as she reached the top step. Kieran followed a few steps behind her with a large cardboard box he was carrying, 'wait till you see this Mary, he said happily as he lowered the box carefully on to the table. Ripping it open he reached in and pulled out a very fancy lookin' Combi oven and grill. 'What d'ya think Mary?' he asked looking at me almost like a school boy would look at his teacher or parent for approval. 'It's really nice Kieran, very modern' I replied 'but we already have an oven' I said pointing to the large gas stove in the corner. 'Yeah, sure we do kid' he said lifting the oven to its new place on the counter 'but these are real good y'know if you wanna rustle up somethin' fast, you girls don't have a lot of time to be cooking'. Kieran then turned his attention to the instruction manual and began waving it in front of Maggie. 'Make sure an' read this good Maggie, I don't want you settin' fire to my apartment.' 'Oh very funny Kieran', Maggie replied 'you must think we're totally clueless, we do have electrical appliances in Ireland you know.' 'Sure you do Maggie and let me guess, you have hotels and highways too,' he laughed.

Chapter 31

Fast Car

I knew exactly where Kieran was heading with his line of conversation. Ever since we met him, we had tried to paint for him a picture of the Ireland we knew. But Kieran, although he listened intently to every story, was like so many other Americans who agreed that although it sounded like a very beautiful country with lush green fields, old medieval castles dotted across the landscape and tiny white washed cottages nestled in the hillsides or beside meandering streams. It was also a backward country and very much behind the times. Kieran couldn't seem to grasp the idea that Ireland was also a place with cities, large detached modern homes and five star hotels. Yes, Maggie and I would desperately try to convince him that we weren't from the 'stone age.' We even have fast cars! But nothing worked, Kieran would just scoff in disbelief and it had become a very touchy subject with Maggie.

Maggie's opportunity to prove to Kieran that we weren't lying came one afternoon while we were relaxing on the sofa between shifts in Kieran and Rocco's apartment. We sat bolt upright in our seats staring at the T.V. guide magazine we had been looking at together. Maggie and I looked at each other and started to smile knowing we were both thinking along the same lines. Advertised for the following evening was an episode of a very popular American detective series called 'Remington Steele' which starred 'Pierce Brosnan' in the lead role. But what really caught our attention the most was, that the magazine claimed that this particular episode was filmed entirely in Ireland. 'Now' Maggie said 'now they'll have to believe us. I don't care what plans Kieran and Rocco have for tomorrow night Mary, they are bloody well going to watch that programme. I'll shut Kieran up once and for all. Oh I can't wait Mary, thank God we're both off tomorrow night.'

It was all arranged. Kieran didn't need any persuasion, anything to do with Ireland or the Irish and he was 'all ears.'

Rocco took a little more convincing and a six pack of beer to prise him away from the stove in the kitchen.

'Now you'll see we weren't telling lies,' Maggie said as we all gathered together on the sofa to watch what we had always remembered to be, a fast paced, action packed detective series. Sadly Maggie's plan did not play out exactly as she had planned it. What we were to witness on the television was probably the best 'plug' the Irish Tourism industry was ever to likely receive. We watched as 'Remington Steele' was summoned by the Irish Police Force to assist them in solving a major crime. He arrived in Ireland with his assistants and he informed them that they would be staying in a hotel for the duration of their stay. But to our horror it was not a three, four or five star hotel with en-suite bathrooms or leisure facilities. But an old crumbling farmhouse, with one bathroom for all the guests; romantic maybe, with its beautiful red rambling roses and certainly picture postcard perfect. It was alas, not the vision of Irish modern society that Maggie and I had predicted in anticipation of watching the programme. To add to our disappointment there wasn't a single motor way to be seen. Maggie lit another cigarette hoping to somehow disguise her embarrassment as we saw 'Remington Steele' give chase after the criminals in an old Morris Minor car, which in Ireland at the time would have been considered vintage, only to be held up by a flock of sheep which were blocking his way. 'Life in the fast lane, eh Rocco,' Kieran joked. 'Oh shut up Kieran' Maggie replied annoyed that her plan had failed. 'It's not like that in Ireland, not where we live anyway' she insisted, but she knew it was not a debate we were about to win when we saw 'Remington Steele' who crashed the Morris Minor being given a ride back to his hotel on a donkey and cart! At that point Maggie and I just looked at each other while Kieran was in convulsions laughing at the expression on Maggie's face. 'Is it any wonder nobody would give us a job?' she said as I, unable to hold it in any more, burst out laughing too.

The day after our move to our new home, Kieran, who had stayed over the night before, left us with an explanation which we had become accustomed to. 'I gotta run, me an' Bob gotta take care of business. Can you girls take the bus to work?' 'Yeah, yeah we'll be fine' Maggie said as she munched her way through a bowl of cereal. 'Ok, catch you later' Kieran said closing the door behind him. Maggie and I caught a bus an hour later then we strolled at a leisurely pace for ten minutes until we reached Colonial Hill and the Little Sicily restaurant. We were both really happy with our new apartment and I was relieved that Maggie had put the whole incident with Rudi behind her and was no longer annoyed with Kieran.

Chapter 32

Let's Get Physical

It was two minutes to ten when we punched our time cards in the cloakroom area at the bottom of the back stairs beside the kitchen. And although the restaurant didn't open for another two hours, at twelve o'clock, we couldn't help notice Rudi's absence as he was usually banging pots and pans around the kitchen by this time or yelling at the person who had the misfortune to be nearest to him. 'With any luck,' Maggie said 'he's got the day off' as we climbed the stairs to the restaurant area and pushed the door open. We had grown accustomed to the 'highly strung' personalities of the Italians and it was not unusual to hear them yelling profanities at each other over the most trivial of disagreements, so when we stepped into the dining area we were not at all shocked to hear our bosses screams coming from around the corner near the podium and front door area. He was yelling at Cindy the hostess, who at twenty years his junior was if rumours were correct, also his mistress. 'Try Benito's number again if you have to, call his friggin mother. I don't care what you have to do, just get him the fuck in here.' We turned the corner to see Cindy frantically punching numbers on the phone while Enzo breathed down her neck and continued to yell like someone possessed until at last, Cindy spoke. 'Hi Benito' she said 'this is Cindy; Enzo needs you to come to work straight away. Rudi has had an accident and he won't be able to work for at least a week. Yes I know it's your day off but we're badly stuck. Please Benito.' Just then Enzo wrenched the phone from Cindy's hand 'if you don't get your sorry ass in here Benito, you're fired you motherfucker.'

'What's up Enzo?' Maggie asked and it was obvious by the way he spun around that he was not aware of our presence until that moment. 'Oh, ah, hello girls,' he said trying to regain his composure and add a more cheerful tone to his voice. 'How are my best workers doin' today?' he asked forcing a smile. 'Fine thanks Enzo,' Maggie replied 'did something happen to Rudi?'

She asked curiously as I nudged her in the ribs with my elbow discreetly in the hope it would remind her to mind her own business. 'Ah nothin' for you girls to worry your pretty heads over, I'm sure he'll be just fine. How was your day off girls?' Enzo asked at a blatant attempt to change the subject. 'Good Enzo' I replied 'Kieran rented us an apartment in Cranston and we moved in yesterday.' I thought Enzo flinched a little at the mention of Kieran's name but I decided it was probably my imagination and after all Enzo was extremely stressed. 'Wow, that's really great. Kieran is such a good guy an' he loves you girls.'

Just then the restaurant door flew open and Benito, the chef, entered looking as if he had just crawled out of bed and another row ensued between him and our boss. I began to set the tables while they screamed back and forth at each other, while Maggie disappeared downstairs to await her first customer of the day.

She had coped well with her position as a valet parker, contrary to the opinion of the male waiters and her over all lack of experience or knowledge of American cars. I was sure however that had the owners of the cars known she was such a novice driver, they would never have entrusted her with their precious vehicles. Her driving wasn't completely without incident though. And one evening while clearing a table near the window I looked down to see what appeared to be a traffic jam running the whole length of the Avenue and Maggie was the cause of it. She had been delivering a car to the parking lot on the opposite side of the street when it had stalled without warning. The old men of the neighbourhood who often stood on the street corners to 'chat' to each other had gathered around the car to offer their advice. There were drivers impatiently blowing their horns, others hanging out of their car windows shouting, 'move the friggin car lady!' Some of the men we're shouting at the drivers who were using bad language, while others were debating with each other how to start the car, while Maggie looked as if she was about to pull her hair out. If it was me, I knew I would have gotten out of the car and left it in the middle of the street. Thankfully, after what seemed like an eternity Maggie's prayers were answered and the car spluttered to life and shot across the road causing the old men to jump to life and out of Maggie's way. I watched as she finally parked the car and sat in the open top convertible smoking what she obviously believed was a well-deserved cigarette. How Maggie coped with all the different cars I'll never know. From the sporty Convertibles to the Cadillac's which were the length of a small bus. Within a few weeks of starting work in Little Sicily Maggie had driven them all. I certainly knew that if it was me, I'd have trouble remembering the Americans drove on the other side of the street!

Enzo, my boss and Benito the chef finally stopped screaming at each other and went their separate ways and not a moment too soon because customers began to file through the door and before long every table was full. I had to put any thoughts of our new home reluctantly to the back of my mind and concentrate on the tasks at hand.

I filled glasses of iced water for the customers and placed complimentary baskets of freshly baked garlic bread on each table. I cleared tables when customers left and re-set them for the next diners. It was also my responsibility to ensure that the salad bar was kept fully stocked, and it was on one of my many trips to the kitchens that day that I overheard a conversation between Nicky and George, two of the waiters. I stopped dead in my tracks on the back stairs when I heard Rudi's name being mentioned. Rudi has gotta be one dumb mother fucker, he's gotta have known she was gonna tell him.' 'Who are you tellin' Nicky?' Not for nothin he's lucky he didn't catch more than a beatin'. You just don't fuck around with those guys, they mean business. Rudi sayin' shit like that about his girl, people have been shot for less.' 'Not for nothin, if he spoke to my girl like that I'd break his legs with a friggin bat.' 'Too fuckin right George, he's only an asshole anyway.' 'Yeah Nicky! One dumb fuckin' asshole.'

I rattled the stainless steel bowls which I was carrying to warn them I was on my way. 'Busy tonight guys' I said as I entered the kitchen. 'Yeah, sure is Mary' George replied 'hopefully that means some big bucks; you need help with that Mary?' 'No thanks George just getting some snail salad, God I don't know how anyone eats them, they're like blubber.' Nicky gave me a big smile 'you need help Mary? All you gotta do is ask. Hey George, we better haul our ass upstairs and make us some cash.' The two waiters disappeared upstairs to attend their customers. But as I filled the bowl with the snail salad I couldn't help but replay in my mind the conversation I had eaves dropped on. Was it true, what Nicky and George had said? Had Rudi really been attacked by someone? They had really sounded serious. I suppose, I thought as I climbed the stairs once more, if you spend your life insulting people it is only a matter of time before you insult the wrong person. Maybe Rudi would now learn to keep his mouth shut. 'Hey Mary', Benito the chef called to me; shaking me from my thoughts 'could you get me some squid from the kitchen? I'm under pressure here.' 'Of course I will Benito' I said grabbing the bowl and taking off once again down the stairs.

I knew my nights work was almost at an end when I saw Kieran walk in and as usual Enzo was 'clucking' around him like a mother hen. 'You nearly done Mary?' Kieran asked practically ignoring the attention being showered on him by Enzo. 'Yeah Kieran, nearly finished now.'

'Mary,' Enzo interrupted 'you've had a long night, you leave anything else for the morning. I'd like to get you two girls and Kieran a drink. Come, sit, sit' he insisted pulling out a stool for Kieran. 'Are you sure Enzo?' I asked surprised. 'Sure I'm sure Mary,' he replied 'I got to look after my best workers.' Where's that sister of yours got to Mary' Kieran asked looking around. 'Oh she's probably in the ladies room counting her tips Kieran; I'll just go and ask her if she's having a drink.' 'Like you don't know the answer Mary; I'm beginning to worry your sisters gotta real problem' he joked. 'Do me a favour Kieran' I asked. 'What's that Mary?' 'Keep your opinions to yourself or you'll be listening to hot tongue and getting cold shoulder all night.'

'Yeah you could be right there kid,' Kieran said smiling 'that sister of yours has got a hot temper.'

I found Maggie, as expected, in the ladies brushing her hair. 'Kieran's at the bar Maggie' I said as I applied a light coat of lipstick and attempted to tame my hair. 'Oh and Enzo let me finish early and has paid for a drink for us at the bar.' 'Jesus, what's come over him?' Maggie asked pushing her long hair back behind her ears. 'How do I know Maggie, but that reminds me, remember he told us earlier that Rudi had an accident?' 'Yeah, what about it Mary?' 'Well, I heard Nicky and George talking in the kitchen and they were saying he'd been attacked and they seemed to know who did it 'because they said he was lucky he wasn't shot.' 'He obviously ruffled someone's feathers which doesn't surprise me, the way he treats people. I'll tell you something Mary; he needn't be expecting any sympathy from me.'

'Hope you got some money for me Maggie,' Kieran said as we pulled up a stool to join him at the bar 'you sure took long enough countin' it, you must be packin' in a small fortune.' Maggie couldn't tell whether Kieran was serious or not and she certainly wasn't about to make a habit of supporting a man financially, she had seen Mam do that for years. 'What do you mean?' she asked. 'Well my funds are gettin' kinda low Maggie, you know how it's tough out there, business is slow' Kieran replied with a sad face and an air of desperation in his voice. Then he winked at me as he watched Maggie rummaging in her handbag. 'Maybe' she said as she opened her wallet 'you'd sell more houses if you had a bit more, you know, charisma. Here, I have fifty dollars I'll give you twenty if that will help.' Kieran didn't comment on Maggie's remark regarding his personality and what she believed was a flaw caused by a lack of 'charm.'

But he looked as if he was regretting ever mentioning the subject of money. 'Maggie,' Kieran explained 'I'm kiddin, don't get so uptight. Do you think I'd ask you or your kid sister for money? You girls are just about surviving, you two should be asking for money?' 'And why would we do that?' Maggie asked a little indignantly, 'we're quite capable of supporting ourselves, you're the one who's obviously short of cash. Do you want this twenty or don't you?' She asked waving the money in front of him. 'Maggie' he said in almost a whisper 'when the bucks are getting low with me it means I'm down to my last ten grand.' 'Well good for you Kieran, but you don't have to brag about it.' Maggie replied as she pushed the twenty back in her wallet. 'Are we going to have another drink here' I asked 'or will we go somewhere else?' 'Oh we'll go somewhere else,' Maggie replied before Kieran had a chance to reply. 'Where are you taking us Kieran? We can't have all that money burning a hole in your pocket!' 'I gotta catch up with Molyneaux in the By Way Maggie, an' Rocco's there too. If you want we can go somewhere else tomorrow night ok.' 'Yeah, the By Way it is then' Maggie replied with a sigh. 'You know, not for nothin' Maggie' Kieran said as we made our way up the street 'for someone who doesn't like the By Way, you got no problem goin' in there most afternoons and you got no business in there on your own.'

'Oh God' I thought to myself 'here we go again.' 'As a matter of fact Kieran' Maggie said stopping dead in her tracks 'I do like the By Way, it reminds me of the small local pubs at home. I just thought it would be nice to go somewhere else for a change and by the way, don't ever think you can tell me what I can or can't do.' Now Kieran was getting annoyed. 'I only friggin said you got no business in there on your own, you don't even know anyone in there.' 'We know Lynn Kieran' I said intervening and wondering if I'd ever get to have a quiet drink and relax 'and I think she likes us, 'cause she's always very nice Kieran.' 'That's what I'm tryin' to say kid, she likes you too much, you know what I mean?' 'Oh right' I said quite dumbfounded and followed him into the bar. Maggie for once thankfully remained silent.

Chapter 33

He Ain't Heavy, He's My Brother

Gerard Molyneaux and Rocco were sitting at the table together and as usual Gerard's other associates, who acknowledged us with a nod, sat at another table near the door. 'Hey Kieran' Gerard said 'we were gonna send out a search party for you. Ain't that right Rocco?' 'Yeah, no kiddin Kieran, we thought maybe you'd bin bumped off.' 'How are the Irish girls doin?' Gerard asked and stood up to give Maggie and I a welcoming kiss on the cheek. 'Good thanks Gerard,' Maggie replied 'will you be having a drink?' 'Nah Maggie, I'm done kid, I was just leavin',' he replied and seemed almost surprised at the offer. 'Everything' ok with you girls? Kieran tells me you girls are workin' a lot of hours.' 'We're fine thanks Gerard;' Maggie reassured him 'hard work never killed anyone.' 'I dunno all about that kid, but if you or Mary need anythin' all you gotta do is ask. I like these girls Kieran, it takes balls to move to a new country, when you don't know nobody, I like that Kieran.' Gerard got to his feet once again and pushed his chair toward me. 'Here Mary, take the weight off your feet' turning toward the bar he called to Lynn. 'Lynn, can you fill a round of drinks for my friends and put it on my tab.' 'Yes sir' Lynn replied 'comin' right up.' 'Girls, catch you later, Kieran walk with me to my car. I need to talk to you about business.' 'Thanks for the drink Gerard,' we called after him. 'No problem girls, anytime.' We were left sitting with Rocco when Kieran went outside with Gerard. Rocco wasn't to say the least a great conversationalist at the best of times; Maggie and I were the ones who initiated any dialogue between us. So we were surprised that as soon as Gerard Molyneaux went away he seemed eager to talk. 'You know Maggie, how you told Gerard that hard work never killed anyone?' 'Of course I do Rocco; I've only had two drinks,' Maggie laughed. 'Yeah, what I'm tryin' to tell you girls is Gerard's two brothers' was killed on a buildin' site some time back an' he took it real bad.' 'Oh my God!'

Maggie and I replied together. 'Kieran never told me that' Maggie continued 'if he had I'd never have made a comment like that.' 'Just so you know' Rocco said. 'What happened to them Rocco' I asked shocked.

'I guess they were workin' on one of them, what d'ya call 'em, high rise buildin's? Word has it one of them slipped and the other brother put his arm out to save him an' I guess they both fell. Gerard doesn't like to talk about it.'

Maggie and I sat in silence for a few moments, each of us thinking about Gerard's double heartache. 'God' I said 'you wouldn't wish that on your worst enemy.' 'I know' Maggie said totally lost for words and decided it might be best to change the subject. Kieran returned about fifteen minutes later just as we were telling Rocco about Rudi being attacked. 'Hey Kieran, come here' Rocco called 'you hear anythin' about a guy gettin' mugged in this neighbourhood? Cause not for nothin' if anythin' happens 'round here, we know. Ain't that right Kieran?' 'Yeah' Kieran nodded 'but Rocco what about that woman who was attacked last night, I ain't kiddin this neighbourhood is gone to the dogs Rocco.' Suddenly Kieran had Maggie's full attention. 'Oh my God Kieran, where on earth did that happen' she asked equally as surprised as I was, because the neighbourhood appeared to be a very safe place to live or work. 'In the car park of the 'Sicily' actually' Kieran replied smiling. 'You've got to be joking Kieran. Jesus, that could have been me' Maggie said with a look of real worry on her face and obviously thinking about all the times she went back and forth each night with people's cars. 'Was the woman seriously hurt Kieran' I asked 'Yeah Mary, word on the street is she won't be doin' any dancin' for some time' Kieran replied with a laugh. 'What's so funny Kieran?' Maggie snapped 'it's not a laughing matter.' 'Yeah Kieran, how can you find that funny?' I said agreeing with Maggie and for the first time feeling a little concerned about Kieran's sense of humour. 'No woman deserves that you know?' 'I dunno,' Kieran finally spoke 'I thought it was funny, how 'bout you Rocco?' Rocco was laughing now and unable to even respond to Kieran while

Maggie and I were becoming more disgusted by the second. 'You're sick Kieran' Maggie snapped as she reached for a mouthful of beer 'you have to be' she continued 'if you think that it's funny for a poor defenceless woman to be viciously assaulted, what in the name of God is wrong with you?' I remained silent and pretty much at a loss for words. 'Actually' Kieran finally responded 'now that I think about it, maybe it was a guy, but he sure was cryin' like a girl, ain't that so Rocco?' 'No kiddin' Kieran' Rocco laughed. 'He ain't nothin' but a pussy.' The mouthful of beer Maggie had just taken from her glass, shot out and across the table and she began to choke. 'Hey Maggie' Kieran laughed 'I told you go easy on the beer' he said as he patted her back.

Very few words were spoken that night when Kieran drove us home. He didn't stay as Maggie explained that she was very tired and was going to get an early night.

But it turned out to be anything but an early night, with so many thoughts going around in our heads. After dissecting and analysing what we had learned earlier Maggie and I were relieved at least to know that Kieran did not find the idea of a woman being abused to be funny. We were shocked when we realised that it was Rudi he had been speaking about and almost sure that he was responsible for Rudi's accident. Maggie also felt somewhat reassured and comforted by the fact that Kieran had, so to speak, defended her honour and I was relieved to know that I was right and that he really did care for her. Rudi on the other hand I was sure was regretting ever opening his mouth and hopefully for his sake would think twice before humiliating anybody else in future.

'Oh my God Mary' Maggie said sitting up in the bed and pulling the covers off me for the umpteenth time. 'What now Maggie?' I moaned. 'Do you think we'll get the sack?' 'I doubt it Maggie' I said. 'But Enzo must know what happened. What makes you so sure he won't Mary?' 'Because Maggie, Enzo like everyone else knows Rudi had it coming. I mean Maggie, from what I can see, not a single day goes by without one of the waiters wanting to kill him.' 'That's true Mary; with the help of God you'll be right. I never meant for Kieran to beat him up Mary even if he is a shithead. Yeah, I better watch what I say to Kieran in future.'

Maggie eventually drifted off to sleep, but I was wide awake. I thought of how I had reassured Maggie that our jobs were safe and although I believed that Enzo our boss, was all too aware that Rudi was a bitter little man who availed of any opportunity given to him to make the lives of the people who worked with him as miserable as possible.

However I also believed that the real reason we had no reason to be concerned about our jobs was that Enzo would not have wanted to suffer the same fate as Rudi. As I lay listening to Maggie's breathing, I also thought of Gerard Molyneaux and the tragic circumstances of his brothers deaths. I couldn't even imagine what that must have been like for him. To lose one family member was heart breaking enough, but to lose two in that way must have been, I thought, soul destroying.

'I feel awful now' I thought to myself for having made judgements about Gerard in the weeks after first meeting him. Maggie and I had sat in Gerard Molyneaux's company on several occasions and although he always made us feel more than welcome. Compared with Kieran who was warm and witty, Gerard was I felt, a totally different kettle of fish. Some people I thought might have described him as being very reserved others I was sure would be less than sympathetic and say he was downright cold. He was like Rocco, more of a listener than a talker and discouraged any inquisitiveness about his personal life by bluntly changing subject. He also had a habit of staring at someone unblinking for what seemed like the longest time, almost as if he were trying to read the person's mind. I had formed the opinion that Gerard Molyneaux was like an iceberg. You only ever saw the tip and that so much more lay beneath the surface. After Rocco told us about his misfortunate brothers I felt so guilty for judging him. 'Sure' I said to myself as Maggie turned in her sleep 'nobody could be a hundred percent after something like that happening to them.'

I arrived to work the next morning bleary eyed and tired from lack of sleep. Maggie who was in a more up-beat mood than me, decided we should take the positive approach and carry on as normal. 'We'll just pretend to know nothing about Rudi' she suggested. 'Sounds good to me Maggie' I replied. 'The less said the better. Don't go asking any ridiculous questions Mary, do you hear me?' 'Me! Maggie?' I replied 'you should take a leaf out of your own book, you never know when to shut up, I never open my mouth.' 'Ok, ok Mary, I'm just saying, there's no need to snap the face off me' she said knowing that I was tired and dreading the long day's work ahead of me.

Chapter 34

Who's That Girl?

'Good morning Enzo' I said as I passed through the kitchen to the cloakroom area at the bottom of the stairs. Enzo didn't respond. He was preoccupied with a discussion he was having with the kitchen porter about water residue marks on the wine glasses and insinuating that the porter had to be blind not to see them. 'Enough already' he shouted 'just be sure those glasses are spotless before they go upstairs, you hear me?' I punched my time card and was just about to climb the stairs when Enzo called me. 'Hold up a minute Mary, I'd like a word with you about something.' My heart started to pound a little faster. 'What if I was wrong' I thought 'maybe he is going to sack me.' 'Yes Enzo' I replied back tracking into the kitchen. 'I was wonderin' Mary, how'd you feel about waitin' tables at lunch time, I'm down a couple of waiters. Vinnie, he's goin' back to college an' can only do weekends and that piece o' shit Antonio just quit. Says his uncle is retirin' from Carmelo's an' he's taking his job. Can you friggin believe it Mary? When I took him on he was a real dumb ass, now he thinks he's a somebody.' I had no problem believing that Antonio, one of Enzo's best waiters, would opt for working in Carmelo's Garden Restaurant next door rather than the Sicily. Unlike Little Sicily, which was only open a year, Carmelo's had been operating very successfully for over fifty. I had often heard the waiters in Little Sicily speak about it and they maintained that if you were blessed enough to get a job there you had it made. It was a meal ticket for life, the tips were so good, it was strongly rumoured that if someone was retiring they sold their job to the highest bidder for thousands. 'If you'd be willing to give it a go Mary,' Enzo said forgetting about Vinnie and returning to the topic at hand 'you can still 'bus' tables at night. How 'bout it Mary?' 'Ah, well,' I stammered 'if you think I can handle it Enzo, I'll give it a go.' 'Good that's settled then' he said rubbing his hands together.

'I was getting worried there for a minute,' Maggie said as we watched Enzo go out the door and I breathed a sigh of relief knowing I still had a job, but terrified at the thoughts of waiting tables. Maggie, obviously sensing my nervousness reassured me, 'You'll be fine Mary, just don't go dropping any plates of pasta on the customers!' she laughed.

Over the next few days even though I was very nervous I managed to muddle through. I had taken one of the menu's home with me and studied it until I knew it word for word. The wine list was another story entirely. Not knowing the difference between Chablis and Chianti, on several occasions I had to ask Giorgio for help. He was more approachable than the other waiters who were definitely of the opinion that Enzo made a big mistake in promoting me. Not because of my lack of knowledge about wine but simply because I was a woman. As far as they were concerned, men were far superior to women when it came to waiting tables. My boss wasn't about to be swayed though and obviously saw me as an asset to the business after several customers praised me for my polite manner and beautiful Irish brogue.

I was nearing the end of my first week as a waitress when my boss introduced me to Jenny. She was a petite girl with walnut brown hair that tumbled in thick waves half way down her back. With big brown heavily lashed eyes and a heart shaped face she immediately caught the attention of more than one of the waiters.

Enzo explained that he had just hired her and we were to work the lunch shift together and asked if I could show her the ropes. I eagerly agreed to give Jenny the grand tour of the restaurant and thought how nice it would be to have a girl about my own age to chat to in a job where the men outweighed the women by about four to one.

I chatted away to Jenny as we polished the silverware in the hope that my friendly manner would put her at ease and help to make her first day a little easier. I did, after all, know exactly how it felt to be the 'new girl.' 'Do you live on Colonial Hill?' I asked as we began ironing a basket of linen napkins. 'Sure do, just across the street, behind Angelina's' she replied. 'Oh that's good, not too far to walk then, have you waitressed before Jenny?' 'Nope, needed a job though and Kieran told me to try here, so here I am.' 'You know Kieran?' I asked delighted to think we had something in common. 'Yeah, you could say that,' Jenny replied and I thought I detected a hint of sarcasm in her voice or was I wrong? Maybe I was asking too many questions and thought it best to stop.

'My mom's heard a lot about you and your sister' Jenny said after a few minutes 'she thinks it's cool the way you both travelled half way across the world.' 'Oh really Jenny' I said surprised 'how did she know that?'

'You kiddin me' Jenny smiled 'you can't do nothin in this neighbourhood and everybody knows about it. I bet the Irish girls were talked about at every dinner table on Colonial Hill when you first got here. And it spread like wild fire when your sister started seein' Kieran.' 'It's the very same in the village where we come from in Ireland Jenny. People would nearly know what you're having for dinner.' 'My mom would love to meet you and your sister Mary. How's' about we grab a bite to eat at Angelina's tomorrow?' 'Ok Jenny, yeah that would be lovely, I'll tell my sister. I know she'll be delighted to go, we were only sayin' the other day that it would be nice to meet some women you know, for a bit of girl talk.

'Who's the new girl?' Maggie asked in a tone of voice that suggested she was veteran of the job for twenty years. 'Her name is Jenny,' I said 'she lives over there Maggie, just behind Angelina's restaurant; she seems like a nice girl. In fact, she said her mother can't wait to meet us and they've invited us to have lunch with them in Angelina's tomorrow.' 'Oh right,' Maggie replied without one ounce of enthusiasm in her voice. 'What's wrong with you Maggie?' I asked 'I thought you'd be pleased to meet them, you know we might even go on a girls night out.' 'Ah, it's nothing Mary, it's just that I was looking forward to meeting Kieran tonight, but he says he has to meet someone in South Boston tonight with Rocco, something to do with work. And I thought he could at least have asked me to go, Boston is supposed to be a beautiful city.' 'Maggie, he probably wouldn't have time to show you around if he's going there on business and you know Maggie, what Mam would say to that.' 'Yeah, I know Mary, never mix business with pleasure.

Chapter 35

For All The Girls I've Loved Before

Maggie and I were no strangers to Angelina's. The cooks had continued to hand out plates of food to Maggie each day and she was on a first name basis with most of them. In return we ate there at least once a week and more if our budget allowed, so it came as no big surprise when we walked in the following day with Jenny, that some of the waiters greeted us and even knew our names. I loved Angelina's. It was a family business that had survived decades. Famous for its no frills, reasonably priced great food and a very friendly laid back atmosphere.

We followed Jenny to the far side of the restaurant, where a woman who appeared to be in her late thirties was sitting in a corner booth. Jenny introduced us 'this is my mom Vanessa. Mom this is Maggie and this is her sister Mary.' Vanessa seemed really excited to meet us and eagerly shook our hands. She was a very attractive, fresh faced woman. Slim in stature with thick shoulder length jet black hair and big brown eyes. Her smile was warm and welcoming and she had a sweet, soft spoken voice. 'You're from Ireland' she said sounding almost envious. 'I've heard it's a beautiful country, why did you leave?' Maggie and I took turns explaining everything in between ordering our food and eating. Vanessa was quite happy just to sit and listen while we told her all about our brothers and sisters and our life in Ireland. Every now and then she would interrupt us with another question. 'Don't you miss your family? Won't your mother be worried? You're both so young. Are you going to go back to Ireland?'

I allowed Maggie to answer the last question as I really didn't have an answer. Maggie certainly hadn't planned on falling in love and as each day passed she mentioned 'home' less and less. 'I don't know yet Vanessa,' she said sounding very unsure 'I suppose that depends on Kieran. He seems serious, but who knows with men?' 'Jenny says you know him.' Vanessa seemed uncomfortable all of a sudden and diverted her gaze away from Maggie to her daughter Jenny, almost as if in a plea for help. 'I told you Ma, this was a bad idea' Jenny said 'but you never listen.' 'Oh God' Vanessa said 'I feel really bad Jenny. You're right I shouldn't have done this. It's just that, you know, everybody has been telling me about you and Kieran and I just had to meet you. I feel really ashamed now because you're both really nice girls and I can understand how Kieran has fallen for you.'

Maggie and I had been looking at each other confused and not knowing what Vanessa was rambling on about but Maggie finally spoke. 'Slow down Vanessa, what's this about?' She didn't respond and was staring at the unfinished food on her plate. It was Jenny who answered. 'What my mother is trying to tell you is that she is Kieran's ex-girlfriend, she was with him for seven years.'

I remember thinking that it was like a scene from one of those 'soap operas on the television. Situations like this one did not occur in Cratloe, Co. Clare!

It was an awkward moment and the silence was deafening. Maggie with all her worldly knowledge was at a loss as to how to react. We had been caught completely off our guard and it was the last thing we would have expected Vanessa to say because even though she was without a doubt a very attractive woman. She was also quite a number of years older than Kieran who was twenty eight.

Maggie finally found her voice. She remained very calm and dignified but I could tell she was really annoyed. 'I think it's time for us to leave Mary,' she said while kicking me in the ankle with her foot. 'Please don't go, I feel really bad' Vanessa begged and genuinely looked on the verge of tears 'Kieran and I split up a long time ago and even though I still care about him, I know it was for the best. I wish now that I'd never listened to my cousin Doris. She lives next door to Kieran and she keeps telling me each time I meet her that she hates you. I just let my curiosity get the better of me and I feel really ashamed now.

You girls are both really sweet and you're young enough to be my daughters. I am so sorry.'

Maggie and I remained seated in the booth and she was no longer kicking my ankle. As I sat there watching Vanessa I couldn't help but feel, with my soft caring nature, a certain amount of sympathy for her. Maggie on the other hand was a less forgiving person but decided to use Vanessa's guilt to her advantage, and, as an opportunity to get answers to some questions that had obviously been playing on her mind.

'Why?' she asked Vanessa 'would your cousin Doris not like us. We say hello each time we see her and she hasn't the decency to respond. It doesn't cost anything to be polite. 'I guess,' Jenny intervened 'it's because my Mom was with Kieran for so long, maybe she was hoping for my Moms sake that they'd, you know, get back together. She knows my Mom took it bad when he left.'

'If that's the case Jenny' Maggie said refusing to back down 'and Doris is concerned about your mothers feelings, why is she continually telling your mother about Kieran and I every chance she gets. Knowing it will only upset her. It sounds to me like she's almost enjoying telling you Vanessa. Are you sure she hasn't got her own hidden agenda? 'Cause if you don't mind me saying so, for someone who should be busy with a young daughter to raise, she seems to spend all her time sitting on the front step fixing her make-up. I'd be willing to bet any money on it, that the reason she's telling you everything is in the hope you will be hurt and start hating Kieran. And the reason she's so ignorant to my sister and I, is pure jealousy 'cause she wants Kieran!'

It was obvious to Maggie and I from the look on Vanessa's face that this thought had never occurred to her, which was perfectly understandable after all. Doris was her cousin but as she sat in silence without objection, it was clear that she was now looking at the whole situation from a completely different perspective. It was Jenny who finally spoke 'Yeah Ma, what is her problem?' She asked realising what Maggie said could quite possibly be true. 'I dunno Jenny' Vanessa replied while looking from Maggie to me. 'I hear all good from people in the neighbourhood about you. It's the Irish girls this an' the Irish girls that, everyone likes you except Doris; she hates you and calls you the 'fat' Irish Mommas!' Maggie and I looked at each other when we heard this and we both burst out laughing. 'She's not exactly an oil painting herself' I said 'she should take a closer look in the mirror.' 'Chalk it down' Maggie agreed 'she's got a nose like Jimmy Durante!' It was Vanessa's turn to laugh and she was obviously enjoying our sense of humour. 'I think we should have some dessert' she said and beckoned to the waiter Guido 'four chocolate puddings please.' 'Who's Jimmy Durante' Jenny asked Maggie who was still laughing at our new title and unable to answer. 'He was a famous actor years ago Jenny,' I volunteered 'and let's just say if he walked in that door right now, his nose would be six inches ahead of him!'

We sat and chatted happily with Vanessa and Jenny until it was time to return to work and by the time we went our separate ways, Maggie and I agreed that Vanessa was a nice person and forgave her for initially deceiving us.

By way of added apology for her behaviour she invited us to her home for dinner on our next available free night and we accepted. Little did we know all those years ago that meeting was the start of a life-long friend ship?

Maggie and Vanessa still meet on a regular basis to this day. I on the other hand, although I have very fond and happy memories of times spent together, failed miserably at keeping in touch.

Chapter 36

Girls Just Wanna Have Fun

It was also about this time that we met Belinda, a relative of Rocco's, she had moved in with Kieran and Rocco, because according to Kieran 'her mother couldn't look after herself not to mind take care of a kid.' Belinda at about fifteen years of age was like most teenagers. She loved music and bopped around the apartment with head phones and her Walkman stereo permanently attached to her hip as if she were on stage. The sweeping brush became the microphone and even when she was washing dishes at the sink her body swayed to the music. In Belinda's mind she was in a faraway place, a superstar playing to a crowd of adoring fans. Wearing sneakers, jeans and cropped T shirts accompanied by cheap colourful costume jewellery she was a real breath of fresh air and I envied her confidence. A friendly girl who was pretty as a picture, I knew it wouldn't be long before boys would be lining up to date her.

One afternoon while on my break from work and relaxing on the sofa at Kieran and Rocco's place, I couldn't decide which was more entertaining, watching the day time soaps with all their drama or watching Belinda doing her usual dance routine. This time in front of a mirror in the living room, while at the same time singing into her hair brush and pausing momentarily to apply an electric blue shade of eye-shadow to her lids. Knowing well that there was no point calling to her because she couldn't hear me with her headphones on, I stood up and tipped her on the shoulder to offer her a chocolate brownie. 'Thanks Mary,' she shouted at the top of her voice and over the sound of the music that was obviously screaming in her ears 'I'm starving' she said taking a huge bite 'I think I got the munchies.' Kieran's bedroom door swung open 'hope you're not smokin' that shit Belinda,' Kieran was yelling 'you wanna end up like your mother with your friggin brain fried?' Belinda couldn't help but hear Kieran because he was yelling right into her face. 'Chill out, I'm only kiddin' Kieran' she yelled back. 'You better be kiddin' Belinda, I find out your smokin' that shit you're gonna get a slap and not for nothin', get that crap off your face 'cause you ain't goin' nowhere.' 'I am too Kieran, I'm meetin' my buddies downtown.' Kieran was doin' his own dance around the sitting room in temper. 'Enough already Belinda, you ain't hangin' out with that gang of no good losers.' 'Don't you call them that Kieran, they're my friends an' you can't tell me what to do' Belinda shouted and started toward the door, ignoring Kieran's roars.

'They ain't your friends Belinda, they're no good' Kieran shouted as she left and slammed the door behind her.

'She thinks those guys are her friends Mary, what am I supposed to do Mary' struggling to calm himself 'There's no talkin' to that kid, she's gonna find out the hard way. An' if they friggin touch her I'm gonna have to kill them. Jesus H. Christ I need this like I need a friggin hole in my head.'

Belinda's stay with Kieran and Rocco was short lived, only a matter of weeks. In that time Kieran took on the responsibility of caring for Belinda, unlike Rocco who seemed totally oblivious to Kieran's concerns for her safety and was, I thought, not exactly parenting material. Kieran tried to lay down the ground rules for Belinda to adhere to, but Belinda, not used to having boundaries set for her, refused to comply and each argument would end with Belinda storming out of the door ignoring Kieran and his orders completely.

'Where's Belinda?' I asked Kieran one afternoon after realising that her 'bubbly' personality was absent from the apartment. 'She's gone back to that 'air head' mother of hers Mary, not for nothin Mary, I tried with that kid, but she wouldn't listen.' It seemed to be a very sensitive subject with Kieran so I didn't pursue it. Kieran was right though and Belinda like most teenagers thought she knew it all and saw no danger and tragically paid a huge price for ignoring Kieran's advice and remaining loyal to her friends. It was several months later maybe even a year when the story spread like wildfire amongst the people in the neighbourhood who had known and loved Belinda. That she had been dragged into the back seat of a car in the down town area of Providence and viciously, physically and sexually assaulted by several of the very 'friends' Kieran had warned her about and 'word' had it that although she survived the attack, the lovely Belinda was never the same again.

Over the following weeks we met with Vanessa on a regular basis. Maggie and I couldn't help but like her because she always made us feel so welcome in her home. At least twice a week we'd sit 'chatting' together for hours, under the grapevine in her tiny courtyard garden and sipping iced tea.

Chapter 37

Gangsters Paradise

Vanessa explained that she had been born and raised in Colonial Hill. She married when she was very young and divorced after a relatively short period of time, but not before giving birth to a son called 'Freddy' and two daughters Jenny and Rena. Rearing three children on her own hadn't been easy. Although she worked whenever she could, money had always been in short supply. Despite the obstacles that were thrown in her path, Vanessa was a very positive person and never gave up. She used the modest rental income she earned from a small one bedroom apartment on the ground floor of her compact two family home to attend evening classes in a local community college. Maggie and I had to admire her stamina. She was determined to do whatever she could to provide a better future for herself and her three children whom she quite obviously lived for and adored.

Vanessa admitted that she had missed Kieran desperately when he left. After all she said life was a lot easier when he was around. He loved spending time with her kids and he was to them, the only father figure they had known. They still loved him and met with him regularly. 'Kieran' she said 'always helped them financially whenever he could.' She also went on to explain that although she and Kieran were together for many years on an' on, off basis she knew in her heart that it wouldn't last. There was a huge age gap between them. 'Kieran' she said 'longed for children of his own and made no attempt to hide the fact that he wanted the mother of those children to be Irish. That' she said for Kieran would be like 'having his cake and eating it'.

Maggie never tired of listening to Vanessa, especially when the conversation involved Kieran. She had long dismissed the idea that Vanessa was a threat to her and Vanessa was always willing to answer any questions she needed answering, which made her a very rare commodity in a neighbourhood where peoples' favourite response seemed to be 'I know nothin'.'

It was during one of those lazy afternoons in Vanessa's back yard that Maggie decided to 'bite the bullet' and ask Vanessa what she most wanted to know. 'Why doesn't Kieran ever talk about work Vanessa? I mean, what's the big deal? Mary and I tell him all the gossip at the restaurant.' Vanessa smiled and took a few minutes before asking 'what exactly has Kieran told you he does for a living?'

'He told me he's a real estate agent, but I don't know Vanessa, he works some really odd hours and he spends most of his days in and out of that men's club on the corner. 'You know Maggie,' Vanessa began 'if I didn't like you and Mary so much I'd let you go on believin' he's working in real estate, but I think you have a right to know the truth.' Just at that moment Jenny stuck her head out of the kitchen window on the first floor above us. 'Shut your mouth Ma,' she called down to her mother 'mind your own business, that mouth of yours is gonna get you in trouble.' 'But Jenny' Vanessa replied in protest, while Maggie and I looked at each other and wondered what the big secret was. 'But nothin', Jenny interrupted 'enough already.' 'Jenny, Maggie has a right to know and anyway Kieran must trust them. How long have we known Kieran? And we didn't know he had an apartment in Cranston.' Jenny didn't respond, a few minutes later she came out of the house, got into her car and drove away. Vanessa stared after her. 'She's just worried about me, people in this neighbourhood don't tolerate loose talk and Kieran is no exception to the rule.' Vanessa took another sip of her iced tea before continuing. 'You have to promise me Maggie, you too Mary that anything I'm about to say is strictly between us, you're not to even think about discussing it with Kieran. I don't want him comin' 'round here yelling at me.' The suspense thickened and Maggie couldn't take anymore. 'What in God's name is going on Vanessa' she asked with more than a hint of concern in her voice. 'Promise me,' Vanessa repeated. 'Yes, yes, ok, we promise' Maggie replied impatiently and obviously wishing Vanessa would get to the point and 'spit it out' whatever it was she wanted to say. Vanessa took a deep breath 'you're right Maggie, to be suspicious, Kieran doesn't know the first thing about real estate. He's, she paused, then glanced around her as if to make sure none of her neighbours were listening and then in a voice no louder than a whisper she said 'Kieran, works for the Mob' When I realised that Vanessa wasn't going to elaborate and after looking at Maggie, and seeing she was none the wiser I asked 'who's the Mob Vanessa?' Vanessa laughed at our total lack of understanding and street smarts. 'You know' she said realising she'd have to explain further 'he's a gangster, have you girls never heard of the Mafia?' 'Oh yeah' Maggie replied 'we've seen the Godfather movie with Marlon Brando, great movie. Those guys were ruthless, you remember it Mary, don't you?'

How could I forget it, I thought, especially the scene with the horses head in the bed, how could anyone be that cruel to an animal? I gave a little shudder, 'yeah I remember it Maggie.' Vanessa breathed what sounded like a sigh of relief and smiled 'at least you know now' she said. 'Know what Vanessa' Maggie asked looking even more baffled 'what has the Godfather movie got to do with Kieran? I swear Vanessa I haven't got a clue what you're going on about.' Vanessa looked at us quite incredulous to the fact that we still couldn't grasp what she had been saying. 'Have I to spell it out for you?' she asked. 'This whole neighbourhood is controlled by the Mafia and Kieran is involved in it up to his neck!' Maggie scoffed at Vanessa and sounded almost annoyed. 'That,' she said 'has to be the most ridiculous thing I've ever heard, the Godfather is a movie, it's not real!' 'You are wrong there Maggie,' Vanessa said in a very serious tone. 'The Mob are as strong as ever in America and Rhode Island is no exception to the rule. Kieran used to say they should never have nicknamed 'Rhode Island' the 'Ocean State' and thought it would have been more appropriate if they called it, Rhode Island, the home of Lobsters and Mobsters! He could be so funny sometimes,' she laughed.

Maggie and I faced work that evening very reluctantly. The conversation we had with Vanessa kept playing over and over in my mind. I found it impossible to concentrate on my work and could only imagine what Maggie was thinking. At the end of our shift Maggie came upstairs to the restaurant to see if I was finished. 'I'm nearly finished;' I said 'is Kieran calling in Maggie?' 'No, she replied bluntly, 'I was speaking to him earlier and I told him we were meeting Lisa for a drink. He offered to give us a ride, but I told him we'd take a taxi.' 'I didn't know we were meeting Lisa for a drink Maggie.' 'We're not, you 'Eejit' Mary, I just told him that 'cause I need some time to think. Did Rudi say anything to you Mary?'

When Maggie and I arrived at the restaurant to begin our shift that evening we were surprised to find Rudi the chef working in the kitchen as there was no sign of his sports car parked outside. It was his first day back after his 'accident' and ten days sick leave. He greeted us with a very enthusiastic hello as we made our way toward the cloakroom. Half afraid to look at him I nodded a response in his direction and couldn't avoid noticing the yellowish tint around his face and eyes. It was Giorgio the waiter, who volunteered to explain the absence of Rudi's car. 'Man,' he said 'Rudi must be real pissed about his corvette.

He stopped at a red light yesterday and what do ya know, this dude walks up to him and pours a can of paint all over him. Man that car ain't worth shit now.'

'No Maggie, not anything nasty anyway,' I said remembering that I did my best to avoid Rudi all night. But when I did run into him, he was uncharacteristically nice. 'He even offered to carry a basin of dirty dishes downstairs for me Maggie.' 'Yeah, same here Mary, he arrived out to where I was standing at the podium, carrying a mug of coffee and some fresh pastries. Two weeks ago he wouldn't have cared if my stomach was hitting my back bone!'

Chapter 38

CAN'T HELP LOVIN' THAT MAN OF MINE

As soon as we entered the kitchen of our apartment in Cranston I reached for the kettle, filled it with water and placed it on the stove to boil. I was glad to be home, it had been a long day and I knew it wasn't quite over, because I could tell by looking at Maggie that she was deep in thought and like me, the events of the day were weighing heavily on her mind. 'Not to worry' I thought 'everything will seem a lot better after a nice cup of tea.' 'What do you make of everything Vanessa was saying to us Mary? It's a bit far-fetched isn't it?'

I knew it would have been a huge relief to Maggie at that time if I decided to tell her that I didn't believe a word of what Vanessa had said and that I thought it was a whole load of nonsense. But I knew that she, like me, had more than likely spent the previous six hours at work playing over in her mind and analysing every moment we'd spent with Kieran. She would also have made comparisons between the characters in the movie and Kieran's lifestyle in general. Maggie would have to be stupid not to notice the all too many similarities. The unorthodox business hours, the expensive clothes, the way people went totally overboard in welcoming Kieran or Gerard Molyneaux when they entered a room and 'fussed' around them constantly to ensure they were happy and had everything they needed at all times. Gerard Molyneaux and his almost scary looking bouncer like associates. All the questions Gerard Molyneaux asked us when we first met him, which we naively mistook for friendliness and Kieran's comment about Gerard Molyneaux believing initially that Maggie and I could quite possibly be undercover cops.

'Maybe Maggie, it's not as serious as Vanessa said,' was the only response I could think of and although I think Maggie appreciated my feeble attempt to 'play down' the situation, I knew she didn't believe that I believed for one minute that it was anything but serious.

'What am I going to do Mary? I mean how could this happen? His father was a lawyer, his mother worked in a bank; they must have been respectable people. He's got real old fashioned values that I really like Mary and he's such a gentleman when we're out.

You've seen the way he stands up when I enter a room Mary, or holds the car door open for me to get in. He only drinks one beer to my three and he doesn't even smoke cigarettes!'

'I know Maggie, you don't have to convince me,' I said. 'He couldn't have been nicer to us or helped us out more than he did. He's sort of a big brother to me and of course it goes without saying that he's crazy about you.' I thought it would help the situation if I reminded Maggie that Kieran loved her, but it unfortunately had the opposite effect. 'Oh my God Mary, do you think if I finish with Kieran he'll have me, you know 'bumped off?' She said almost knocking over her cup of tea. I had to laugh. Maggie could be a real drama queen at times. 'Don't you think you're over-reacting a bit Maggie? I said Kieran loves you, I didn't say he would be willing to do life for you!' 'What makes you so sure Mary? I mean if Vanessa is right, and the Godfather movie is anything to go by, those guys don't accept rejection very well!' I decided to fill the kettle again for another cup of tea. Something told me it was going to be a very long night. 'I'm not sure of anything Maggie apart from one thing and that is Kieran Hennessy wouldn't harm a hair on your head.'

'Mary, you better not go sayin' anything to Mam about it when she calls. I've already told her I'm seeing a real estate agent and she sounded really pleased. I can't exactly dash her hopes now and say 'I'm in love with 'Al Capone!' Oh God, what am I going to do?'

I started to laugh as I remembered a line from a 'Laurel and Hardy' movie that seemed appropriate. 'I dunno Maggie, all I can say is, 'another fine mess you've got us into!'

Over the next few days' information continued to flow from Vanessa. She said Kieran had already spent some lengthy time in prison. One conviction was for the possession of counterfeit money. On one occasion when the judge asked if he had anything to say before sentencing, Kieran had allegedly thought that it might help to lighten the sentence if he mentioned that his deceased father was a lawyer. But allegedly the judge was disgusted with Kieran for bringing shame on his family and the Irish community in general and sentenced Kieran to serve his time in a prison where the vast majority of the population were black. 'By all accounts,' Vanessa continued 'Kieran didn't have an easy time of it.

Rocco Del Monte she explained had served time with the 'Boston Strangler' and was also she said responsible for an associate of his being handed the death penalty. Rocco, Kieran told her, had been entrusted with the job of getting a man, who was on the run from the law, to a safe house. But Rocco, having no sense of direction got lost and stopped a state policeman for help, who recognised them and arrested them on the spot. Fortunately for the man in question, while waiting on 'death row', Rhode Island State abolished 'The Death Penalty' and the man's life was spared. Gerard Molyneaux's family had connections to the 'Mob' for generations and in Vanessa's opinion Gerard would never have known any other way of life. His brother Tommy was serving a life sentence for robbery. The reportedly large sum of money which was taken in the heist was never recovered and the word on the street was that Gerard, who was also involved, had stashed it. Vanessa also 'backed up' Rocco Del Monte's story about Gerard's other two brothers' tragic deaths.

'Yes you're right' Vanessa nodded to Maggie, confirming her suspicions. 'That scar on Kieran's chest is a bullet wound. He had a narrow escape but he gained a lot of respect within the high ranking elders in the 'Mob.' 'Why was that?' Maggie asked, struggling to comprehend what she was being told. 'Because,' Vanessa replied 'when the police arrived on the scene to the bar where it happened, Kieran wouldn't talk. He

was sitting upright on a chair and refused 'point blank' to tell the cops who shot him!'
Maggie and I found it almost impossible to believe that Vanessa was talking about the same man that we had come to know. The Kieran who we spent countless happy hours with, the Kieran who we told Irish jokes to until he cried with laughter, the Kieran we played practical jokes on , and most of all, the Kieran who although had a fiery 'Irish' temper, was always to us, kind, considerate and caring. We quite simply couldn't believe it! Maggie even considered that it was quite possible that Vanessa was trying to frighten her away from Kieran and back to Ireland. 'I think Vanessa still 'holds a candle' for Kieran Mary' she said one day while we sat having a quiet drink in the 'By-Way. She says it's over between them but I'd bet any money she would take him back in a heartbeat!'

I couldn't dispute Maggie's opinion because like Maggie, Vanessa never seemed to tire of speaking about Kieran but considering everything she told us about him, she never appeared shocked or angry. Everything was said as if it were very much matter of fact.
Kieran knew, like he seemed to know everything else, what was happening in the neighbourhood that we spent quite a bit of time at Vanessa's house and if it ever bothered him, he never said. Instead he joked 'I hear you've met my 'French Gang.' 'Who's that?' I asked. 'Freddy, Jenny and Rena' he replied. 'Oh yeah,' I said remembering that Vanessa had told us that her ex-husband was French. 'They're real good kids Mary,' he said with a hint of sadness in his voice.

Chapter 39

Private Eyes

It turned out that Vanessa was right when she told Jenny that Kieran must trust us because as the days rolled by, Kieran began to let his guard down more around us, and on each occasion he was less than subtle. The first example of this occurred when Maggie and I called to Kieran and Rocco's place to relax between shifts. It had very quickly became the 'norm' in our daily routine and the apartment had become very much like a second home. Maggie and I would joke about feeling quite spoilt, with a choice of two 'pads', Kieran and Rocco's place in the city and our apartment out in the suburbs. We were happy and very content in our relatively simple routine.

That afternoon after letting ourselves in through the unlocked back door, Maggie headed straight to the bathroom to take a shower, claiming that the humidity was killing her. While I collapsed onto the sofa and 'tucked in' to a salami filled 'sub' I had bought a few minutes before in the delicatessen across the street from the restaurant. A few minutes later Maggie emerged from the bathroom and went into Kieran's room to get dressed. 'I wonder where he keeps the hair dryer' I heard her say to herself through the closed door. A moment later, dressed, but with a turban shaped towel wrapped around her wet hair, she stood in front of me waving two packets of ladies nylon stockings in her hand.

'Look at these Mary', she roared, 'I swear to God if he's seeing someone else, I'll kill him,' she continued shaking with temper. 'Shit' I thought if anyone should be worrying about being 'bumped off' it was Kieran. Maggie was furious, and I didn't get a chance to say anything because Kieran had returned and was standing right behind her. 'What's up with you Maggie?' He asked looking highly amused. 'What's up with me?' She screamed and waved the packages in his face. 'I'll tell you what's wrong with me, what are these doing in your chest of drawers? Who do they belong to?' 'They belong to me' Kieran replied calmly and took the stockings from her. 'Oh of course they're yours' Maggie said sarcastically. 'You'll be telling me next that you wear them.' 'Sure do' Kieran replied walking into his bedroom and shutting the door behind him. 'You don't fool me Kieran', Maggie shouted at the closed door. 'I'm not an Eejit you know.' Maggie sat on the sofa deep in thought, arms folded in front of her and a look of defiance on her face. 'He's not going to make a fool out of me Mary; I haven't a notion of speaking to him 'till he explains himself.'

Maggie didn't move a muscle when Kieran's door opened behind her a few minutes later, and she didn't notice my mouth drop open when I looked at Kieran and watched him raise his finger to his mouth, urging me to say nothing. Kieran pounced on Maggie and she almost jumped out of her skin with fright when she saw him. Kieran was wearing the nylons on his head as a mask. 'Told you they're mine Maggie' he said. Then burst into fits of laughter at the expression of surprise on her face. When Maggie finally got over the shock of seeing Kieran's contorted face squashed against the nylons, she decided to look on the situation with her usual optimism. 'At least I know now,' she said to me 'he's not foolin' around.'

It was later that evening after our usual 'night cap' in the 'By Way' and Kieran made his usual offer to drive us home that something happened that made us realise, that what Vanessa had told us was closer to the truth than we had ever anticipated. Despite the fact that we had been hoping it was an elaborate fabrication or that Vanessa at the very least was suffering from and all too vivid imagination.

While driving down Lincoln Avenue, we came to a stop at a red traffic light. Although it was past midnight there was still quite a lot of traffic due to the amount of restaurants on the street. As I sat in the back seat, I noticed that Kieran kept looking in the rear view mirror. 'Watch those assholes' he said and without warning opened the car door and leapt out. There were several cars behind us waiting patiently for the lights to change colour, but Kieran only seemed interested in the occupants of the car which was second in line behind his. 'Just so you know' he shouted through the closed window at them 'I'm going to Cranston.' The lights had turned to green and Kieran seemed oblivious to the fact that cars were honking at him in an effort to remind him that he was holding up traffic. The driver of the car that Kieran had been yelling at, swerved out of line, then drove at a snail's pace past Kieran's car allowing Maggie and I an opportunity to see two very clean-cut looking gentlemen in suits staring back at us.

'See you later guys,' Kieran called after them before sitting back into the car. 'What was that all about?' Maggie asked. 'Are you normally in the habit of holding up traffic while you speak to your friends?' 'Maggie,' Kieran replied 'they ain't no friends of mine, even if, like you, they seem to really enjoy my company. They're F.B.I.' It was all too much for Maggie.

'I just want you to know Kieran' she said 'I have my reputation to think of and if you end up getting arrested, you needn't be expecting me to show up at a police station to bail you out, you can just 'fuck off!'

Kieran almost lost control of the car when Maggie swore at him. It wasn't like her to use bad language. 'What's that supposed to mean?' He asked looking at a now familiar defiant expression on Maggie's face. 'What's what supposed to mean Kieran? Have I to spell it out for you?' 'What does 'fuck off' mean?' Kieran asked, mimicking my Irish accent. 'It means', Maggie growled through clenched teeth 'you can get lost!'

Kieran struggled to keep the car straight he was laughing so much. 'Fuck off', he kept repeating it over and over to himself. 'You're killin' me Maggie,' he managed to say 'I just can't wait to meet my 'buddies from the F.B.I. again, I'm gonna tell them to 'fuck off!'

I made myself scarce when we finally reached home. I climbed into my sleeping bag on the sofa, leaving Maggie and Kieran sitting at the kitchen table. Kieran might as well have been sitting on his own; because even though he was speaking to Maggie she was giving him the 'deaf ear.'

As I lay on the sofa cocooned in my sleeping bag, I thought about Maggie, Kieran and the events of the day. 'Was this it?'

I asked myself. 'Was Maggie going to finish with Kieran?' I thought of how hard Maggie had worked at her education over the years and she had already completed three years of college. Would she be willing to jeopardise all that for Kieran and risk losing out on the career she had dreamed of? Could she face visiting him in prison if it came to that? Would Kieran ask or expect her to? So much had happened in such a relatively short space of time. Everything seemed to be moving so fast. I deliberated long and hard that night, and felt sure that Maggie was going to finish with Kieran. She wasn't cut out for the life style that seemed almost inevitable if Kieran continued on the road he was travelling. We had never even met someone who had been to prison, apart from Paddy who had been removed from our home on a few occasions to find himself 'sobering up' in a cold cell in the local Garda station and getting a stern warning from the Sergeant the following morning for being drunk and disorderly. I was sure Kieran would be devastated when Maggie broke the news to him and I hoped he would understand.

I also thought how I would miss his friendship, but as my eyes became heavy I consoled myself with the unrealistic and naive possibility that maybe we could all remain friends.

Chapter 40

JAIL BIRDS

I woke the next morning to Maggie's hand on my shoulder and her voice calling me as she shook me. 'Mary, are you awake? I've made you some tea. Are you awake Mary?' 'I am now' I managed to say while thinking to myself that Maggie, who was anything but a morning person, sounded quite chirpy. 'Here's a cup of tea for you,' she said determined not to let me fall back to sleep. 'What's up with you Maggie?' I asked while trying to wriggle out of my sleeping bag. 'Guess what Mary?' I was barely awake and was not in the mood for guessing games. And with all that had transpired in the previous weeks, anything was possible. 'What Maggie? Just tell me.' 'Oh Mary, Kieran wants me to meet his mother, that means he must be serious right?' Maggie didn't wait for my response. 'We're both invited to his mother's house for dinner at the weekend. You can tell by the way he talks about his mother that he thinks the world of her. I get the impression that introducing me to her is a really big deal for him. Oh Mary, I'm so excited, what will I wear? I want to look my best.' 'I'm sure you'll find something Maggie,' I said yawning. 'After all, today is only Wednesday.' 'I know, I know Mary, but it's important that I make a good impression.' Maggie turned on her heels, happy that she had succeeded in waking me up and sharing her good news with me. 'I'm making French toast for Kieran, do you want some Mary?' she asked as she left the living room. 'Yes please Maggie, I'll be out in a minute.'

Standing in the living room sipping my tea and staring out the window at the street three floors below, I thought how wrong I had been in my assessment of Maggie. She had obviously made the decision that she was in the relationship with Kieran for the 'long haul', and I trusted that she had given all aspects of it careful consideration. 'I'm sure she knows what she's doing' I said aloud, 'Sure isn't she the one with the brains?' Who knows what the future holds, maybe Kieran will give up whatever it is that he's doing. Maybe, just maybe I thought, Maggie might be the one to get him back on the 'straight and narrow.'

Enzo our boss didn't argue when Maggie and I told him that we wouldn't be available for the lunch shift that Sunday. We hadn't taken a day off for two weeks so we were more than entitled but knowing what I knew by then, I doubt he would have objected even if we weren't due a break.

Kieran called us early Sunday morning to remind us we were to be at his mother's for one o'clock. 'He's picking us up at a quarter to Mary,' Maggie said as she hung up the phone and rushed back to the bathroom. She had been there since the 'crack' of dawn, showering, washing her hair, styling it, painting her fingers and toe nails, but come twelve o'clock she was no closer to being ready. I saw Kieran's car pull up on the street outside the house, he was with Rocco and another man whom I didn't know. They began talking with Danny, Kieran's brother. 'Kieran's outside', I called to Maggie who was putting on her make-up in the bathroom. 'I'll never be ready Mary,' she replied nervously. 'Well, changing your clothes three times didn't exactly help Maggie,' I said feeling totally unsympathetic to her plight. I had endured a morning of questions, 'how does this look Mary? Do these shoes go with this or will I wear the others? Is this skirt too short?' On and on she went; she wouldn't have gone to as much trouble I thought if she was meeting the President.

Kieran gave a quick tap to the kitchen door before opening it, 'you two decent?' He asked smiling. 'Maggie's in the bathroom Kieran.' 'I'm nearly ready Kieran,' Maggie shouted. 'Take your time,' he called back to her 'I gotta take care of some business, I'll be back, half hour the latest, ok?' 'Ok Kieran, see you in a while,' I said thinking Maggie would be glad of the extra time. No sooner had Kieran gone when Maggie began swearing in the bedroom; 'Shit, shit, I can't believe it, I have a ladder in my nylons. Shit, what am I going to do now?'

I knew that this was enough to send Maggie over the edge and I was about to suggest that I run to the drug store two blocks away to buy her some new nylons when I noticed Kieran's car was still parked outside on the street. They must have taken Danny's car I thought. 'Kieran's car is outside Maggie; you could go to the drug store and buy new ones.' 'Oh thank God, come on, let's go Mary, you can run in and get them for me.' Maggie had been driving Kieran's car on a regular basis, so she knew that he always left the keys in the ignition.

We were to and from the drug store in less than ten minutes and as Maggie pulled the car into the driveway and stopped by the front door, she let out a sigh of relief. 'Problem solved,' she said and we ran back up the stairs. Little did we know at the time that our problems were just starting.

Maggie dressed quickly and she was sitting at the kitchen table when we heard the screeching of tyres outside. I ran to the window to see what was happening. I saw that Kieran had returned and was reversing his own car at top speed back out on to the street where he had originally parked it, and the car that they left in, fly into the driveway to the side of the house. The three men jumped out and there seemed a lot of commotion. Kieran was swearing and all of a sudden ran toward the house. He bounded up the stairs so fast I hadn't time to warn Maggie. He burst into the kitchen, swearing and waving his arms frantically. He was six foot two and broad, a big man, but now in the relatively small kitchen he seemed larger than life. 'Who moved the friggin car?' He was yelling at Maggie, knowing that I couldn't drive. Both Maggie and I had grown used to Kieran's occasional outbursts and paid them very little attention. They never lasted very long and reluctant as Maggie was to admit it, Kieran usually had good reason. This time however it escalated to a whole new level, because Maggie, who was already stressed at the impending visit to Kieran's mother, was not going to tolerate it and began screaming back at him. 'I moved the car' she roared 'I had to go to the drugs store to buy 'panty hose', what's the big deal anyway?' 'What's the big deal?' Kieran said repeating the question. 'Yeah, what's the big deal Kieran?' Maggie repeated. 'One minute you're playing the 'good fella', saying I can drive the car whenever I want, now you're freakin' out. You'd want to make your mind up Kieran. In fact, you can keep your bloody car, you needn't worry about me driving it again.' Maggie paused to light a cigarette and Kieran saw his opportunity. 'You girls are driving me crazy, two dim-wits I'm dealing with it. I can't friggin believe you moved the car.' 'Don't dare speak to me like that Kieran Hennessy', Maggie spat at him. 'If this is the way you treat women you're only a shit head and I don't want anything to do with you.'

Maggie I knew, although close to tears was not going to back down. 'Will the two of you just calm down' I said, hoping but not believing for one minute that either of them would heed my advice. 'Just calm down' I repeated. 'An' Kieran, Maggie is right, if you didn't want her to drive the car you should have said.' Maggie was off again, 'you've got another thing comin' Kieran, if you think I'm going to your mother's house now.' Maggie was cryin' now and Kieran was at a loss for words and as usual regretting his outburst. 'You think I like giving you a hard time Maggie?' He said as he watched tears roll down her face.

'Let me tell you this not for nothin', if the cops pulled you over in that car today, you and your kid sister were gettin' life!' 'Yes Kieran,' Maggie replied fighting back more tears and determined as always to have the last word, though she was visibly shaken at what Kieran had said. 'And whose bloody fault would that have been?' She screamed. Then jumped to her feet and went into the bedroom slamming the bedroom door so hard the walls shook.

It was three days before Maggie agreed to speak to Kieran again. And although she shuddered to think what had been in his car that day she never asked. I didn't want to know either and believed that the Italians of the neighbourhood were 'rubbing off' on me. My attitude was 'if I don't know, then I can't say.' It was a habit that has stayed with me to this day.

Chapter 41

Time To Say Goodbye

The summer days were drawing to a close and although the weather was still quite warm compared with Ireland, the tell-tale signs that told you Autumn was near were everywhere. Leaves of gold, red and copper abseiled aimlessly through the air and landed at our feet wherever we walked. The squirrels that inhabited most of the city streets seemed busier than usual as they scurried around gathering their hoard which they hoped would see them through the freezing winter until spring returned once more.

Mam had called three times the previous week, but thankfully for once, it was Maggie she was yelling at and not me. All I could hear was Maggie's answers to Mam's questions. I didn't need to hear Mam, I knew why she was calling. She wanted to know when we were coming home. 'Yes Mam,' I heard Maggie say 'I know I've three years done. Yes I know I'll have my degree after one more. I don't know Mam. Yes I like him a lot, Yes, I know I've only known him a few months.' Maggie didn't want to leave Kieran, and I was surprised when after answering Mam's third call, that I heard her say 'Alright Mam, I'll be home next week.

Maggie placed the receiver back on the wall and slumped into a chair at the kitchen table. 'When did you decide to go home?' I asked her and handed her a cup of tea. 'Just now Mary, Mam thinks I'm going back to college but I'm not. I still have to go home though. I need to inform the college that I won't be returning, collect my exam results and tie up any loose ends.' 'And then what Maggie?' I asked still surprised. 'I'll work my ass off Mary. I'll get two jobs if I have to, but I'll be back here by the New Year.' 'Does Kieran have any idea that you're leaving Maggie?' 'No Mary, but he'll just have to get used to the idea. I'll be back before he knows it. 'Sure 'tis the end of September now, yeah I'm sure he'll be fine.' Maggie didn't sound all to confident that Kieran would take the news well and as I sat

there hoping the 'tips' at work would be good in the coming week, and worried that I might not have enough money for my plane fare, Maggie announced her new 'brainwave' idea. 'I was thinking Mary that you might consider staying on here. I mean, you like it here and what have you got to go home for?' It was more of a statement than a question. 'And then Kieran would have to believe I was coming back if you're still here.'
Maggie sounded desperate and I knew how difficult it would be for her to leave, so it was agreed, she would go home and I would stay. 'And you could let me know how he's gettin on' she concluded. Which really meant, you can spy on him Mary and let me know if he does anything wrong. 'Now' I thought, all she has to do is break the news to Kieran.
All things considered, Kieran took the news of Maggie's decision to return to Ireland well. He understood that she had some commitments at home and that she wanted to explain things to Mam, face to face, rather than over the phone. 'She's a braver woman than me' I thought as I pictured Mam's face when Maggie told her she was quitting college. All that said, it didn't mean that he didn't try to change her mind. 'Your mother could come here for a vacation Maggie, an' you could write to the college, yeah they could post your exam results. What do you even need those for?' 'Ah, so I can resume my studies here Kieran. You hardly believe I'm going to spend my life parking cars. I want a career and a nice home.' Kieran tried a different approach. 'Ain't you worried about leavin' your kid sister on her own?' 'Mary will be fine, won't you Mary?' Maggie said as if she had every confidence in me. 'Yeah, I'm sure I will,' I replied feeling not too sure at all. I had never lived on my own before and although I wasn't afraid, I just didn't know how to do things like write a cheque or pay the household bills and I was too embarrassed to ask.
Kieran made one last ditch effort to sway Maggie. 'You know Maggie, you're gonna miss 'Frank Sinatra' in concert on New Year's Eve. We got front row tickets, it's a great show, we go to see him every year in Atlantic City, don't we Rocco?' Kieran

had obviously been hoping for a little back up from Rocco, but he just nodded his head and grunted.

The last week of Maggie's stay flew by a lot faster than she wanted. She and Kieran spent the entire last day and night together. It was decided that Maggie was to take a Greyhound Bus from Providence to Logan Airport in Boston. And Kieran was to drive her to the bus station. I decided that Kieran should go alone with her and that I'd stay behind thus giving them the last few minutes alone. Maggie and I hugged and said goodbyes in the yard of Kieran and Rocco's apartment under the watchful stares of Doris, who was, as usual, perched on her front steps.

I'll always remember Kieran's face when he returned from the bus station that day. Although he stepped out of the car almost immediately, he stood for what seemed like the longest time just staring into space. And I would not have been one bit surprised at the time if I saw Kieran jump back into the car and chase after Maggie, in the hope of getting her back. 'You ok Kieran?' I asked seeing the sadness in his eyes. 'Don't worry Kieran,' I said when he didn't answer. 'I know my sister and if she says she'll be back, then she will be back.' Kieran looked at me and managed a faint smile. 'You think so Mary?' He asked swallowing hard. 'Kieran,' I said hoping to reassure him 'I know so!'

It was at that moment that Rocco came outside, obviously curious to know why Kieran was standing in the yard for so long. He must have read Kieran's mind, which wouldn't have taken a psychic to do so, because the pain on Kieran's face was plain to see. Right there and then all my reservations and suspicions about Rocco were proved to be well founded. 'Hey Kieran' he said 'not for nothin, you wanna forget about her, you gotta be dumb not to know she's gone back to her boyfriend. I bet she's got maybe half a dozen and she ain't gonna be cryin' any tears for you, jus' forget about her.'

I remember thinking at the time how downright nasty Rocco was, but I couldn't understand why, and it was some years later before I did. Rocco wasn't so much envious of the time that

Maggie spent with Kieran, but he was worried. He had seen Kieran in other relationships but if other people, like Lynn the bar lady, could see how much Kieran loved Maggie, there was no doubt in my mind that Rocco could see it too. Rocco had invested a lot of time and energy into teaching Kieran the tricks of the trade. Kieran was Rocco's meal ticket. He was in his sixties and was depending on Kieran to support him in his old age. He knew Kieran was so proud to be Irish and that Maggie represented everything that Kieran knew he should have been, had he not been groomed and led into a life of crime by him. Rocco was not going to run the risk of Kieran going 'straight' or worse, disappearing out of his life altogether if Kieran decided to marry Maggie and start anew somewhere else. I'm quite sure Rocco would have been of the opinion that if Kieran did want to get married, it would be far more beneficial to him if Kieran married a nice Italian girl.

Maybe someone from the neighbourhood, who knew how things worked; It would also help strengthen Kieran's standing within the Mob, the Italians would, I believe, have preferred if Kieran was with one of their own.

Chapter 42

On My Own

In the days that followed Maggie's departure I missed her a lot and the novelty of having the apartment to myself soon wore off. I knew it would be difficult to manage the rent and my utility bills on my own, so I was delighted when Enzo my boss, offered me some extra hours. I was to start work each morning at ten rather than eleven and do all the cleaning before the restaurant opened. It was also a relief to me to have to spend less time on my own. I called to see Vanessa quite a lot and she always made me feel welcome. She often told me she'd love to have me as a daughter in law. If only her son Freddy would ask me out and I'm sure it was only because of Vanessa's coaxing that he finally did. I liked Freddy a lot. He was very gentlemanly and really handsome. On our first date Jenny and Rena came along to 'break the ice.' I think we both needed a bit of support. Rena, Vanessa's youngest daughter was very nice and had obviously inherited her mother's warm and friendly personality and Jenny and I got on well together at work. We went to a bar and we all sat around 'chatting' together for a while, then Jenny and Rena joined the company of some of their friends so Freddy and I had a chance to get to know each other. Everything was going quite well until I insisted on paying for a round of drinks. Freddy couldn't believe it and sounded almost insulted, 'you're not payin' for the drinks Mary'; he objected 'round here we know how to treat a lady and it's the man who pays.' Freddy lost the battle, but sadly I lost the war. We went on one more date after that and he told his mother I was more like a sister to him. A polite way I thought of saying he wasn't 'into' me. There was no animosity though and we remained on good terms. I didn't blame Freddy for deciding to call it quits. I was, at the best of times, nervous around men and found it difficult to make conversation. Freddy was, as Kieran put it, 'a good kid.'

I didn't call to Kieran and Rocco's apartment much after Maggie left because I didn't want him to think that I was checkin' up on him. But I often 'bumped' into him on the street. On one of those occasions I spotted him on the corner of Nimnuc St and Avenue where he lived. He looked as if he were waiting on someone. I knew he hadn't seen me and I decided to surprise him by creeping up beside him, but it was I who was surprised. Kieran was startled when I pounced on him and swung his arm out as if in defence, and if I hadn't have reacted as quickly as I did to avoid the blow I would surely have been knocked out cold.

Kieran got a bigger shock than I did knowing what he had almost done, 'Jesus H. Christ Mary,' he yelled obviously shaken, 'don't ever creep up on me like that, I can't see nothin' out of this eye. Jesus H. Christ Mary, I could have killed you!' 'Well, you didn't Kieran, I'm fine' I said trying to reassure him. 'What do you mean your blind in one eye Kieran? What happened you?' 'Ah it was somthin' that happened a while back Mary. I got into a fight with this guy an' he whacked me with a bottle an' I gotta piece of glass stuck in my eye.' 'That's awful Kieran', I said grimacing at the thought of how painful that must have been. 'And you lost your sight because of it?' 'No it wasn't the glass Mary. I could see after that happened. Someone called the cops and I got arrested and cops got a doctor to check out my eye. I guess his sight wasn't too good either 'cause he stuck some friggin thing in my right eye.' 'What?' I said in horror imagining the agony of it. 'But it was an accident Kieran. You don't think he did it deliberately?' 'Who knows Mary? The cops ain't what you'd call my best friends. Just forget about it and don't go jumping out on top of me ok.' 'No I won't Kieran, I'm sorry I didn't know.' 'Don't worry about it kid, I gotta go now, I'll see you later.' 'Ok Kieran, take care,' I said as I watched him cross the street to where Gerard Molyneaux was sitting in his Cadillac outside the men's club. Just as I was about to turn and walk away, Kieran called to me across the street. 'Hey Mary, don't be a stranger, call around to me an'

Rocco whenever you want.' I waved and nodded to him as the car pulled away.

I called to Vanessa's house that afternoon and over a cup of tea I told her what Kieran told me about his eye. 'Yes, that's true Mary,' she said confirming Kieran's story. 'And do you know who hit him with a bottle Mary?' I looked at Vanessa and shrugged my shoulders. 'It was that dirty old man who sold Maggie those shoes.' 'Oh right' I said remembering Kieran's explosive outburst on the night in question. 'So' I said 'Kieran blames him for losing the sight in his eye.' 'No Mary, Kieran hated that man long before that happened because the guy had a reputation for dating girls young enough to be his Granddaughters and Kieran told him exactly what he thought of him to his face. That's what caused the fight that night.'

I decided a few days later to take Kieran up on his offer and call around to the apartment to say hello. As I had done at least a hundred times before, I went to the back door, gave it a tap to announce my arrival and walked in.

Rocco was standing on the far side of the kitchen and I could tell he was surprised to see me, as it was my first visit in a number of weeks. I was even more surprised though to see the kitchen table completely covered in about six inches deep in a green grassy substance, I could only assume was Marijuana. There were some plastic bags containing a white powdery substance which I realised many years later wasn't flour! That wasn't the only surprise though. All of a sudden an arm went around my throat gripping me in a headlock and I felt something cold and metallic press against my temple. Frozen in fear and unable to see who was holding me, all I knew was that I didn't recognise the man's voice which sounded almost hysterical. 'Who the fuck is she?' He screamed at Rocco, who was waving his hands and shouting back at him. 'Hey, hey cool it, put that thing away', he said pointing to whatever the man was holding to my head 'are you fucking crazy?' 'Who the fuck is she?' The man screamed again. 'She's ok, enough already' Bobby replied 'that's Kieran's buddy, she's one of the Irish girls.'

The man reluctantly loosened his grip on me and I was free to walk away. I didn't look behind me to see who had been holding me. I walked across the kitchen thinking that at any moment my knees were going to buckle. I kept going through to the sitting room and it was only when I reached the front door that I turned to Rocco and said 'tell Kieran I just called by to say hello.' I walked around the corner to the By-Way bar and surprised Lynn by asking for a large scotch. 'It ain't like you to be drinkin' this early Mary, rough day?' 'Yeah, something like that Lynn' I said gripping the glass with both hands to steady it.

I don't know if Rocco ever told Kieran what had happened. If he did, Kieran never mentioned it and I'm certain I was never in the company of that other man again because without a doubt, I knew, I would never forget his voice!

Maggie called me religiously every week and wanted to hear all the news but it was never long before she got around to her real reason for calling, Kieran. She wanted to hear every snippet of information and the conversation was more like an interrogation. Had I seen him? If so when and where? Who was he with and where was he going? Had I been speaking to him and had he asked about her?

I explained to Maggie about working the extra hours and that because of the extra work load I hadn't been calling around to the apartment as much.

I didn't mention the ordeal that I had endured only a few days before, because I felt there was no point in worrying her and after all I thought, that had nothing to do with Kieran. I told her that anytime I had seen Kieran he was on his own and if he wasn't he was with Rocco or Gerard Molyneaux and no, he hadn't mentioned her apart from occasionally asking if she had called.

'What do you think of that Mary?' was always her favourite question. 'Don't you think it's strange that he doesn't ask about me? 'No I don't Maggie' was always my reply. 'How many men do you know Maggie who discuss their relationships with their girlfriend's sisters? You know Maggie that Kieran wouldn't do that.' 'Yeah I suppose Mary but'. On and on the questions would flow until I'd hear Mam yelling in the background. 'Maggie' I hope you know you're the one who's going to be paying the phone bill.' Then she'd say 'give me that phone, I want to have a word with Mary.' Maggie would say a reluctant goodbye and I knew Mam had to prise the phone out of her hand. I knew Mam would be asking me the same questions she asked since Maggie had returned home. 'Mary what in the name of God are you doing over there on your own? Why don't you come home? Can't you at least come home for Christmas?' Each week that passed Mams pleas became more and more difficult to listen to and her tactics had changed.

'The boys and Barbra miss you and Barbra thinks you've forgotten all about her and 'Rogue' hasn't stopped running around the house looking for you since the day you left.' Eventually, like Maggie, I gave in. 'Mam I'm not promising anything' I said 'but if I can save enough for the plane fare I'll come home.' 'Will you Mary? Oh that would be great and with the amount of hours Maggie told me you're working, you must have plenty of money.' 'I'll talk to you again next week Mam' I said not wanting to tell her the truth, which was, that I was struggling to make ends meet, without the added pressure of trying to raise the price of a plane ticket. 'You're sure you're ok Mary' Mam would ask before hanging up. 'Yeah, I'm fine Mam' I would lie 'don't worry about me.'

Chapter 43

Someone To Watch Over Me

A few days later I was faced with another problem. I went to work as usual. Having finished the cleaning and confident that the restaurant was in 'ship shape', I went downstairs to open the door for the lunch trade. There was a man standing at the door waiting to be left in. He appeared to be in his early sixties and was like most of the restaurant customers, well dressed. I smiled and said 'Good Morning' as I held the door open for him. 'Well, aren't you the pretty thing' he replied smiling 'you're not from around here.' I spoke to him politely as we climbed the stairs together, explaining that I was from Ireland and that I had been working in Little Sicily for a number of months. 'You'll certainly be seeing me here more often' he said as I showed him to the bar. He was true to his word. For the next week, he was the first customer in the door each day and the last one to leave at the end of the lunch trade. Each day he would call me over to where he was seated at the bar and I would politely answer any questions he asked me. And every day before he left, despite the fact that I'd never waited on him, he would leave twenty dollars with Bobby the bartender to give to me. I explained to the man that there was no need to 'tip' me because he wasn't eating. But he would just say 'don't worry about it sweetie, there's plenty more where that came from.'

By the fifth day I was beginning to feel a little uneasy. He was demanding more and more of my attention and I couldn't help but notice that he was constantly staring at me and no matter where I went in the restaurant he eyes seemed to follow.

On the first day when we met, he asked me where I was living and innocently I had told him the name of the street. But five days later he wanted to know which house and my 'gut' feeling was not to tell him. My heart began to beat faster as I tried to think of a valid excuse. 'You know' I said quite innocently 'I've only lived there a few weeks and I can't remember the number on the door.' I knew it was the lamest excuse ever and I thought

if the man did believe me, he would also have to realise that I was really stupid, but this was the one time that I didn't care if someone thought I was an 'Eejit.' 'I go by that street every morning Mary and it's gettin' pretty cold out there, you know I could give you a ride to work.' 'Oh God no,' I said as nicely but firmly as I could. 'The fresh air wakes me up.'
'Ok' he replied 'the offer still stands if you change your mind.'
I was so relieved when he accepted my feeble excuse.
The next morning I made the ten minute walk to the bus stop. A freezing rain had begun to fall and my hair was dripping wet. Cold and miserable, I didn't pay any attention to the car which was parked about twenty feet from the bus stop, so I got the shock of my life when just as I was about to pass it, the door swung wide open and the man from the restaurant stepped out. He was practically blocking my way. 'Hop in' he said smiling. 'No, really I'm fine' I replied nervously. The man wasn't taking 'no' for an answer. 'Get in' he said in a voice that sounded more like he was giving me an order. 'Enzo would be really pissed if I let one of his staff out in this rain.' I didn't know what to do, I didn't want to get into the car but I was afraid that if I insulted the man who had been spending a lot of money in the restaurant, Enzo might be really annoyed with me. For all I know I thought he could be Enzo's best friend. Reluctantly and feeling very frightened I got into the car.
I knew I'd made a big mistake within minutes of the car pulling away from the kerb and the ten minute drive to work seemed like an eternity. The man kept taking his eyes off the road to stare at me. 'You're such a pretty little lady' he said with a look that made my stomach turn, 'did anyone ever tell you that?' I didn't respond, I was too afraid to open my mouth in case I threw up all over his car. The man began to rub his hand up and down my leg and as he did, nightmarish memories of a hellish experience I'd suffered at the age of fifteen at the hands of two men in their fifties who also said I was pretty, came flooding back. Mam or Maggie knew nothing about it at that time. 'Come to Florida with me' the man said interrupting my memories 'I'll show you a really good time, you can have it all,

clothes, money, jewellery, every woman likes diamonds right? You'll be lookin' like a million dollars.' 'I don't know' I said finally finding my voice 'I'll have to think about it' I lied. 'You do that honey' he said as he swung the car into the lot at the restaurant.
I was shaking when I walked into the kitchen of the restaurant, so much so that Enzo, who was doing a stock take, even noticed. 'You ok Mary?' he asked seeming, for once, genuinely concerned. 'You look like you've seen a ghost.'

'I'll be alright Enzo, but I think I might be coming down with something, could I take twenty minutes when I'm finished cleaning to go to the drug store.' 'Yeah, sure Mary, you take your time, Jenny will be here by then and she can cover you for a while.'
I set about my cleaning duties on the verge of tears. 'Suppose he's at the bus stop again tomorrow' I thought, my heart skipped a beat and my stomach turned. 'Suppose he finds out where I'm living.' There was something about that man that really frightened me and what made it worse was he seemed to know it. I was more afraid of that man than I was of the man with the gun, because with a bullet I knew that the damage, although fatal, would be minimal. The pain instantaneous but brief and the end would be death. Which would come quickly compared with the hurt and damage a man can inflict on a young girl that can leave her emotionally scarred, maimed and suffering for a lifetime.
I didn't go to the drugstore on my break. I ran the short distance to Kieran's apartment and prayed he would help me. I knocked on the back door and waited. 'Who's there?' I heard Kieran's voice. 'It's me Kieran' I replied opening the door. 'Hey Mary' he called from the bathroom where he was standing in front of the mirror shaving, 'whataya doin' knockin' on the door? You know you don't have to do that?' And then as he noticed my red eyes and less than happy demeanour he asked me as he dried his face 'what's up with you kid?'

For a moment I hesitated and I thought of Rudi and what had happened to him when Maggie complained him to Kieran, but decided that I didn't care if the man got a beating. I didn't know what else I could do; I just wanted the man to leave me alone. So I told Kieran what was happening. 'Maybe this guy just likes you Mary. Is he good lookin?' 'Kieran' I almost screamed 'he looks older than Rocco!' The smile disappeared from Kieran's face and he realised I was in a panic. 'I just want him to leave me alone Kieran, I don't want him touching me' I said as my eyes filled up with tears. 'Hey Mary, don't let this guy bust your balls, if he calls in today, you just tell him you can't go out with him 'cause your boyfriend will go crazy.' 'Oh very funny Kieran' I said feeling hurt at Kieran's apparent flippancy 'you know I don't have a boyfriend' I yelled almost crying at the realisation that Kieran didn't seem to see the seriousness of the situation.

'Mary listen to me, you tell this guy that your boyfriends name is Kieran Hennessy.' 'What?' I said shocked, but then I understood what Kieran was saying. 'Oh, ok' I said finally. 'You get what I'm saying Mary?' I nodded. 'I gotta go now Mary,' Kieran said buttoning his shirt 'you let me know how you get on ok.' 'Thanks Kieran.' 'No problem Mary, you dry your eyes an' don't you worry about nothin.'

I returned to work feeling a little better and relieved that as yet there was no sign of my 'stalker.' I began serving the customers and for a brief time forgot my troubles. I even managed a little smile when a couple beckoned me to their table and the woman asked in an all too audible voice. 'Hey honey, come 'ere', in an accent that wasn't familiar to me. 'Is it true that this neighbourhood is controlled by the Mob? Have you ever met any real-life gangsters?' I responded in true Colonial Hill fashion, I've absolutely no idea what you're talking about; you shouldn't believe everything you hear.' 'You see Marg' the woman's partner volunteered. 'I told you, you were watchin' too much TV. As I turned away from the table to attend to another customer I saw that the man I dreaded was once again installed at the bar. I pretended to be very busy when he waved and smiled in such a way that it made my skin crawl. I could see that the man's expensive suits and aftershave couldn't disguise the fact that he was a predator who preyed on the young and vulnerable, lured them with money and the promise of a better life. And if they were unfortunate enough to fall for it, he could then, do with them as he wished. My fear turned to fury and my blood began to boil as the man continued to leer at me. But I knew I had to keep a calm and even 'sweet' demeanour if Kieran's plan was to work.

As my lunch shift drew to a close, I strolled nonchalantly over to where the man sat at the bar. And having rehearsed what I was going to say over and over in my head, I was feeling almost confident. 'Please let this work' I prayed.

'How are you?' I asked giving him a big smile. 'Hey sweetie' he replied 'I was beginning to think you weren't talkin' to me.' And he displayed a 'mock' hurt expression on his face. 'Why wouldn't I talk to you?' I smiled through gritted teeth 'In fact I've been thinking about what you said earlier about having dinner and maybe even going to Florida, and I'd love to have dinner with you.' The man's face lit-up with obvious excitement. 'I'm just worried' I continued 'that my boyfriend will find out, maybe' I said 'we could discuss your plans for Florida.'

I knew at that point that I had him just where I wanted. 'To hell with your boyfriend sweetie' the man said leaning closer to whisper 'what you need is a man to show you a good time. Who is he anyhow? Some kid from around here I bet.' 'Oh yeah' I said in a voice full of innocence, while I quietly savoured the moment. 'He lives just around the corner, but I don't think you'd know him.' 'You'd never know Mary, it's a small neighbourhood. What's this guy's name? I might, you know, have to give him a few slaps, to let him know you're with me now.' 'Oh I don't like violence' I said sounding shocked. 'Just tell me who he is' he said as he reached out and grabbed my arm in a firm hold. 'Oh ok' I said 'his name is Kieran Hennessy.'

The 'look' on the man's face was worth a million dollars to me and I had to stop myself from laughing. Although he still had a hold of my arm, it was no longer to intimidate me, but instead, to prevent him from falling off his seat. His face had taken on the grey waxy pallor of a corpse and he stuttered and stammered before finding his voice. 'Kieran Hennessy from Nimnuc St?' He finally managed to say. 'Oh isn't it a small world?' I said, 'so you do know him?' I thought for a moment I'd have to call an ambulance for him, but he managed to find his feet. 'I didn't mean nothin by it, please, don't say nothin', he said imploringly, 'I gotta get outta here.' 'But what about Florida?' I called after him as he made his way unsteadily toward the door.

'I think I deserve a drink after that' I said to Bobby the barman who had witnessed the whole scene. 'Oh you are bad Mary' Bobby said laughing. 'That guy has just lost ten years of his life, but he deserved it. I've been watchin' the way he looks at you for days. He's a real sleaze bag.' 'You don't have to convince me Bobby' I said 'I know.' 'Here, this ones on me Mary' Bobby said as he slid my drink across the bar. As I raised my glass to my lips I said a silent prayer 'Thank you God for Kieran.'

I never saw the man again but I was told that he ran for Mayor unsuccessfully the following year.

As I lay in bed that night I felt relaxed and secure in the knowledge that my 'stalker' wouldn't be bothering me anymore and once again thanked God for Kieran. It was a great comfort to know that there was someone I could turn to if I needed help, and it was indeed a luxury Maggie or I hadn't been accustomed to before.

With our father dying when we were very young and more often than not, better off on our own than to have Paddy as a father figure, we fought all our battles alone. There were very few extended family to turn to if we needed help and the ones that did exist never seemed interested. Maggie and I spent our childhood watching out for Mam and our younger siblings. But there was nobody watching out for us. Having Kieran as a friend was a totally new experience for me and not one that I took for granted. It was a great feeling, just feeling safe, and I believe that was also one of the reasons Maggie was so drawn to him.

Chapter 44

In The Still Of The Night

I slept soundly that night and woke to see six inches of snow on the ground. It was like a scene on a Christmas card and really beautiful to watch from my window. But I knew it wouldn't be so nice when I had to make my way to the bus stop with no coat and canvas shoes that were meant for far more clement weather. I had been meaning to buy some winter clothes, but I was also trying to save money for my plane fare. 'I'll be fine' I said trying to convince myself, as I put on a second pair of socks and pulled a long sweater over my tuxedo jacket. That coupled with running through the snow to the bus stop kept me warm, and before I knew it I was at Kieran and Rocco's back door. I wanted to thank him for his help and reassure him, as he'd asked, that I was alright.

I could hear Kieran inside, but as I opened the door my heart skipped a beat when it only swung open a few inches before hitting something and coming to a sudden stop. I was about to close it again as I remembered the man with the gun, but then I heard Kieran's voice. 'That you Mary, wait up a minute, I gotta move some stuff around. Rocco pull your finger out o' your ass an give me a hand here a minute.' I stood in the small hallway and listened to Kieran and Rocco arguing amongst themselves. 'Kieran, I'm tellin' you, that ain't gonna fit there.' 'Rocco, gimme a break here, don't you know nothin', just move the friggin chair.' I smiled to myself knowing Rocco was not a man to exert himself. Rocco's idea of work was stirring a pot of sauce on the stove so it didn't burn. The door finally opened and Rocco stood before me wiping sweat from his brow with a towel.

'You gotta excuse this place Mary, it's a mess' Kieran said as he watched me looking around at the rails of clothes that were standing where the kitchen used to be. 'I gotta take care of this stuff for a buddy of mine who's opening a store. I should be rid of it in a couple of days.' 'Oh right' I replied as I looked from one rail to another and saw the designer labels hanging from every sleeve. 'I just called 'round to tell you Kieran that I did what you told me and it worked. I don't think I'll be seeing him again. I have to go to work now, but thanks for your help; I was really scared of that guy.' 'Anytime kid,' Kieran replied sincerely. 'Hey Mary,' Kieran called as I turned toward the door 'why ain't you got no coat on? It's freezing out there.' 'I know it is Kieran,' I replied 'I'm going to buy one in a few days when I get my pay check.

I'm fine though Kieran, once I keep moving.' Kieran turned to Rocco, 'not for nothin' Rocco is this kid somethin' or what?' Come 'ere Mary, you take a look at these,' he said pointing to the rails of clothes 'an take whatever one you like.' 'Are you serious Kieran?' I asked 'I don't get paid for another few days, but I really don't think I can afford any of these' I said, running my fingers along the soft luxurious leather, suede and tweeds. 'Who said anythin' about money Mary? Don't worry about it. Just pick one, I can't have you freezin' to death, your sister would kill me. Here, what about this one Mary?' Kieran suggested holding up a full length double breasted herring bone tweed coat in steel grey. 'Try it on Mary' he insisted 'I bet it looks real good on you and it will keep you real warm, it's a hundred percent wool you know.' The coat fitted me perfectly. 'It's lovely Kieran' I said and did a little twirl. 'I feel warmer already. Thank you so much Kieran, my mother won't recognise me at the airport.' 'I didn't know your mother was comin to visit,' he said enthusiastically 'you never said Mary.' 'Oh no, she's not Kieran, I'm going home for Christmas.' Rocco had left the kitchen to watch TV in the living room and although I couldn't see him, I could hear him. 'Told you Kieran, you're one 'dumb fuck' if you think her sister's coming back to you.'

Much as I tried to reassure Kieran that Maggie meant what she said and was working two jobs to get her plane fare, I couldn't help but see the resignation in his face and feel that Rocco was winning him over with his way of thinking and I wished that Rocco would shut his mouth instead of 'chipping' away at Kieran's all to obvious lack of confidence in regards to Maggie. The following week I slept over at Vanessa's house at her insistence. It had snowed hard for several days and although the buses were still running, the ten minute walk to and from the bus stop was painstakingly difficult. More and more I had found myself walking along the street where the snow and been flattened by traffic at the risk of being hit by a car, rather than trudge through the twelve inches of soft snow on the footpaths in my canvas shoes which offered little protection against the freezing cold.

I was relieved when it stopped snowing and although Vanessa very kindly made it quite clear that I was welcome to stay as long as I wanted, feeling that I had been a burden for long enough and not wanting to outstay my welcome, I was anxious to return to the apartment which I now considered home. I accepted her kind offer to drive me home that evening at eleven o'clock when I finished work. I thanked her and watched her drive away from Kieran's brothers' house. I climbed the stairs and was happy to be home after almost a week away and decided to have a hot bath to ease my aching muscles before going to bed. It was almost an hour later after my fingers took on the appearance of prunes that I persuaded myself to get out of the bath. I filled the kettle to boil it for tea and headed into the living room to turn on the TV. The words to the song I'd been singing to myself fell silent on the air as I stared at the radio equipment that was strewn on the floor next to the sofa and even I knew it was not any ordinary run of the mill stereo system. Not wanting to disturb anything I decided to make my tea and drink it in the bedroom while I organised my clean clothes for the morning.

I was deep in thought about the radio equipment and wondering what on earth Kieran needed it for when I opened my underwear drawer to see two guns sitting on top of my knickers! I had never seen real guns before apart from the shotguns some of the farmers in Cratloe used for shooting pheasants or rabbits. Although tempted to pick one of them up, just to look at, I resisted the urge and listened to my 'gut' which was telling me to leave 'well enough alone.' So I prised my underwear out from underneath them, slammed the drawer closed and dived into bed.

I was to get a bigger fright the following night when I returned home. I was fumbling around in the dark trying to find the kitchen light switch, when all of a sudden I could hear noises coming from the bedroom. It was the sound of somebody snoring. I was sure, as I tip-toed across the kitchen floor toward the bedroom, that whoever was sleeping in there would be woken by the sound of my heart beating against my chest. I pushed the door gently, praying that it wouldn't creak and it opened just enough for me to see the shape of not one, but two bodies. I couldn't see who they were because they were almost completely covered by the bedclothes. But what I could see was that one of them had long wavy brown hair. One of them was a woman.

I decided the best thing for me to do was to get out of there fast. Kieran I thought had obviously given some friends permission to stay there and had forgotten to tell me.

What if he forgot to tell them about me? I thought a little annoyed, as I crept back across the kitchen toward the back door with my mind racing expecting at any moment to be pounced upon or worse, shot as an intruder!

I was never so relieved as when I managed to reach the bottom of the stairs without waking anyone. I stepped out of the house and onto the street where the freezing night winds hit me in the face. I had no other option but to return to Vanessa's house and I ran in the dark to the bus stop ten minutes away, hoping that, at well after midnight, I'd be able to catch a bus.

I woke the following morning after a very restless night sleep in Vanessa's house and for the first time was really annoyed with Kieran. I decided to make it my business to see him and tell him how I felt. After all, I thought, I was paying the rent.

I was nearing the end of my shift when I saw Kieran entering the 'Men's' club at the far side of the parking lot. I ran across the street and boldly knocked on the door. I wanted to be sure there would be no more surprises when I went home. The door of the clubhouse was answered by a man whose face was familiar to me from the neighbourhood, but I didn't know his name. 'You lookin' for Kieran?' he asked before I had a chance to say anything. 'Ah, yes I am' I replied wondering if the man was a mind reader. 'Hey Kieran' the man shouted 'there's a kid here at the door, wants to talk to you.' 'Who is it?' I heard Kieran ask. 'It's one of the Irish girls Kieran' the man replied. Kieran appeared a few minutes later and stepped out of the doorway and onto the street. 'Hey Mary, what's up with you? You don't look too good, something wrong?' 'Well actually there is' I replied. 'Kieran, why didn't you at least warn me that there would be people staying in the apartment last night?' Kieran seemed a little uncomfortable and took a moment to say anything. 'What are you talkin' about Mary?' 'Kieran' I repeated 'when I got home last night from work, there were two people asleep in my bedroom. I got the fright of my life Kieran. You could at least have told me. I had to catch a bus back into town and stay at Vanessa's house.'

I was waiting on some form of an apology from Kieran, but the response I got was totally unexpected and I couldn't but notice the sarcasm. 'Mary, how the hell was I supposed to know you'd be stayin' at the apartment last night?

The way I'm hearin' it, you and Vanessa are pretty tight, you're over at her place so much, I thought you'd move in.

I stood on the street and for a few minutes, I was totally lost for words. It was obvious that Kieran resented the fact that Maggie and I were friendly with Vanessa and I had to admit that I understood it was a bit unusual. 'But why now?' I thought. He had been fine about it all along. 'Kieran, why didn't you say that it bothered you?' I asked. 'Mary' he said 'it ain't none of my business what you do. You're goin' back to Ireland in a couple o' weeks anyway.' With that said Kieran walked in the door of the club house and slammed it behind him.

There was something different about Kieran that day and I just couldn't put my finger on it. Had Rocco said something? Was Kieran really upset that I was friendly with Vanessa? Had my decision to go home upset him that much or did my departure to Kieran; signify the end of things between him and Maggie? These were the questions I asked myself over and over again. But I had no answers just a niggling feeling in my gut that told me something had changed.

Chapter 45

Hey, Big Spender!

The days turned into weeks far too quickly and although I called to visit Kieran on several occasions he was never home. Rocco was, but each time I asked if Kieran would be back soon or where he was I got the same response. 'I dunno Mary' he would say with a shrug of his shoulders. 'I guess he's got things to do y'know.' With Rocco's lack of enthusiasm for conversation, I never stayed long, but asked him before leaving each time, to tell Kieran that I called and even though he nodded his head in agreement each time, I wasn't too confident that he would. There was no more that I could do so I turned my thoughts to my own situation and I was regretting telling Mam I'd be home for Christmas. Thanksgiving had long since come and gone and I was no nearer by buying my plane ticket. The lunch trade had been painfully slow for a number of weeks and there were days when I barely made enough to cover the price of bus fares and something to eat. Most days my diet consisted of left over garlic bread which I helped myself to in the restaurant and at home at the end of the day my main meal consisted of 'Ragu' tomato sauce poured over spaghetti! It was filling but not exactly 'haute cuisine.'

'It's always like this in November Mary' Enzo, my boss said in an effort to console me. 'People gotta save their bucks for Christmas.' 'I realise that Enzo, but I really need the money now' I explained 'I'm finding it hard to make ends meet with Maggie gone, and my mother is expectin' me home for Christmas.' 'Yeah I know Mary' Enzo said but seemed more interested in sampling the new house wine. 'I'll tell you what I can do Mary' he said, just as I was about to give up. 'I'm short a waiter for Saturday night if you're interested. I'm sure it's gonna be real busy. Are you up for it?' 'God, yes Enzo,' I replied not too sure that I was, but I wasn't going to miss out on an opportunity to make some desperately need cash.

Saturday night arrived and I was a nervous wreck and it didn't help to know that the other waiters weren't exactly overjoyed to see me. I set up all my tables and polished each glass and piece of cutlery till they sparkled and I decided to ignore the comments I couldn't help but overhear. 'Enzo must be crazy to have her workin' a Saturday night' Raymundo said as he looked at himself admiringly in the mirror while adjusting his bow tie.

'You're tellin me?' Nicky the headwaiter and most chauvinistic man I'd ever met replied; 'I might be good but I don't have time to be babysittin' her. I wanna make some money.'

By nine o'clock I had served about six parties without incident. I still struggled with the wine list especially when a customer asked me to recommend a wine to complement their veal, fish or chicken entree. But I managed to scrape through. While the customers were studying the menu's I would study Nicky's tables and recommend whatever wine his customers had ordered under his guidance.

'You're not doing so bad Mary' Nicky finally said after refusing to even acknowledge my presence for hours. 'That is' he added 'for a woman I mean.' 'Thanks Nicky' I said knowing that this was about as close to a compliment I was going to get. 'You makin' some money Mary' 'Oh yeah' I said quite pleased with myself 'I've made over fifty dollars and the night isn't over yet.' 'Fifty bucks' Nicky scoffed 'it wouldn't be a Saturday night if I didn't clear a hundred bucks.'

I knew Nicky was more than likely telling the truth, he was very good at his job and because of that was always assigned the larger tables. He was just so smug, not just about being the best waiter but he continuously bragged about how well 'connected' his family were in the neighbourhood, and because of this I was reluctant to praise his already inflated ego.

I was just about to walk away from Nicky to clear one of my tables when he said, sounding nervous and excited 'this night just keeps gettin' better and better Mary. See that guy who just walked in, he is the main man, you don't wanna mess around with that guy. Strange to see him in here though, he usually eats at Carmelo's next door. It must be my lucky night eh? He never leaves less than a hundred bucks of a tip.' I watched my boss 'flap' around Gerard Molyneaux like a moth who was drawn to the light but afraid to get too close in case he got burned. He complimented the women in Gerard Molyneaux's party of ten, and then offered to take their coats while at the same time almost yelling at Nicky to set up the long table in the back near the bar. I watched as Gerard Molyneaux made his way through the restaurant, stopping at almost every table as people stood up to greet him, pat him on the back or shake his hand.

His appearance as usual was immaculate and he could easily be mistaken for a leading politician or famous celebrity. 'Here we go,' Nicky said taking a deep breath as he smoothed back his hair and almost stood to attention.

'Hi Gerard,' I said grinning as he was about to pass me by 'how's it going?' 'Hey Mary,' he replied smiling back 'I nearly missed you there kid. These guys got me surrounded.' Gerard threw his arms around me and gave me a big hug. 'How've you been doin? I've been tellin my buddy's here Mary that I gotta call in an' see how my Irish friend is doin. Enzo' he called to my boss who was opening bottles of Dom Pérignon 'I want my good friend Mary to wait on my table, you got it?' 'Certainly Mr Molyneaux' my boss replied as he struggled to steady his hand and pour the champagne.

One look at Nicky and I knew that at that precise moment a melon could quite easily have fitted in his mouth and I knew what he was thinking, the same as all the other waiters who stood and stared. 'How could a girl from Ireland who was only working in the neighbourhood a few months know 'Gerard Molyneaux?' To add insult to injury, Enzo my boss ordered him to assist me whenever I needed help. Nicky looked as if he had just been asked to clean the toilets.

I treated Gerard Molyneaux as I would any other customer and made polite conversation with his guests. But I couldn't resist the urge to joke with him as I'd always done, especially when he ordered my boss to keep the champagne flowing. Much to my bosses dismay and the guests at the table I said

'Gerard, I'd say it's far from champagne you were reared.' A silence descended on the table and my boss looked at me as if he were about to faint. Much, it seemed, to the relief of Gerard Molyneaux's entourage he began to laugh. 'I told you guys' he said 'not for nothin', this kid cracks me up.

That night Gerard Molyneaux left me a hundred dollar 'tip' but not before I agreed to have a drink with him before he left. 'When are you leavin' for Ireland Mary' he asked just as one of the women in his group said 'Gerard, we're waitin' to leave.' 'Hey' Gerard said giving the woman an icy stare 'can't you see I'm talkin' to my friend here? You guys go on without me; I'll see you in 'Vinnie's' later. Don't worry, you can tell them to put the drinks on my 'tab.'

'I'm leaving on the twenty second Gerard' I replied as I watched the woman walk away like a scolded child. 'It will be good for you to spend Christmas with your family Mary. If I don't see you before you leave, you have a safe journey.' Gerard stood up to leave and gave me a hug. 'Have a good Christmas Mary, you sure as hell deserve it, you're a good kid.' 'Thanks Gerard' and then he turned and said, 'you tell that sister of yours I said 'hello.' 'You can tell her yourself Gerard,' I said 'she'll be back here in a couple of weeks.'

I treated myself to a taxi home that night and I was feeling a sense of tremendous relief knowing that because of Gerard's generous 'tip' and the money I'd managed to hide away in Kieran's secret drawer in the apartment, I at last had enough money to buy my plane ticket. As the taxi driver made his way through the dark city streets towards Cranston I gazed dreamily out of the taxi window at the brightly coloured displays and twinkling lights of every window. As I did, I remembered Christmases gone by and the memories they held for me, very few of them were happy ones. But I really felt privileged compared to Gerard Molyneaux. To have lost so many close family members through such tragic circumstances, Christmas for him I thought must have been a time that evoked memories of happier times spent with his brothers. 'God,' I thought 'Christmas must be a very sad and lonely time for him'.

Chapter 46

Let It Snow, Let It Snow, Let It Snow

As it happened, I did meet Gerard Molyneaux again. It was the twenty second of December and the day of my departure. Vanessa had very kindly offered to drive me to Logan Airport in Boston. I explained to her that before leaving I wanted to call to Kieran and Rocco's apartment to say 'goodbye' and give them a Christmas gift, a small bottle of aftershave lotion each, which I'd just about managed to scrape the money together to buy.

Gerard Molyneaux' Cadillac was parked outside the apartment so I knew he was inside. I climbed the snow clad steps at the front and I noticed the door was ajar. Tapping lightly on the living room door, I opened it and went in. Gerard was sitting on the sofa with one leg covered with plaster of Paris, which was outstretched and resting on the coffee table and a pair of crutches were lying on the floor beside him. 'Hi Gerard, what in the name of God happened to you?' I asked surprised. 'Aw it's nothin Mary, slipped on the friggin ice, that's all. Hey Rocco' Gerard called in the direction of the kitchen 'how long does it take to get a cup o' coffee 'round here, I'm dyin' of thirst here. Mary I thought you said you were goin' home for Christmas?' 'Yes I am Gerard, I'm leaving in an hour, I just came over to say goodbye and give Kieran and Rocco a Christmas gift. I'm sorry I have nothing for you Gerard' I said embarrassed. 'Don't you worry about me kid; Hey Rocco, get in here' Gerard said sounding a little agitated. 'Here you go Gerard, just how you like it' Rocco said placing the mug of coffee on the table in front of him. 'You want anything else Gerard?' He asked as he turned toward the kitchen again. 'Here Rocco, this is for you 'Happy Christmas' I said handing him the small gift wrapped box. 'Is Kieran here Rocco? It's just that I have to leave soon and I didn't want to go without sayin' goodbye.' 'Nah, he ain't here Mary' Rocco replied with his usual shrug and didn't even acknowledge the gift I had just handed him. 'Hey Rocco, where you goin' now?' Gerard asked as Rocco walked away 'ain't you got no manners Rocco? Show a little respect here. This kid just walked over here in the snow an' when's the friggin last time a lady bought you somethin?' Gerard didn't wait for a response from Rocco. 'An' you gotta know where Kieran is, what the fuck is wrong with you?' 'Hey I'm sorry Gerard,' Rocco replied nervously 'I didn't mean nothin' by it. I dunno where Kieran's at.' 'Are you tellin me Rocco, he didn't know Mary was leavin' today? Did you tell Kieran you were leavin' today Mary?'

Rocco glanced at me nervously knowing that I'd asked him time and time again to tell Kieran. 'I don't know Gerard' I lied, 'I just thought he knew.' Rocco just looked at me and was surprised at my response and knew that I knew, he hadn't bothered to tell Kieran, but I decided to keep my mouth shut and say nothing. 'Look, don't worry about it' I said as I watched Gerard scrutinizing Rocco. 'I've got to go, I'll leave Kieran's gift here and you can give it to him later, can't you Rocco?' 'Oh yeah, sure I will Mary,' Rocco replied enthusiastically, but was struggling to look me in the eye 'uh, an' thanks Mary.' I knew it wasn't the gift Rocco was thanking me for. Gerard silently stared at Rocco, unblinking, but eventually turned to me, 'you wanna walk me to my car Mary? Rocco tell Kieran I'll see him later.' I linked Gerard's arm as he fumbled with the crutches. 'I hope you're plannin' on stayin' in Ireland Mary, I can't have the Irish Mob takin' over my neighbourhood' he joked. 'Well blast your cheek Gerard' I replied with mock annoyance. 'I hope you fall and break the other leg!' Gerard, who was concentrating all his efforts on getting down the steps, stopped dead in his tracks and stared at me; 'What did you say to me kid?' 'You heard what I said Gerard,' I replied 'What's wrong, can't you take a joke?' Gerard continued to the last step then smiled, 'it's a good thing I like you Mary, people have been killed for less', 'Yeah Gerard,' I laughed looking at the crutches 'but you'd have to catch me first.'

Chapter 47

The Green, Green Grass Of Home

On the flight home I thought about the previous six months and what an adventure our trip to America had been. I certainly hadn't earned a fortune as Maggie initially predicted when she persuaded me to go. In actual fact I knew that financially I would have been far better off had I stayed at home. I had ten dollars to my name when I boarded the plane in Logan Airport, but I had six months of unforgettable memories that were to me, priceless.

I thought of Lisa, Maggie's friend and the weekend we spent with her and her boyfriend in the little cabin by the lake. I thought about Long Island and our sunburn ordeal. I thought of the many heated arguments Maggie and I had while searching for work under the blazing summer sun. I thought of Vanessa, how kind she had been and how genuinely sad she was at the airport to see me go. I thought of Gerard Molyneaux, cool, calm and collected. One could be forgiven for thinking he was a quiet man. He could, I thought, best be described as an 'iceberg.' You only ever saw the tip, but if you looked a little closer you would find a lot more hiding beneath the surface. I thought about Rocco and how his relatively welcoming approach to Maggie and I in the beginning had changed when he realised how serious Kieran was about Maggie. Kieran obviously thought the 'world' of Rocco, and I knew that for whatever reason and no matter how misguided his loyalties were, Kieran would stand by him. Surely, I thought, Rocco, if he cared at all about Kieran would want him to be happy. Surely he wouldn't want Kieran spending his life in and out of prison as he had done. Surely I was wrong in thinking that to Rocco; Kieran was just a meal ticket for him in his old age. I thought of Kieran and how very vulnerable Maggie and I would have been in so many situations if it had not been for him. I thought about the things that Kieran considered most important in his life. Family, friendship, loyalty and all things Irish, and I thought of all the times we had spent together when we laughed 'till we cried. I wondered if Kieran realised that in meeting Maggie, he had arrived at one of the most important cross roads in his life, and I prayed he would find the wisdom and courage to take the right turn!

Most of all, as I gazed out the window at the patchwork of fields of the Clare countryside beneath me, I thought of Maggie.

I knew from our frequent telephone conversations with each other since she had returned to Ireland that her feelings for Kieran hadn't changed. If anything they had grown stronger with the distance between them. I also knew Maggie was ambitious and determined to have a successful career, and she dreamed of having a beautiful home and a loving husband to share it with. I knew Maggie well and believed that sometimes I knew her better than she knew herself and there was nothing I was more sure of, as, the 'fasten your seatbelt' sign flashed before me and that was, Maggie was no more suited to being the wife of a criminal than she was suited to being a farmer's wife. As the plane touched down in Shannon I wondered what the future held for her.

Little had changed at home in Cratloe since I'd left. Rogue my dog looked a little greyer around the muzzle. The boys and Barbra were a little taller and Mam looked a lot older than I'd remembered. The only major change was Maggie. I had hardly recognised her when she stood beside Mam in the airport. She looked like a million dollars, she was about twenty pounds lighter and had an hour glass figure that any young woman would have died for and the blonde highlights she'd put in her hair made her eyes look bigger and bluer than ever. Standing in the airport in four inch heels and looking very much like a 'Barbie Doll', she was oblivious to the many admiring looks she was getting from people as they passed by. 'Oh my God Maggie' I said after giving Mam a hug 'look at you, you're like a model.' 'Yes' she replied 'I lost a lot of weight Mary, that's what working two jobs does to you, but at least when I go back to America, Doris won't be calling me a fat Irish Momma.'

Chapter 48

My Heart Is In Ireland

I saw very little of Maggie in the days that followed apart from the initial, what could best be described as an interrogation by her in regards to Kieran on my first day home. She was rarely home, trying to hold down two jobs and with me reinstated in my old one, we were just like ships in the night, either running past each other on our way out the door, or on the verge of exhaustion on our way to bed. Maggie had booked her flight to America for the fifth of January and by the time that day arrived she had a whole new wardrobe of clothes to go with her new streamlined figure. But the purchase that took pride of place when she was packing was a sweater she bought for Kieran. It was an 'Aran' sweater, hand knit by the women of Aran, who came from a small cluster of Island's off the Galway coast, where for hundreds of years the inhabitants of the island derived a meagre income from fishing. The wives and mothers of the fishermen knit the sweaters from fleece of local sheep, to protect their husbands and sons from the bitter and unforgiving extremes of the Atlantic Ocean. People say each family had their own intricate and distinctive pattern, so that in the event of a tragedy at sea, the bodies could be easily identified by the sweater they were wearing.

As the tourism business flourished in Ireland so did the demand for the 'Aran Sweater.' It became a much sought after commodity among visiting tourists from all around the globe, but especially the Irish-Americans.

'That must have cost you a small fortune Maggie,' I said knowing that she had spent the best part of a hard earned week's wages on it. 'It did Mary,' she agreed 'I don't mind though, I think it will mean a lot to Kieran.' 'Oh yeah Maggie, he'll be over the moon with it' I said, as I imagined Kieran's face when she handed it to him.

When Mam and I stood in Shannon Airport and watched Maggie until she disappeared through the departure gates, I wondered when we'd see her again. Certainly I knew I wouldn't be 'jetting off' anywhere for quite some time, and it would take me several months of saving if I did want to return to America. But I also wondered if I had the money, would I want to? While I loved the experience of being independent in America and the people I'd met there, I also loved the fields, streams and narrow country roads of home.

Since returning from America I had slipped back into my old routine of spending hours with 'Rogue' my dog, walking the Cratloe Hills.

At work, I had become somewhat of a celebrity with co-workers who were eager to hear all about life in America and while I shared some of my experiences with them, I omitted to mention that Kieran was a 'mobster' and stuck to the more sobering 'real estate' story. It wasn't because I was ashamed of Kieran but I knew there was no point in trying to explain to them, they just wouldn't have believed it. Also, with all the new attention I was getting because of my time spent living in America, I was enjoying my new found popularity and I didn't want to risk being called an Eejit for telling 'tall-tales.'

Chapter 49
I Will Survive

Two days after Maggie returned to America, the telephone rang at home. I wasn't in any hurry to answer it because I was getting dressed and was sure Mam would, because she was nearer to it. But she didn't, because she and the boys were having one of their family discussions in the kitchen which sounded like World War Three was about to break out. Running down the stairs to reach it before the caller gave up I thought 'God will they ever shut up!' I was worried that when I picked up the receiver the caller would hear the utter pandemonium in the background.

'Hello, 97240, who's speaking please' Mam always insisted that we answer the telephone in a 'proper manner.' 'Mary is that you?' I heard Maggie's voice struggling to be heard over the crackling sound of the long distance line. 'Yeah it's me Maggie,' I replied 'I didn't expect to hear from you so soon. How are you?' 'Mary, Kieran finished with me' I heard her say and knew she was crying. 'Did ye have a fight Maggie?' I asked remembering all the disputes they'd had in the past which never lasted very long. 'No, no, nothing Mary' she said as the line cleared enough for me to hear her strike a match and light a cigarette. 'But,' I stammered, quite speechless 'what happened? What did he say?' 'He called to the apartment last night Mary. I had been over to his place twice the day I got back and Rocco kept saying he didn't know where he was. I was really 'pissed off' Mary that he wasn't there to welcome me back. But I forgot how annoyed I was when I answered the knock on the door last night. I was just so delighted to see him Mary. So I immediately gave him the sweater.' There was a pause and I could hear Maggie blowing her nose. 'And,' I said impatiently. 'He told me he was seeing someone else and that it was over between us.' Maggie sounded as if she were on the verge of hysteria. 'Was that it Maggie? Did he say anything else?' 'Oh yeah Mary, he said my life was going somewhere

and his wasn't. What the hell is that supposed to mean? I gave up so much for him Mary, I feel like killing him!'
I didn't know what to say to Maggie, but my mind flashed back to the night I discovered the guests in the bedroom and the woman with the long brown hair. 'Did he tell you who he's seeing Maggie?' I asked nervously not wanting to upset her any more than she already was. 'Oh, that's the best part Mary, guess who it is?'
'I don't know Maggie', I replied praying it wasn't Vanessa, the woman we'd both grown so fond of. 'Just tell me Maggie.' 'It's Jimmy Durante' she spat. 'Who?' I asked having a momentary loss of memory. 'Jimmy Durante, you know Mary, Doris, Vanessa's first cousin.' 'Oh my God, you were right all along Maggie. You always said she fancied him. Imagine Maggie, Vanessa used to cry on her shoulder when Kieran left her and she wanted him all the time.' 'I know Mary, nice cousin eh? God only knows how Vanessa's feeling right now.' 'I'm shocked Maggie, what are you going to do now? Maybe Kieran will change his mind.' 'Oh no Mary,' Maggie replied sounding stronger, defiant and more like her usual self, 'she's welcome to him, he's only a shit!' 'Are you going to come home Maggie?' I asked, thinking how lonely it would be for her without Kieran. 'No way, I haven't a notion of it Mary', she said stubbornly 'I'm going to make a go of it here and if anything what he's done will only make me all the more determined to succeed than ever. So don't you say a word to Mam Mary, the last thing I need to hear right now is her telling me 'I told you so.' 'Ok Maggie,' I promised before hanging up the phone.
We are all wiser in hindsight and the mistake Maggie made all those years ago at the young age of twenty, in regards to Kieran was, she should never have 'upped sticks' and returned to America for him. She should have insisted that he go to Ireland with her. If he had refused there and then she would have at least known where she stood with him. But if he agreed to go, who knows? Life for Kieran just may have turned out a lot different than it did.

Over the course of the next few months, Maggie phoned home regularly, once, sometimes twice a week. Considering the shock she got when Kieran finished with her, she was coping quite well and I had to admire her courage. She focused all her time and energy on work. She was waitressing in the Little Sicily full time and she also tended bar in a new upmarket lounge called 'Garibaldi's' on Colonial Hill. She was also gathering information about available courses in the local colleges in the area and told me she planned on resuming her studies in the 'fall.'

Every now and then a phone call would come and I knew by the sound of Maggie's voice on the line, that she was very low. The reason for her 'down beat' mood was always Kieran. If she saw him on the street or 'bumped' into him at a bar or restaurant, the result was always the same.

She would repeatedly question her own judgement and then she would question me about her conclusions. 'Mary, was I stupid to believe he loved me? Do you think he loves her Mary? Was I crazy to think we could have a future together?' My answers were always the same. 'No Maggie, you weren't stupid to believe that he loved you. Anyone who saw you together could see he worshipped the ground you walked on. As for Doris, I doubt very much that he loves her. She, Maggie, was just the easier option and I don't think you were crazy to believe you had a future together. But Kieran isn't stupid Maggie, he knows you weren't going to accept his present lifestyle and he knew you would expect him to 'turn' his life around, to make a complete break and start with a 'clean slate' somewhere else. That's what I mean Maggie, by the easy option; Doris strikes me as a person who can't see beyond her nose, if you'll pardon the pun Maggie. I'd say she's a woman with limited ambitions and expectations. I mean she must have bed sores on her backside from sitting on her front step!

She was born in that neighbourhood and chances are she will die there too, let's face it Maggie she must be divorced a few years now and she still hasn't got off her backside to look for work and provide for her daughter. She's got exactly what she

wanted, someone to support her and her daughter. She would have known from listening to Vanessa that Kieran was good to her children.' 'Yeah you're right Mary.' 'I know I'm right Maggie and I know I'm also right when I say that she will measure Kieran's love by what he gives her. As long as she's dressed in furs and diamonds, everything will be 'rosy' in the garden, and she won't care where he gets them.'
Maggie was always looking for more answers than I could give, given the fact that I'd never been in a relationship myself didn't help but I tried my best. 'I'll never understand it Mary,' she said during one of her routine calls 'what really boils my blood is the fact that every time I do meet him, he goes out of his way to talk to me and he's all smiles asking how I am. Is he stupid or something Mary? He's the one who finished with me. Does he really think that I actually want to speak to him? What's he playing at Mary?'

'Maggie,' I said 'I can only hazard a guess as to why he finished with you. It could be that he believed Rocco, when Rocco told him that you had loads of boyfriends in Ireland and that Kieran was a fool to believe you were coming back to him. Maybe Kieran threw in the towel when he realised I was leaving too. It could be, if we're to believe everything we're told, that Kieran thinks he'll have more power within the Mob if he's with an Italian woman. Or, Maggie, it could be as simple as Kieran said. That you have a future and he believes he hasn't. I just don't know Maggie. But what I do know is that he will probably miss you for the rest of his life. I swear to God Maggie, I feel like getting on a plane, going over there and shaking him.'
'Are you coming back Mary?' Maggie asked excitedly. I knew she missed me and needed all the emotional support she could get. Despite this I wasn't too sure if I wanted to go back and I knew it was all to do with my own lack of self-confidence. The one thing that struck me when I was living there was how educationally orientated the Americans were. Everyone was either going to University or at the very least doing some kind of course. Even the waiters in the restaurant were only waiting

tables as a 'stepping stone' to something better. This caused me a huge amount of embarrassment especially when time and time again customers would ask what I was studying and looked at me as if I were on drugs when I told them I wasn't.

Chapter 50

Breaking Glass

I decided while out one evening having a drink with my friend Sharon to tell her about my dilemma and hoped she could offer some advice as to what I should do. I was glad that I did. 'If you're not sure' Sharon suggested 'that you want to go back to America permanently, why don't you go back in the summer for a holiday? I'll go with you; I'd love to see America.' It was decided, we would go for three weeks in August and although we were already in April I felt confident that I could save the money for the plane fare and even though I wouldn't have a lot of money for spending, I knew I'd get by. Maggie was delighted with the news when I called her. 'You'll be here for my twenty first birthday' she said, really excited. 'Oh, I can't wait Mary; we'll have a great time.'

The day Maggie collected Sharon and I from Logan Airport it was obvious she was delighted to see us. But it was also obvious as we moved at a snail's pace through the bumper to bumper traffic of Boston, that she was very stressed. 'There just isn't enough hours in the day for me,' she said as she blew the horn at a guy in a pickup truck who pulled out in front of her, cutting her off. 'I moved to a new apartment yesterday and all I managed to do was dress the bed and hang a few pictures and kitchen stuff. There's boxes all over the place, so you'll have to excuse the mess.' 'Don't worry about that Maggie' I said 'Sharon and I can help you.' 'That would be great if ye could because I have to catch the ferry at five, I'll be gone for the weekend, I'm working on Block Island for the summer, so once you and Sharon have had a few days to settle in ye can come to Block Island for a week or so, it's really beautiful there.' 'Sounds good to me,' Sharon said as she stared out of the car window.

When we reached the apartment, Maggie handed me the front door key. 'Let yourselves in,' she said 'I'm just going to pop 'round to the convenience store and buy a few groceries.'

'Ok,' I said and watched her drive away. 'Maggie' I thought to myself 'was doing ok and her hard work was paying off. She was driving her own car, not one that you'd look twice at but a car none the less.'

'What do you think so far Sharon?' I asked as we unpacked our clothes.' 'Mary, I don't care where I am as long as it's hot and it's certainly that', she said smiling.

'I'll take you on a little tour of the neighbourhood this evening, after we've got this place sorted out Sharon. I can't believe how much 'stuff' Maggie as accumulated in such a short time, she's even bought all her own furniture, even if it is second hand.'

'So Mary is this Colonial Hill, the place you told me about?' Sharon asked. 'Yep, this is it Sharon, it's a nice neighbourhood Sharon, really quiet all things considered. But remember what I said Sharon. People don't take kindly to being asked a lot of questions.' 'Yeah, yeah,' Sharon replied then started laughing. 'What would they do, shoot me?' I had tried to explain to Sharon about Kieran, Rocco, Gerard Molyneaux and the neighbourhood in general. But, like Maggie and I the year before when Vanessa tried to explain, Sharon didn't believe it either.

Having finished unpacking my clothes I was just about to make a start on opening some of the cardboard boxes which were strewn haphazardly around the living room. When the screen door flew open and Maggie ran in carrying two bags of groceries and looking like she was about to pee in her pants with fright. 'Oh Jesus, Mary and Joseph I think they're going to come over here and kill me' she said and practically threw the bags of groceries into my arms. 'Who's going to kill you Maggie? What happened?' I asked as I watched her slam the front door and lock it. 'Danny' she replied as she stared out the living room window from behind the curtain. 'I passed him on the street and he started yelling at me, said that if I didn't give back his brothers TV that they were going to come over here and wreck the place.' 'Who's Danny,' Sharon asked innocently. 'He's Kieran's brother Sharon. Which TV is he talking about Maggie?' 'That one there Mary, the one on the floor' Maggie said then turned her attention back to the window. 'And what are you doing with his television Maggie?' 'When Kieran finished with me, he told me I could keep that television until I had the money to buy my own, probably to ease his guilty conscience.' 'So why don't you give it back to him Maggie, you have two other televisions?' 'No-way Mary, after what he did to me, he owes me.' 'But Maggie is it worth the aggravation?' 'Yeah' Sharon intervened 'is it worth dying for?' She asked and started laughing again. 'What did you say to Danny, Maggie?' 'I told him if he or his brother came near my home I'd call the cops.' Not the brightest move out of you Maggie I thought but decided to keep it to myself.

'They won't come over here Maggie; Kieran wouldn't wreck your apartment.' 'Yeah, you're probably right Mary', Maggie agreed and finally moved away from the window. 'Is it always this exciting here?' Sharon asked. 'Sharon' I replied 'you've got no idea.' Maggie left an hour later and once again handed me the keys. 'Make sure you lock up when you leave Mary, just in case. See you Sunday, bye.'

Sharon sat for a while on the front step trying to catch the sun, determined as Maggie and I were the year before to get a tan. 'This is the life' she said to me through the screen door as she drank from her ice cold bottle of beer and stared up that the blue cloudless sky. 'Are you hungry Mary? I'm starving' she said after about an hour. 'Yeah me too Sharon' I said as I removed the last of the tableware from a box and placed them in one of the kitchen presses. 'I know just the place to go Sharon; my mouth is already watering just thinking about it. Come on' I said and we made our way to Angelina's. After eating our way through three courses we finished our first evening with drinks in the Sicily where Enzo, my ex-boss even bought us a drink. By the time we got back to the apartment we were definitely a little worse for wear and we collapsed into Maggie's double bed.

I fell into a deep sleep but was woken and brought to my senses abruptly by a noise coming from the kitchen. In the stillness and silence of the night, it sounded like an explosion. 'What was that?' Sharon whispered as I listened to the sound of glass breaking. 'Be quiet Sharon', I managed to say as fear gripped me. 'Maggie was right,' I whispered 'they're wrecking the apartment' and I expected at any moment to see the bedroom door fly open. 'But they can't do that' Sharon whispered naively, 'they'll be arrested.' After what seemed like the longest time, silence returned but I was sure that my pounding heart would waken the neighbours next door. 'I think they've gone Sharon' I said almost afraid to move. 'Go out and see Mary' Sharon suggested without moving a muscle. I was about to refuse and thought about staying where I was till morning. But the sudden urge to use the bathroom meant it wasn't an option. I tip-toed toward the door in slow motion and turned the handle, hoping it wouldn't squeak. As I entered the kitchen, I had all but stopped breathing and expected any moment to be hit with a baseball bat. The light switch I knew was on the far wall and as I crept my way toward it I could hear the crunch of broken glass under my slippered feet with each step. I hit the switch and was momentarily blinded by the flood of light.

Is there anyone there?' I heard Sharon call from the all too imaginary safety of the bedroom. 'I'm going to fuckin kill Maggie' I heard myself say 'I'm just going to kill her; she has my nerves at me.'

Sharon, who could tell by the sound of my voice that I was no longer afraid, but furious, stepped into the kitchen to see a spice rack which had held about a dozen small glass bottles lying broken on the floor and the bottles that hadn't smashed on impact when hitting the ground had rolled aimlessly to the four corners of the room. Realising that the spice rack was one of the items that Maggie; in her busy schedule, had hastily nailed to the wall. Sharon said 'Maggie would want to 'brush up' on her DIY skills.' I laughed and laughed from sheer relief, while feeling a little ridiculous for believing that Kieran would ever hurt me.

Maggie wasn't wrong about everything though and three days later Kieran came looking for his television. Maggie had returned from Block Island that morning and after having breakfast with Sharon and I, said she was going to visit Vanessa. 'I'll be back in an hour or so Mary and if you like we can go to the mall to do some shopping before we catch the evening ferry.' 'Righto' I replied 'Sharon and I can pack the clothes we're bringing while we're waiting for you.' Maggie was gone less than ten minutes when the phone rang. 'Is he there?' I heard her whisper before I had a chance to say hello.' 'Is who here Maggie?' I asked. 'Kieran!' she replied in such a way that suggested I should have been inspired. 'I was stopped in traffic on my way to Vanessa's house when I saw him running towards me' she continued. 'What did he want Maggie?' 'How the hell do I know Mary? Probably his television, but I just put my foot to the floor and took off. He was running down the street like a lunatic after me!' Somehow I wasn't quite convinced that Maggie was telling me the whole truth. 'Are you sure you didn't say anything to him Maggie?' I asked knowing well, that at times, Maggie could be as Mam put it 'brazen as brass!' 'Well' she began 'I did give him the finger and called him a shit head as I drove past him.' 'Maggie, why don't you just give him back the television? After all it was good of him to allow you to have it for this long,' I said. But knew Maggie wouldn't share my point of view. 'Oh big deal Mary, just lock up the apartment and don't answer the door if he knocks', she said ignoring my advice. 'Call me back if he shows up Mary, I'll wait here at Vanessa's. He'll kill me if he catches me.' 'He's not going to kill you Maggie' I said to myself, because Maggie had already hung up.

So I began to rush around closing all the windows as Maggie had instructed. 'What on earth are you doing Mary?' Sharon asked. 'It's like an oven in here.' I had just finished explaining to Sharon when the front door flew open and there standing in front of me was Kieran with Rocco about two steps behind him. 'Shit' I thought I never locked the door. One look at Kieran and I knew it was not the time for greetings or introductions. 'Your sister thinks she's a real wise ass huh Mary.' It was more of a statement than a question. 'Take a look at this Rocco' he continued 'can you believe it Rocco? She's got three friggin televisions and my mother's got none. Un fuckin believable!' He said as he reached for the nearest television, turned and was gone out the door. 'So that's the Kieran I've heard so much about?' Sharon said as we watched him speed away. 'Yep, that's Kieran,' I replied feeling a little sad knowing I probably wouldn't see him again. 'God' I thought 'how things have changed in just a year.

Chapter 51

She Wore An Itsy Bitsy Teeny Weeny.........

Block Island was a beautiful place. It was heaving with holiday makers from all over the East Coast. Maggie was working in a hotel called 'The Shamrock' which sat on the water's edge. A family orientated hotel with a calm laid back atmosphere. 'Do you want to work?' Maggie asked Sharon and I on our second day. 'No way,' Sharon replied adamantly, determined to relax and enjoy every moment of her stay. 'What kind of work?' I asked Maggie, thinking some extra money would come in handy. 'They're short of people to clean bedrooms, the pay isn't great but you'd be finished early enough to go to the beach every day.' I agreed and for the next several days I watched Sharon armed with bath towels and swimwear, head off happily on her half mile trek to the beach, while I nearly died in the heat of the hotel bedrooms.

It was our last day at Block Island when staring out one of the hotel bedroom windows and feeling the perspiration trickling down my back as I watched the crystal clear water of the ocean just fifty feet away, that I decided I was going for a swim immediately after work and I counted the minutes until my shift ended.

When my work was finally done I ran the short distance to the beach hut Maggie considered home for most of the summer. I quickly changed into my swimsuit and grabbed a towel, thinking I'd never reach the cool water and felt like I was passing out. I made my way along the stone pier which stretched about fifty yards out into the ocean. I had never seen water so clear or calm before and when I dived in, I thought I'd died and gone to heaven. I had the whole place to myself, although I could see hundreds of people sitting along the sea-front under their umbrellas in the distance. Apart from them, there wasn't a single bather in sight. After all the hustle and bustle of the busy hotel it was a real sanctuary and I felt truly blessed to have such a heavenly place all to myself and wondered why people opted to walk half a mile in the blazing sun to the other beach when they had paradise literally on their doorstep.

The answer came from a voice which at first I thought came from heaven as I drifted along on my back only to realise there was a man shouting to me from two hundred feet away on the pier. I began treading water and strained to hear what the man was saying. Then I really thought I was hearing things when I finally grasped what the man was yelling. 'Sharks! Get out of the water lady.'

Sharks! I thought he had to be some kind of crazy person, but when he continued to yell, I instinctively looked around me and realised that I was surrounded. 'Get out, swim, swim lady' I heard the man again. I watched in horror as the sharks which were about six foot long and too many in numbers to count swam around me close enough for me to touch. I started to swim and didn't stop or look around me until I reached the pier where the man grabbed me and pulled me shaking from the water. He was still shouting. 'Are you crazy lady? Do you want to be eaten alive? Don't you know the sharks come in here every evening for the waste food from the hotel?'

'How was I supposed to know that?' I replied almost crying and realising how close I'd come to death. 'Did anyone around here think to put up a sign? I can read you know and' I continued almost hysterical as I pointed to the crowds of people sitting and sipping cocktails, oblivious to my near death experience 'could they not have warned me?'

When Maggie and Sharon found me two hours later I was sitting at the bar in the hotel, sipping what must have been my fourth or fifth drink and still in shock after my ordeal. 'Are you drinking all afternoon?' Maggie asked. 'You should at least have gone for a swim.' 'Go for a swim? Go for a swim?' I barked. 'I did go for a swim and was nearly eaten alive!' 'What's got you in such a bitchy mood Mary? Did you step on a crab?' Maggie asked as she nudged Sharon who was a little taken aback with my uncustomary bad humour.

As I called for a drink for Maggie and Sharon, I explained to them about my near death experience. 'Were they big Sharks?' Maggie asked trying to keep a straight face. 'All I know Maggie' I said reliving my experience 'is that their mouths were bigger than my size three feet!

In a way that only the Irish know best, Maggie and Sharon showed their sympathy and support by falling around laughing! 'I'm glad ye find it so amusing' I said smiling and beginning to see the funny side to it also. 'At least I know now that I could win a gold medal in the Olympics for swimming.' 'Yeah,' Maggie and Sharon answered together 'if there were sharks chasing you!'

Chapter 52

THERE MAY BE TROUBLE AHEAD

We spent ten glorious days on Block Island before we returned to Providence and with little more than a week left in our holiday, we decided to sit down and discuss how best to spend the remainder of the time. 'I'd love to go to a concert' Sharon said as we sat drinking tea in Maggie's kitchen. 'Diana Ross is in the civic centre this weekend' Maggie suggested 'I don't know if tickets are sold out, but you could call the ticket desk and ask.' 'Oh I'd love to see her in concert' Sharon said 'she's one of my favourites.' 'Come on so Sharon, let's go' I said thinking of the number one hits she had. 'Do you two want to meet me later for a drink in Garibaldi's?' Maggie asked as we were about to leave. 'Ok,' we both answered not needing much encouragement 'we'll see you there at eight.'

I liked Garibaldi's, although it was small in size, no bigger than the average living room. It was decorated to such a high standard that you almost felt like you were sitting in a grand country home rather than a neighbourhood bar. The seating consisted of several expensive looking sofas which were strategically placed around the horse shoe shaped bar which was hand crafted and carved from the finest wood. A beautiful piano took pride of place in the far corner and on each wall there were oil paintings of every famous landmark in Italy. It was the type of place a man might take a lady on a first date if he wanted to impress her and I did wonder if it hadn't been for the fact that Maggie worked there, would we even be welcome. Sharon and I had to admit that we stuck out like a sore thumb when we walked in wearing tee-shirts and jeans and received a few strange looks from some of the customers who were either dressed in suits or designer cocktail dresses. But we didn't care; we were in great spirits having succeeded in purchasing two tickets for the concert.

As we sat in Garibaldi's sipping our drinks Sharon and I discussed our plans to go to New York on a day trip. I would have preferred to go to Boston and tried to convince Sharon that I was convinced she wouldn't like New York, but she was adamant that her holiday in America would not be complete without a visit to the 'Big Apple', so I surrendered.

Just as Maggie stood to go the bar, the door opened and two burly looking Italians stepped inside closely followed by Gerard Molyneaux who was surrounded by four heavily bejewelled ladies with model like figures who were competing with each other for Gerard's undivided attention. They were all very attractive women but I couldn't help but think that they'd need a chisel to remove the make-up from their faces at the end of the evening.

As the owner of the bar almost ran to take their drinks order, the women bickered amongst themselves as to who would have the honour of sitting next to Gerard. Maggie called to him, knowing that with all the commotion the ladies were causing he hadn't even seen us. 'Well snob, aren't you even going to say hello?' Gerard looked and recognising Maggie, jumped to his feet. 'Hey Maggie, how you doin?' You lost a lot of weight eh? You're lookin' real good' he said holding her at arm's length before giving her a hug and a kiss on each cheek. 'Hey Mary, when did you get back? He asked surprised and genuinely pleased to see me, 'you back to stay this time Mary?' He asked giving me a hug. 'No Gerard my friend and I are just here for a few weeks,' I replied introducing him to Sharon. 'It's really good to see you kids' Gerard said lifting his own drink from the tray the owner was carrying and he sat down to join us, much to the annoyance of his lady friends, who gave us some disapproving stares.

'Now' he said making himself comfortable 'what's happenin?' At the time, Maggie and I couldn't understand why Gerard Molyneaux would choose our company over that of such glamorous looking ladies, but when I look back now I believe it was simply that we were honest with him. We said what we meant and we meant what we said and I think he really appreciated it. At that time unknown to us, Gerard Molyneaux was a man who was used to sitting in the company of people who agreed with him regardless of whether they believed him to be right or wrong. When he was serious they nodded with sombre faces and when he laughed at some joke he was telling, they laughed as if it was the funniest thing they had ever heard. Whereas in our company Gerard heard our honest opinion whether we thought he would approve or disapprove. That night Gerard's opinion of us was put to the test in a situation that we realise now could have quite easily ended with a completely different outcome. It was about halfway through the night when Gerard Molyneaux brought up the subject of the I.R.A.

The 'Hyde and Regency Park' bombings had occurred only a few weeks before Sharon and I flew out to America and were still very much world news. Gerard was clearly in support of the I.R.A. and their plight against the British. He said 'he himself hated them and believed they should all be wiped out.' 'You don't know what you're talking about Gerard' I said hating the fact that the conversation had turned to politics and also having this need to defend Sharon, who was born in England, a fact Gerard Molyneaux was totally ignorant of, even though I felt sure at the time he would notice the difference between Sharon's accent and mine.

'Sure I know what I'm talking about kid. The I.R.A. should kill every last one of those motherfuckers.' 'How Gerard; is killing innocent bystanders and dumb animals going to improve things? If anything' I said 'it will only result in creating negative feelings toward the I.R.A.' 'I'm surprised at you kid, are you defending those bastards? They left your people starve to death in prison.' 'No Gerard, I'm not defending the British hierarchy, I'm defending the ordinary British person who is getting caught in the cross fire and totally innocent of any wrong doing. 'Nah' Gerard persisted 'just wipe them all out, every last one of them' he suggested as he signalled to the owner to fill another round of drinks. Sharon knew I was getting really annoyed, 'leave it go Mary' she advised, but I was determined to make my point. 'So you're telling me

Gerard that even though you don't know them, you hate every single British person and if you had your way you would kill them. Is that it?' 'Sure would Mary' Gerard replied calmly as if he were discussing swatting flies. 'Well' I said 'you'll have to kill Sharon so,' I said 'cause she was born in England.'

Gerard looked at Sharon, then me and finally at Maggie, who was nodding her head confirming what I had said to be the truth. 'You English?' Gerard asked Sharon after a long silence. 'Yep, my parents are Irish, but I was born in England' Sharon replied unashamedly. 'Well,' I said staring at Gerard in anticipation of his response. 'Ok kid' Gerard finally replied 'I get your point; maybe your friend Sharon is ok. Yeah, she's ok I guess.' 'Thanks Gerard, I just wanted you to realise that you can't 'tar' everyone with the same brush!'

I excused myself and went to the ladies, happy in the notion that I'd proved my point, but relieved that the conversation was now over and we could return to the more light hearted banter we were sharing before the subject of the I.R.A. came up. But it wasn't to be. When I returned to my seat Maggie was trying to say something to Gerard who was refusing to listen and was shouting over her. 'Maggie, you don't know what you're talkin' about. You're talkin' out of your ass.' 'But' was all Maggie managed to say. 'But nothin', Gerard replied cutting her off once more. 'Shut your mouth Maggie, you don't know nothin' Gerard continued and waved his hand in a gesture as if to dismiss her.

To this day I don't know what they were talking about, all I know was that I looked at Maggie and knew she wasn't about to back down and that she wouldn't take too kindly to being told to 'shut up!' The song 'there may be trouble ahead' sprung to mind and all of a sudden Maggie, in all her wisdom and in a voice loud enough to be heard by everyone in the bar said 'Gerard Molyneaux, you're only an asshole!'

The next ten minutes unfolded as if in slow motion. At first there was silence as people stared in open mouthed horror at Maggie. The owner of the bar seemed frozen in fear as if his brain was refusing to process what he had just heard. Maggie was stubbornly staring at Gerard while he was staring into space, just sitting there motionless as if turned to stone. The owner, who had found his voice began pleading with Maggie to apologise, then regretted saying anything to her a few moments later because Maggie had no intention of 'backing down.' 'I will not apologise' she said adamantly 'he is an asshole.' The owner proceeded to apologise on her behalf. 'Mr Molyneaux, I'm so sorry. I'm sure she doesn't mean it.' 'I do mean it' Maggie interrupted his grovelling. Gerard's lady friends approached Gerard in a show of support and suggested he should join them at their table while each of them glared at Maggie with contempt. Sharon and I just sat there and I quietly hoped Maggie would apologise. But I knew that hell would freeze over first. I wondered as I watched Gerard's bouncer like associates wait patiently for instructions from Gerard as to which plan of action they should take, would we ever get to see 'Diana Ross!' After what seemed like an eternity Gerard finally spoke as he waved his lady friends and minders back to their table. 'Forget about it, she thinks she means it, but I know she didn't.' It was as if God had spoken and miraculously everything returned to normal.

The night didn't end there. Gerard asked if he could leave with us when it came to going home and once again the disappointment was evident on the faces of his lady friends who had waited patiently, but in vain, for his attention all night.

Gerard insisted that Maggie drive and having gained so much experience as a valet parker the year before; she handled the huge Cadillac with ease, which didn't go unnoticed with Gerard. 'You're a good driver Maggie, you know that?' He said as we made our way through the Colonial Hill streets to her apartment. 'I know Gerard' Maggie replied with her usual self confidence. 'I'm not just a pretty face.' Gerard was further impressed when we got out of the car when he noticed that Maggie had parked with the front wheels turned out toward the street. 'Hey, I like that Maggie' he said smiling as he pointed to the wheels. 'Where d'ya learn to do that?' 'Kieran'

Maggie replied bluntly. Gerard obviously realised he'd touched a raw nerve with Maggie and to lighten her mood said 'Yeah, not for nothin' Maggie, 'the next time I need a getaway driver, I'm gonna come lookin' for you'. I smiled to myself as I painted a picture in my mind of Maggie as a getaway driver. 'No' I thought that would never work; there was no way Maggie would wear a balaclava over her head because it would ruin her hair-do.

As usual, Maggie volunteered my services to make 'Irish Coffees' that night and we sat around talking about everything and nothing until the early hours of the morning. 'You know girls, I had a real good time tonight,' Gerard said as he sipped the cream from what must have been his third coffee and was obviously in no hurry to leave. 'So Gerard,' Maggie asked 'am I forgiven for calling you an asshole?' 'Forget about it, it ain't nothin' Maggie' Gerard replied smiling. 'I don't think Gerard, your friends were too impressed with me, if looks could kill, I'd be dead.'

'Do you really think Maggie, those people are my friends. They ain't no friends of mine, not one of them. They'd stab me in the back if they thought they'd get away with it. Yeah, no kiddin' girls, they'd love to see me dead.'

I watched Gerard and I could tell that he believed every word he was saying. 'But Gerard' I said 'if you feel that way why do you speak to them and always buy them drinks?' 'You got a lot to learn Mary, about life,' Gerard said giving me one of his intense stares. 'You an' your sister are good people, but you dunno nothin''. If you're lucky enough an' you got friends, keep them close, but you gotta keep your enemies even closer. You get me kid?' I nodded. 'But' Sharon asked, 'how do you know who's your friend and who's your enemy?'

'It ain't easy' Gerard replied 'so I treat them all good, 'cause you never know who you're friggin' friends are until your back is to the wall.'

I don't know what time I finally drifted off to sleep that night, but I woke the next morning beside Sharon who was curled up on the opposite end of the sofa. Maggie was sound asleep in her bed and Gerard Molyneaux was gone. I never met Gerard again, but many times over the next thirty years I remembered the advice he gave me that night. Which time and time again, I ignored, much to my detriment, as people I considered to be my friends 'kicked me in the teeth.' But I always consoled myself with the belief that I'd rather care for and trust someone at the risk of being hurt, than be like Gerard Molyneaux who trusted nobody and went through life very much on his own.

Chapter 53

Reach Out And Touch

Three nights later Sharon and I went to see Diana Ross in concert as planned. She gave a fantastic performance and we enjoyed every minute of it. But the icing on the cake for Sharon and I was that we actually got to meet her in person and speak to her briefly. It wasn't during the concert and we certainly weren't among the chosen few who got back stage passes. The encounter with Diana occurred after the concert as Sharon and I made our way back to Colonial Hill. We were chatting away to each other delighted in the fact that we had such a great evening. The street was practically deserted as most of the traffic from the concert had dispersed onto the nearby highway and pedestrians were very few and far between, so we were a little startled when a young boy of about twelve years of age appeared out of the shadows and jumped out into the street in front of a huge white stretch limousine that was approaching. Sharon and I came to a standstill on the footpath as we watched the scenario unfold. 'Miss Ross, Miss Ross' the boy yelled as the tinted back seat window rolled down and revealed a smiling Diana Ross. The young boy was suddenly rendered speechless as Diana reached out of the limousine to shake his hand and he wasn't alone. I couldn't quite believe it. I heard the chauffeur reminding Diana that they needed to leave 'we're running late Miss Ross.' But Diana was undeterred. 'Just give me a minute' she insisted. 'Where are you girls from?' She asked turning her attention away from the star struck boy who was gazing adoringly at her. 'We're from Ireland,' Sharon and I answered together. 'Oh Ireland' she smiled 'I'd love to go there someday. I've been told it's a beautiful country.' 'You should' Sharon advised 'you've got thousands of fans there.' 'Did you girls enjoy my concert?' Diana asked ignoring the pleas from her driver. 'Yes, it was fantastic' I replied. 'But' Sharon added 'meeting you has really made our night, our friends won't believe us when we tell them.' Diana sat back in her seat 'it's been a pleasure meeting you girls. I love your accents,' she said as the window began to roll upwards and the limousine slipped away from the kerb.

'Oh my God Mary' Sharon screamed 'I can't believe we just met Diana Ross.' 'I know' I said staring at my hand and remembering her warm handshake. 'I don't think I'll ever wash this hand again Sharon,' I said laughing.

It was definitely the highlight of Sharon's trip to America and our visit to New York paled in comparison. It wasn't that the day was uneventful because it was, but not for the right reasons and I think Sharon regretted not heeding my earlier advice when I had suggested visiting Boston instead.

We arrived by Greyhound Bus into Port Authority Terminal New York around mid-morning and already the temperatures were in the high eighties. The humidity, the crowds, the traffic and the noise was exactly how I remembered it. Sharon had made a list the evening before of all the places she wanted to see and our first port of call was the Empire State Building where each of us stood in different poses so the other could take photographs. We bought hot dogs and sodas from one of the many street vendors and sat happily on the edge of a fountain eating as we watched the people of New York go by. Everyone seemed to be in such a hurry, nervously checking the time on their wristwatches as if they were late for some important event. I watched men carrying expensive leather briefcases in one hand and a neatly folded copy of the New York Times in the other, ladies teetering in rather uncomfortable high heels struggling to keep up. Everybody was in a hurry to their own destination, that is, with the exception of the dozens of homeless people and drug addicts who were perched like rag dolls on every street corner hoping for a few cast off coins from a sympathetic passer-by.

'Watch that man there' Sharon said interrupting my thoughts 'do you thinks he's dead Mary?' She asked pointing to a man who was lying face down in the gutter at the pedestrian crossing. 'I don't think so Sharon' I replied, but thought he

might as well be as I watched hundreds of well-polished heels step over him as if he didn't exist.
Little did I think then, that twenty five years on, I would see similar scenes on the streets of Limerick and every other Irish city when heroin took its toll and destroyed whole families.
We finished our lunch and made our way to 'Macey's' where Sharon bought some gifts to bring home to her family. After that, Sharon and I decided our next stop would be the Statue of Liberty. That was the plan, but we never actually got there. While on route, Sharon stopped suddenly outside a rather dingy looking record store.
'Look Mary' she said pointing to the records displayed in a window that looked as if it hadn't been cleaned in decades 'Janis Ian's Greatest hits Mary, I have to get that for Tom.' 'Sharon, I think we should stick to the bigger department stores' I said and for some strange reason Kieran Hennessy popped into my mind. 'Are you girls friggin crazy?' I imagined him saying as he had so many times in the past. 'Let's go somewhere else Sharon' I insisted, but to no avail. Sharon, fearless in her naivety pushed the shop door open and went inside. With little other option I reluctantly followed Sharon into the dimly lit store and while she searched through the dusty display of records, I searched for other customers and could see none. We were alone in the store apart from two Hispanic looking men dressed in sleeveless vests and heavy gold chains, standing behind the counter. My attention was then drawn to the sound of voices coming from the rear of the property. In what was meant to be an office, through thick clouds of cigarette smoke I could see at least three more men sitting around a table drinking beer and playing cards. 'Oh God I feel sick' I thought not feeling at all comfortable with the store or the people in it. 'Sharon, will you hurry up' I whispered not wanting the men to hear our accents and realise we were tourists. 'Sharon, I just want to get out of here!' 'Will you relax Mary, what's the rush?' Sharon replied loud enough to attract the attention of the men in the office, who all of a sudden seemed more interested in us than in playing cards.

'Right Mary, I'm ready. I'll buy these' Sharon said much to my relief and stepped up to the counter to pay.
'Where are you ladies from?' one of the men behind the counter asked as he reached out to take Sharon's money, and I noticed was taking his time giving her, her change. 'We're from Ireland' Sharon replied mistaking his leering stare for friendliness. 'My friend here and I could take you ladies out, yunno, show you the sights.' The man said still holding Sharon's change in his hand. 'Oh no,' I replied before Sharon got a chance 'we couldn't do that, we're here with our boyfriends' I said giving Sharon a sharp nudge in the ribs to keep quiet. 'We've got to go now, they're waiting for us outside', Sharon held her hand out for the change. But instead of handing it to her the man grabbed Sharon by the arm and pulled her over the counter toward him and before either of us had the opportunity to react, he planted a firm but sloppy kiss right on her mouth.
Sharon was horrified and looked quite ill as she managed to break free from the man's grip and we both ran for the shop door. She was still wiping her mouth and spitting ten minutes later.
'I just want to go home' she moaned practically on the verge of tears. 'I tried to warn you Sharon,' I said as we boarded an early bus back to Providence and the relative safety of 'Colonial Hill.'

Chapter 54

I'll Be Home For Christmas

Before I knew it, our holiday had come to an end and we were waving goodbye to Maggie at Logan Airport. Maggie waited and watched until we reached the departure gates. I handed my boarding pass to the stewardess and as I turned to wave one last time to Maggie, I thought how much her life had changed in the previous twelve months.

I thought about the summer before and the fact that if we had succeeded in finding work on Long Island as originally intended we would never have heard of Colonial Hill. Maggie wouldn't have dropped out of university and would now have her degree instead of holding down two jobs to make ends meet. Most of all I thought she would never have met Kieran or have had her heart broken by him. Not that Maggie would ever admit to being broken hearted, she was too proud and stubborn to admit that, and it was these very attributes that kept her from taking the easy option, which would have been to tuck her tail between her legs and return home to Ireland. The saying 'Hell hath no fury like a woman scorned' best described Maggie all those years ago and the fury would prove to be the force that sustained her and kept driving her forward toward her goal of a successful career. Despite the fact that I knew Maggie still loved him, I also knew that even if Kieran wanted, the odds were she would never give him a second chance.

'No' she had said definitely when I asked her 'Kieran had his chance Mary and even if he doesn't already, I know that someday he will regret finishing with me. Yes Mary it will be his loss not mine' she almost scoffed. But as her sister, she couldn't fool me and the hurt in her eyes was all too plain to see.

I believed Maggie's prediction that Kieran would regret leaving her, but he had for whatever reason made his decision and Maggie would have to draw a line under the whole situation, move forward and try to believe there was a reason why everything had gone so horribly wrong. Yes, I thought to myself as the plane readied itself for the take-off, Maggie would have to forget all about Kieran as he had, it seemed, forgotten her. He was out of her life and that was that!

I couldn't have been more wrong. In the months that followed my return to Ireland, it became clear to me that Kieran had not forgotten Maggie.

He would turn up out of the blue at her place of work or stop her in the street to enquire about her general wellbeing or make idle chit chat before going on his way again. Each time he did, a phone call would come from America and Maggie would relate every minute detail of their encounter. One of these phone calls came about a week before Christmas that year. 'Is that you Mary?' Maggie asked sounding really excited on the other end of the line and before I got a chance to respond she announced 'I'm coming home for Christmas Mary.' 'That's fantastic Maggie; I thought you said you couldn't afford to come home?' 'I can't Mary' she replied and sounded really thrilled at the prospect of seeing everyone and not at all concerned about her finances 'It's not costing me one red cent Mary, Kieran gave me the money.' 'What Maggie?' I gasped in surprise at the mention of his name 'are you back together?' 'No way Mary,' she replied indignantly as if I were an Eejit to even suggest it.

As I stood in the freezing hallway in Cratloe I listened as Maggie explained. 'I was working behind the bar in Garibaldi's last night Mary and who do you think walked in?' 'Kieran' I replied thinking that was a no-brainer.' 'Yes' Maggie agreed 'but he wasn't alone, he had 'Jimmy Durante' with him. I could have cried Mary, she practically hit me in the face with her full length fur coat as she paraded past me and believe me Mary she had more jewellery on than Mr T, and there was me looking like a 'shit on a slate' behind the bar.' 'I'm sure you looked fine Maggie' I interrupted in an effort to console her. 'I didn't' she almost screamed back 'I've been so busy with work and college I haven't even had time to get my hair done in months. I kept thinking Mary as I filled their drinks, how horrible he was to flaunt her in my face. I mean, there's plenty of other bars they could have gone to.' 'Maggie' I said 'will you get to the point? My hands are ready to snap right off with the cold! Why did he give you the money?' 'Well' Maggie continued 'they stayed for about an hour and a half and although Kieran was being very polite to me, I just couldn't bring myself to look at him.' 'Did he seem happy Maggie?' I asked much to my regret. 'Who gives a shit Mary whether he is or he isn't?' she snapped. 'Although now that you mention it Mary' she continued 'Doris was the one doing all the talking, he barely opened his mouth.

Anyway Mary, they were making their way toward the door to leave and I pretended not to notice, there was no-way I was going to say 'have a nice day', then I overheard Kieran practically order her out to the car and after protesting vehemently but unsuccessfully, she reluctantly left and soon as she did Kieran walked across the bar to where I was standing grabbed my hand and handed me a rolled-up bundle of notes!' 'Just like that Maggie? I mean, he must have said something.' 'Oh yeah, he did Mary, he said that I shouldn't be on my own for Christmas and that I should go home to Ireland and spend time with my family!'

I was delighted for the fact that Maggie was going to get home for the holidays and secretly grateful to Kieran for realising what a lonely time it would be for her alone in America and for giving her the money. I didn't argue with Maggie when she refused to admit that it was a nice gesture on Kieran's part, and preferred to adopt the attitude that Kieran 'owed' her and that his conscience was probably bothering him. If it helped her to cope with what had happened then, so be it I thought and was just glad that she would get to spend Christmas with family despite the usual chaos in Cratloe and it would also be an opportunity to meet with all her old friends which I felt certain would be sure to give her a much needed 'lift.'

Maggie's visit home was of great benefit to her and by the time the holidays had come to an end she looked rested and was also excited about a trip some of her old work-mates were planning to make to America that summer. They would, they promised, spend a few days in Rhode Island with her. 'It was,' she said 'something she would really look forward to.'

Once again and all too soon, we waved Maggie off at the airport with wishes of a Happy and Prosperous New Year' and those wishes obviously came true because four months later Maggie managed to secure a small mortgage. She was buying her first home. The house was on Lime St. on Colonial Hill, a three-apartment family house with a small one bedroom cottage in the backyard.

Maggie's goal was to rent the three apartments in the main house which would pay her mortgage and thus enable her to live rent-free in the cottage. Although both houses needed cosmetic work and major updating this didn't deter Maggie. 'Rome wasn't built in a day Mary,' she said 'but hopefully I'll have the cottage re-vamped in time so the girls can come and stay in the summer.

Chapter 55

PHONE CALLS FROM AMERICA

Maggie had a gruelling schedule and for the following number of months the phone calls from America were few and far between. She worked full time in a restaurant called 'Andy's' on the East Side, she bartended at the weekends in Garibaldi's and she attended college full-time. In between all of this, anytime she did have was, for many months, spent either painting or wallpapering. She did however decide to take some time out one evening to visit a friend who was working in the 'Merlin Hotel.' She had been looking forward to the well-earned drink and the opportunity to catch up on all the news with her friend and as usual she called me the following day to tell me all about her night out.

'I was sitting at the bar Mary' Maggie explained in between puffs of a cigarette 'minding my own business, when all of a sudden these two women who were sitting just a few feet away started yelling at me and calling me names.' 'Did you know them Maggie?' I asked concerned. 'I never saw them before, but one look at them and you knew they were looking for trouble. It was obvious they had been drinking for some time and I think the fact that I was on my own I was an easy target.' 'What did you do Maggie' 'To be quite honest Mary I didn't know what to do. I was afraid to leave in case they followed me to my car.' 'So what happened Maggie?' 'Mary, you probably won't believe this, but I was about to ask for the manager to make a complaint about the women when Rocco Del Monte appeared out of nowhere. Walked right up to the women and told them they had no idea who they were messin' with!' 'And what happened then?' I asked hardly able to believe my ears. 'He told them if they didn't want to deal with Kieran Hennessy, they'd better 'hit the road.' 'I bet that worked Maggie' I said remembering with a shudder, my stalker at Little Sicily. 'Oh yeah Mary, they left very quickly and very quietly. Rocco even followed them to the door to make sure they left.' 'God you were blessed Maggie.' 'I guess I was Mary 'cause it was the last place I would have expected to see Rocco, hotels aren't exactly his scene. Anyway Mary I have to get off this phone, I have so much to do before the girls arrive tomorrow. 'Will you take some time off work while they're there Maggie?' 'No, can't afford to, but I'll meet up with them at night after class. No doubt Mary, we'll hit the town. I went shopping today so the refrigerator is full and top of my list was a large carton of cream.

All I need now Mary, is you here to make Irish Coffees!' Yes, I thought to myself, as I hung up the receiver. Making Irish Coffees was one of the very few things I excelled at!

Two days later the last person I expected to hear on the telephone line was Maggie when I answered the call at eleven o'clock in the morning. Not only was it rare for Maggie to call twice in one week, but being eleven o'clock in the morning in Ireland meant it was six in the morning in Rhode Island. My heart skipped a beat when I heard her irate voice and thought something awful must have happened. 'He has got some nerve Mary, who the hell does he think he is?' Maggie yelled in an awful temper. 'What's wrong? What's happened?' I asked panicked at the sound of her voice.

'He thinks he can do whatever he bloody well likes' she continued. 'He must be a bit slow' and then there was a pause as I heard Maggie strike a match and light a cigarette. Now was my chance I thought. 'Maggie, will you calm down? You're not making any sense. Start at the beginning.' 'Ok, ok' she replied taking a deep breath followed by another puff on her cigarette. 'The girls arrived yesterday as planned Mary. I collected them from the airport and brought them to their hotel. I explained that I had classes until nine but that I would meet them at 'City Nights Night Club' on the waterfront at about ten. I rushed home from class, changed into a new outfit that I'd bought so I'd look my best and walked into the club. I just couldn't believe it; I thought I was seeing things. All the girls were there as planned, but who was sitting in the middle of them only that Eejit!' 'Who's that Eejit Maggie?' 'Kieran of course Mary'

Maggie replied in a way that suggested I should have known 'can you believe it, I swear to God Mary, I'll swing for him!' The girls obviously didn't know who he was but had mentioned that they were visiting with their friend 'Maggie' who lived on Colonial Hill.

'Did he say anything Maggie?' 'Oh yeah, wait till you hear this Mary. He asked me if I would like to join them for a drink and if I was going to the bar he would have a Jameson!' I could only imagine the expression that must have been on Maggie's face at that point in time and knew she must have nearly needed sedation. But also knew that Kieran would have seen this as an opportunity to 'wind' her up. I just couldn't help but laugh. 'I don't know what you find so funny Mary, it's not a laughing matter and that's not the best part. As if to add insult to injury he tells me he's been invited to a party, with a big stupid grin on his face.' 'But wasn't that a good thing Maggie?' I asked a little confused 'I mean, at least you knew he wouldn't be staying very long.' 'Yes, that's what I thought Mary until I asked him where the party was on. I was just making polite conversation with him Mary because I didn't want to be arguing in front of the girls and ruin their night out.' 'And Maggie, what did he say?'

'Well Mary, he obviously realised that I was only 'sweet talkin' him to get rid of him, which of course he found highly amusing and was hardly able to sit straight, he was laughing so much. Mary, I'm telling you I could hardly control myself with temper and I told him he should 'fuck off' to his party if he was going.' 'And did he leave Maggie?' 'Nope Mary, he said he couldn't leave without us because the party was on in MY house!'

Maggie was screaming down the line, as I proceeded to cover my mouth so she wouldn't hear me laughing. 'I mean Mary, who the hell does he think he is?' 'So did he actually go to your house Maggie?' 'Oh yeah Mary, he was the life and soul of the party and if it weren't for the fact that he's still with 'Jimmy Durante' I'd have to say Mary, it was like 'old times.' 'What did your friends think about the whole situation Maggie?' 'Oh they thought he was lovely, a real gentleman and that he couldn't seem to take his eyes off me. He only left an hour ago, insisted on driving the girls back to their hotel, God only knows where he's going to tell Doris he's been all night.'

'Did he say anything when he was leaving Maggie? You know, about the two of you, any kiss goodbye?' 'No, nothing Mary, he hasn't touched me or mentioned the word 'us' since he finished with me eighteen months ago, which is fine with me Mary. I wouldn't touch him now if my life depended on it.'

I knew Maggie was lying about not wanting to touch him. What she should have said, if she were being a hundred percent honest was, that she wouldn't touch him as long as he was with Doris. Maggie may have convinced her friends that she had no feelings for him but I being her sister, wasn't fooled that easily and I knew that underneath the brave facade, Maggie still missed Kieran.

I was proved right. In fact Maggie missed Kieran so much that a few days before Christmas that year and almost two years after they split up, in her wisdom after several drinks with friends and feeling very low she decided to write him a letter. Somewhere between missing him and one too many drinks her mood had obviously altered and instead of writing romantic terms of endearment as she had originally intended, she listed all the things she disliked about him including calling him a loser. 'Oh that's definitely going to win his affections' I said sarcastically into the phone 'what in the name of God possessed you to do that Maggie?' 'I don't know Mary' Maggie replied sorrowfully. 'It's all a bit fuzzy. I do remember putting the letter in his mailbox though with 'shit head' written in bold capital letters on the envelope. Oh God, do you think he'll find it Mary?' 'Of course he will Maggie, unless of course you drive over to his apartment and set fire to his mailbox! All you can do now Maggie, realistically, is wait for him to show up on your doorstep.' 'Jesus, Mary an' Joseph, he'll be out for blood Mary, do you think he'll murder me?'

'Stop being so dramatic Maggie, of course he won't. Just tell him you were upset.' 'Yes you're right Mary and I have good reason to be. Why should I worry about him, he's so full of shit he's eyes are turning brown.' 'And I suppose you told him that as well Maggie?' I said trying to hold in a laugh. 'Ah – yeah, I did Mary.' 'Well I'd be willing to bet any money Maggie, you'll be getting a visit from Kieran in the next few days.' 'Oh God Mary, what am I going to do? I'm never drinking again.'

Chapter 56

Santa Clause Is Coming To Town

Whatever Maggie had written in the letter, it certainly got Kieran's immediate attention. He called to her house that very night and she called me the next morning to tell me all about it. 'Is that you Mary?' 'Yes Maggie' I yawned 'Oh did I wake you Mary' she asked knowing well that she had. 'Why would you think that Maggie it is after all, six o'clock in the morning?' 'Sorry Mary, I just had to call you, Kieran was here a while ago.' 'I take it he didn't murder you then Maggie?' 'Ah, no Mary, but I really don't think he's the 'full shilling.' 'Why Maggie' what did he do now?' 'Well Mary, I went to bed around ten thirty and I was reading a book, it's a true story Mary, you should read it, it's called'. 'Maggie, will you get to the point' I interrupted I'm blind with sleep here.' 'Oh ok Mary, there's no need to snap the face off me. Anyway I heard the yard gate swing open and I knew instinctively it had to be Kieran. I turned off the bed side lamp hoping he wouldn't notice, but then came the knock on the door. I kept praying 'please God, let him think I'm not home.' But my prayers went unanswered Mary because he then started calling my name. 'Maggie open the door, I know you're in there' on and on he went. I swear to God Mary, I thought I was going to get a panic attack.' 'Maggie, will you stick to the story' I urged, half sorry I'd answered the telephone. 'Mary, I opened the door and Kieran was standing there holding a big black refuse sack, my two knees were rattling Mary. I was sure he was going to murder me and stuff my body in the bag.' I rolled my eyes up to heaven at Maggie's all too vivid imagination. When I thought, was she was going to realise that Kieran had never stopped loving her?' 'Mary, I asked him if he had come to kill me and he just brushed past me into the kitchen.' 'And', I said impatiently 'what did he say?' 'He said 'Ho! Ho! Ho! Merry Christmas!'

I smiled to myself and tried to picture Kieran's impersonation of 'Santa.' 'Don't you think that, that's a little crazy Mary?' 'Oh yeah Maggie, almost as crazy as you believing he was going to kill you. And what was in the refuse sack Maggie?' 'Christmas gifts Mary, several of them, all individually wrapped, just for me. Kieran put them under my Christmas tree and made me promise not to open them until Christmas morning and then he just left. Would you blame me Mary for thinking he's not the 'full-bob?' 'Maggie, you know, you may be right, maybe Kieran is a little crazy. But one thing's for sure and that is, his heart is in the right place.'

Maggie and Kieran were in my thoughts all that day. It was now two years since Kieran finished with her and despite the fact that there was no intimacy between them, it had never quite ended. Maggie missed Kieran, in my opinion; he loved Maggie or at the least thought of her often. But never asked her to give him a second chance, in fact, he never asked Maggie for anything. Did his heart get the better of him every now and again and he just couldn't resist seeing her? Or, did he just need the reassurance that she was 'doing' alright? I believed it was a little bit of both. Seeing Maggie may have been enough for Kieran. But for Maggie though, it was understandably an impossible and seemingly fruitless situation and I was very much aware that it was only a matter of time before something had to 'give.'

Chapter 57

Diamonds Are A Girl's Best Friend

1984 was a year of change for both Maggie and I. For Maggie the change came in the form of Alex, a young lawyer who people claimed had a very bright future ahead of him. For many weeks he showered Maggie with compliments and bouquets of flowers at the restaurant where she worked. She rejected all requests to date, made by him initially but after weeks of resistance on her part, his charm and persistence paid off and she finally agreed to see him. He certainly knew how to impress, she told me, the best tailor made suits, a flash car and insisted that only the best restaurants would suffice.

It was a whirlwind romance and within a few months there was talk of marriage and children and all necessary introductions were made to his parents who seemed to approve of their sons choice.

'Do you love him Maggie?' I asked during another long distance call. 'Course I do Mary, let's face it, I'd be crazy not to. Alex has even told me there will be no need for me to work, imagine that Mary, me, a lady of leisure.' 'Yeah, sounds great Maggie,' I replied, but I didn't feel so sure. I just had this niggling feeling that would not go away. 'Do you worry at all Maggie that you and Alex come from such different cultural backgrounds?' 'God Mary' Maggie replied sounding shocked 'I'd never have expected you to be a racist.' 'No, it's not that Maggie' I said knowing she was referring to the fact that Alex was Lebanese 'it's just, well, that they often have different ideas about women and you know you're so independent.' 'Don't be so ridiculous Mary, Alex was born and raised in America, not in a tent in the desert surrounded by camels! I have a feeling Mary that he is going to propose tonight, he wouldn't tell me where we're going but he gave me money to get my hair done and told me wear something special, so wish me luck Mary.'

Maggie was right, Alex did propose that night and she called me at six o'clock the following morning just to tell me. I practically hit off every wall in the hall as I stumbled sleepily with one eye open to answer the persistent rings of the telephone. 'Oh, shit, Hello' I said as I answered after stubbing my toe on the leg of the hall table. 'Is that you Mary?' I heard Maggie say in a voice that sounded close to tears. 'You obviously didn't get engaged Maggie' I said but was surprised with the response.
'I did Mary, the most beautiful ring you could imagine with a solitaire diamond the size of a rock.' I stood in the hallway as night gave way to morning and listened as Maggie spoke. 'He slipped the ring on my finger Mary while violins serenaded us, it was so romantic and the ring was so beautiful, just perfect. I was picturing my friends' faces when I showed it to them. I really thought all my Christmas's had come together but.' Once again Maggie sounded as if she were about to break down in tears and I would have been forgiven for thinking it was because she was overwhelmed with joy. I heard her blow her nose. 'But what? Maggie,' I asked confused. 'Mary' she practically screamed down the line 'wait till you hear this Mary, it's got to be one for the books. He tells me, 'Maggie I only ask one thing of you and that is, when we have children you are not to tell them of their Irish roots, I will however allow you to travel to Ireland to see your family, but you will do so alone.' 'You've got to be joking Maggie' I said suddenly awake. 'No Mary I'm not.' 'What did you say to him Maggie?' 'What do you think Mary? I told him if he knows what's good for him, not to darken my door again. Mary, he must have thought I came down in the last shower!' 'What about the ring Maggie?' 'Oh Mary, I stormed out of the restaurant but not before throwing the ring back at him, last time I saw him he was crawling around on his hands and knees looking for it!'

Chapter 58

Welcome Home

I got married in April of that year and returned to America with my husband two months later and two months pregnant. Maggie agreed to rent us a two bed roomed apartment on the second floor. There was nothing glamorous about it but I knew with a little work and a few bits and pieces I could turn it into a real home. I was really excited as it was our first home. Finding work was a struggle though, people understandably were reluctant to hire a pregnant woman, but with help from one of Maggie's friends I started work in a family run factory where they produced all types of badges for the Police and Fire Department. My husband also managed to secure a job in another factory, thanks to another one of Maggie's friends, a fellow student and native of Limerick called Richard Sullivan. It was three days to our first pay check and we had no money and I knew I couldn't ask Maggie for a loan 'cause she had spent what cash she had paying a fine for having her car clamped for illegal parking outside the house that morning. I was in dire straits and there was only one person I could think of that might be willing to help me, and that was Kieran.

As I turned onto Nimnuc St. where Kieran lived, I wondered nervously what his reaction would be. It had been two years since we last met and Maggie hadn't heard from him since the previous Christmas when he had arrived with the gifts.

I wasn't in the habit of asking people for money. But I had no choice. Just as I reached the front door of the apartment it swung open. It was Kieran. He seemed a bit startled and then realised it was me. 'Hey Mary, how are you doin?' He asked and threw his arm around my shoulder. 'Come on in Mary' he said. I hadn't anticipated being invited in and wasn't quite sure if I should. 'Ah no, I don't think that's a good idea Kieran,' I said hoping I wouldn't sound ungrateful. 'Come in kid' Kieran said refusing to take no for an answer and ushered me into the all too familiar living room. Dorothy, Doris's younger sister was relaxing on the sofa and I don't know who she was more shocked at, me for being in her sister's boyfriend's apartment or Kieran for inviting me in.

'Hey Dor,' you remember Mary, don't you?' Dorothy didn't even respond, obviously has the same charming personality as her sister I thought. She just stared at the television as if I didn't exist. 'I hear you're a married lady now Mary and you're expectin' a baby.' 'Yeah that's right, 'I've another while to go yet though Kieran, I'm not due until February.' 'That's good news Mary, I gotta meet this husband of yours, take him out for a few beers. You think he'd like that Mary? Yunno, show him the neighbourhood.' 'Yeah, I'm sure he would Kieran, anyway I'd better be going Kieran, he'll be wondering where I am. I just wanted to say hi. It's been good seein' you Kieran.' I had lost my nerve. It wasn't that I was afraid to ask Kieran, but it was embarrassing enough to have to ask him for money without having to ask him in front of Dorothy.

'I was halfway down the street when Kieran came running after me. 'Hey Mary, wait up a minute' he called after me. 'You got enough money Mary?' Oh my God I thought is there anything he doesn't know, he must have read my mind. 'Kieran' I said struggling to get the words out 'my husband and I don't get paid for another few days, I hate asking you, but if you could loan me fifty dollars I promise I'll pay you back next week, I'm really sorry for asking'. Kieran pushed a hundred dollar bill into my hand 'tell that husband of yours I'll be over to take him out Friday night ok Mary.' 'I will Kieran and thanks so much for the money. I won't forget it.'

True to his word and much to Maggie's surprise, Kieran arrived on the Friday night. Maggie was watching television in our apartment, something that had become the 'norm' since my return to America. 'Sure, he mightn't turn up at all Mary,' she said. 'He's about as changeable as the Irish weather.'

There was a knock on the back door and Kieran walked in smiling from ear to ear. 'You ready to paint the town red?' He asked my husband when I introduced them. 'Yeah I'm ready' my husband replied 'I just have to go to the bathroom first.'

Maggie was doing to Kieran as Dorothy had done to me a few days before. Staring at the television and giving him the 'cold shoulder.' 'Hey Maggie' Kieran said knowing she was ignoring him 'ain't your sister lookin' good, you're gonna be an aunt soon.' 'Yes' Maggie said dryly 'I had noticed.' Kieran smiled then winked at me.

'It's just you'd better get a move on Maggie, you ain't gettin' any younger, you know what I mean?' Maggie turned and stared Kieran straight in the face 'that's rich comin' from you Kieran,' she snapped 'but then again, you'd know all about older women!'

Kieran laughed knowing that Maggie had always been able to match his wit and decided to leave while the going was good. So he turned his attention to my husband 'hey Chris, what's takin' you so long? He called through the bathroom door 'you shaving' your legs or somethin?' Maggie couldn't help herself and burst out laughing. She always loved his sense of humour. My husband didn't stay out very long that night; he called me from a payphone asking if I knew the phone number for a taxi company. 'Isn't Kieran driving?' I asked. 'He is but I don't want to ask him and I've got to get out of here, my stomach isn't feeling very well.' 'How's your stomach now?' I asked him when he walked into the bedroom where I was reading twenty minutes later. 'You look fine.' I didn't believe the story he'd given me on the phone about being sick. 'My stomach is fine now' he growled 'did you know those guys carry guns Mary? I mean they look like gangsters.' 'Well Chris,' I said as I reached out to turn off the bedside lamp 'the next time I tell you something you just might believe me. Did you honestly think I could just fabricate a story like that out of thin air?' My husband like anyone else I had tried to explain to; had put my tale of America down to watching too much television.

As promised, a week later I returned the hundred dollars Kieran had given me. He was reluctant to accept it but I insisted. 'You're gonna need all the money you can get Mary' he said trying to push the money away. 'You've got a baby on the way.' 'I know that Kieran,' I said 'but I'm fine really and if

I didn't pay you back I'd never be able to ask you again, just take it,' I insisted and pushed the hundred dollar note into his hand. Kieran looked at the crumpled note and then at me, 'you know Mary, if everyone I know was like you, I'd be a friggin millionaire. I've given money to so many people, every friggin' day they're bangin' on my door 'Kieran I've a problem with this, an' Kieran I need money for that, but you and your sister, you guys are the only ones that ever paid me back.'
'Well I'm sorry Kieran' I said 'but I don't understand that at all, if someone is kind enough to help you out when you need it, you shouldn't, how would you say? Screw them over.
Maybe Kieran you should choose your so-called friends more carefully because the way I see it, if they aren't good enough to repay their debt they won't be there to help you if your back is to the wall. People like that Kieran, have very short memories.'
'Ah forget about it. How are you feeling Mary?' He asked in an attempt to change the subject. You gotta take good care of yourself now. I hope you ain't workin' too hard at that factory?' 'No, I feel fine Kieran,' I replied noticing the sincere concern on his face. 'You need anything Mary, all you gotta do is ask.' 'Thanks Kieran, I appreciate that and actually there is one thing you could do for me.' 'Yeah sure Mary, what's up?' 'I was wondering Kieran if you would be Godfather to the baby when it's being baptized?'
Kieran was momentarily dumb founded, 'who me Mary? You want me to be Godfather?' He managed to say sounding almost emotional. 'Yes you Kieran, look, whatever happened between you and Maggie I don't know. I can only trust you had good reason to do what you did. But, you've always been a good friend to me Kieran, I don't forget. But if you don't want to be Godfather I'll understand. 'No, no Mary, sure, I'd love to be Godfather.' Kieran was smiling from ear to ear. 'That's settled so Kieran, I'm glad you've agreed'. 'Let's face it Kieran', I joked 'it is after all no doubt, the only kind of Godfather you're going to be!' Kieran laughed 'you sound like your sister now, a real wise ass, get outta here.' As I made my way home that day I smiled to myself, happy that I'd asked Kieran to

be Godfather and I knew it meant a lot to him. Kieran did not take responsibilities to family and friends lightly, and I felt certain Maggie wouldn't mind.

Chapter 59

PLEASE REMEMBER ME

Before I knew it Christmas had come and gone and I was just waddling around believing that if my stomach got any bigger it would explode, and counting down the days to my due date which was only a week away. Maggie and I were equally surprised and excited to hear that Mam was making the trip to America so she could be present for the birth of her first Grandchild. Aunt Maureen had loaned her the money.

It was on the second night of Mam's visit while we were relaxing in the living room and listening as Mam told us all the news from home that a knock came to the back door. 'I'll get it' Maggie volunteered and then I heard her say in a surprised voice 'what are you doing here?' It was then that I heard Kieran's voice 'don't worry Maggie, I ain't here to bust your balls, I hear your mother is visiting and I just wanted to meet her!' 'Oh did you now?' Maggie replied. 'You'd better come in so.' When Kieran walked into the living room it was clear he had a few drinks on board. He was by no means drunk just 'merry.' He was wearing a big smile and carrying a bottle of Jameson whiskey which he held at arm's length for all to see. 'This is like old times ain't it Mary?' He said before turning to shake hands with Mam, whom he seemed to hold in the same high esteem one would afford the parish priest or the family doctor. 'Kieran, this is my mother Margaret, Mam this is Kieran Hennessy' Maggie said with the same enthusiasm she would display if spending her last fifty dollars on a bill. 'Pleased to meet you Ma'am' Kieran said 'Maggie has told me so much about you. You know, I got a sister called Margaret, ain't that somethin' another thing we got in common Maggie.' 'Actually' Maggie sniped 'I'd say it's the only thing we have in common.'

Mam looked a little confused and I could hazard a guess as to why. 'Wasn't this the man Maggie had dropped out of university for three years ago only to have her heart broken?

Were they back together again and nobody had bothered to tell her? These were the questions I was sure were on the tip of Mam's tongue and she was about to open her mouth when Kieran spoke. 'Hey Maggie, how about we have some 'Irish Coffees' to celebrate your mothers arrival?' 'Yeah ok,' Maggie agreed, then asked 'Mary can you go to the store and buy some cream?'

I nodded and proceeded with the now familiar struggle of lifting myself out of the armchair only to 'flop' back down again as I watched Kieran in his huge frame lunge from one side of the living room to the next in one step to where Maggie was lounging in a rocking chair. 'I don't friggin believe it' he almost yelled and I knew from experience it was only the presence of Mam that kept him from doing so. 'Your kid sister is about to give birth and you want her to walk to the store in the dark, you go.' 'Ok, ok' Maggie said a little startled 'Jesus, what's eatin' you? Mary loves to walk, ok Kieran I'll go.' But just as Maggie reached for her car keys Kieran grabbed them, I'll drive,' he insisted. When Kieran and Maggie left, Mam saw her opportunity 'are they back together Mary?' 'No Mam' I said not wanting to say too much because I didn't know how much Maggie had told Mam about Kieran and there wasn't the time to explain because it only took a few minutes to reach the nearest store so I decided to keep it simple. 'Mam, it's been like this for years. They have this love, hate thing going on. I don't think it's ever going to end; it's as if they have unfinished business.'

They arrived back from the store about fifteen minutes later and Kieran placed the carton of cream in my hand. 'No Irish Coffee for you Mary, you shouldn't drink in your condition.' 'I know that Kieran' I replied 'I haven't had a drink since my wedding day.' 'Good for you kid' Kieran replied as I shuffled past him to the kitchen where Maggie was filling the kettle. 'I swear to God Mary,' she whispered as she watched Kieran in the living room, happily chatting to Mam. 'I think he has lost the plot.' 'He's not crazy Maggie' I said 'what makes you say that?' 'Mary, on our way back here he turned the car into a dark laneway, switched off the engine.' 'Did he kiss you Maggie?' I interrupted. 'No Mary, he said it was a good night for a murder.' 'What Maggie' I asked almost spilling the coffee as I poured it into long stemmed glasses. 'Did he say who's?' 'Yeah he did Mary, mine!'

I had to admit Kieran often displayed what the Irish would describe as a black sense of humour, but once again I reassured Maggie that he was not going to kill her and that if anything he still loved her. 'He's got a funny way of showing it Mary.' 'Well it's not like you to go out of your way to be nice to him either Maggie. Ye're constantly sniping at each other.' 'No, I'm not Mary' Maggie replied as Kieran called from the living room, 'You need any help girls?' 'No Kieran we're coming' Maggie replied picking up two of the glasses 'no need to get your knickers in a twist!'

For the next three hours Kieran seemed more than content just to sit and listen as Maggie and I reminisced about our childhood in Ireland. We told him of the freedom all children shared in the safety of the Irish countryside. We told him of days we spent picking blackberries along the hedgerows of the winding country roads and of times when we snuck into neighbouring orchards to steal a few apples which would sustain us till we reached home. Maggie and I smiled when we related stories of warm summer days spent paddling in shallow streams and the evenings spent sitting around blazing bonfires cooking sausages on sticks which were held over the flames till they turned golden brown.

Mam, who was normally very reserved also got her speech after her Irish Coffee and Kieran seemed fascinated and quite in awe of what seemed like an unending but amazing knowledge of Irish history. She spoke of the famine and how the Irish in their hundreds of thousands braved the wrath of the Atlantic Ocean in ships unfit for cattle in the hope of finding a better life in America. The horror and heartbreak of leaving loved ones behind in the knowledge that in all probability they would never see them again and the people who were left behind who, if they didn't starve to death waited in vain, for a letter or sometimes a snippet of information to console them that their departed families had survived the journey. 'It's not like today,' she said 'when you can jet home from America in a few hours for less than two weeks wages. No, in those days when you said goodbye on the quay side, it was final.'

I made a second round of Irish Coffees and offered one to Mam. 'Oh no I don't think I should' she said 'I'm feeling very flushed' she continued fanning her rosy cheeks. 'I don't usually drink Kieran and I'm splitting ye're heads talking.' 'That never stops your daughter,' Kieran said laughing as he looked at Maggie, who stared back at him and if looks could kill he'd have died there and then. 'No really,' Kieran said averting his eyes away from Maggie's glare and back to Mam 'I'm really enjoyin' listening to you; it reminds me of my father. He used to tell me stories about the Irish all the time.' Mam took a sip from her glass before continuing.

She spoke of the heroes of the 1916 Rising, of the men who had either died in battle or were executed at the hands of the British, some of them, no more than boys who had given their lives in the fight for justice and freedom for their fellow countrymen. 'It didn't end there Kieran' she said 'what was to follow was one of the saddest times in Irish History.

The Civil War, which turned brother against brother and father's against sons. There was a bitter rift' she explained 'between the people who supported De Valera and the people who supported Michael Collins. My own Grandfather provided a safe house for 'Collins' at the back of his pub in Wickham St.' 'You never told us that before Mam' Maggie interrupted. 'Oh yes, that's true Maggie, Aunt Molly, your Grandaunt, spoke of it several times and do you know that your Granddad, my father, didn't speak to his brother in law for years?' 'No I didn't Mam, why was that?' Maggie asked all of a sudden just as interested as Kieran was in listening to Mams stories. 'Because his brother in law, your Granny's older brother made your Granny who was just a girl, carry bullets in her bodice, across Sarsfield Bridge in Limerick which was being heavily patrolled at the time. 'Did she get caught Mam?' I asked intrigued. 'No Mary she didn't, if she had been, she wouldn't have survived, they would have shot her on the spot. 'That's amazing' Kieran said 'you know my father told me the Irish didn't have it easy when they came to America.' 'He was right,' Mam nodded 'some shops even had signs up on their doors saying 'No Dogs and No Irish.' 'Yes they fought their battles here too Kieran, that's how they earned their name "the fighting Irish" I suppose. They worked hard; some people even say they built America'. 'Yes' Mam concluded 'for such a tiny nation we have so many people we can remember with pride.' It was at that moment the evening took a turn for the worse. I looked at Kieran to ask him if he would like one more Irish Coffee before calling it a night, only then did I see he was crying. Tears rolled silently down his face and the more he tried to control them, the faster they flowed. Maggie, who after a few moments also noticed, took off to the bathroom, unable like most of us Irish to cope with such an outburst of emotion. Kieran got to his feet and while trying to hide his embarrassment and dry his eyes complained to Mam of suffering from hay fever as he said his goodbyes. There was no sign of Maggie returning from the bathroom as Kieran made his way to the door with his head lowered. 'Are you ok Kieran?' I asked concerned because I had never seen him looking so low. 'I'm good Mary,' he replied not too convincingly as he opened the door 'I'll see you later Mary, you take care.' 'Yeah, you too Kieran, I'll see you soon.'

'Is he gone Mary?' Maggie whispered from behind the half open door of the bathroom. 'Yes, he's gone Maggie' I replied a little annoyed that she had left me in such an awkward situation. 'Why did you run off like that Maggie? He was really upset.' 'So what Mary, did he care how upset I was when he decided to dump me? Let him go home and cry on Doris's shoulder.' 'Aren't you even curious as to why he was so upset Maggie?' 'Not really Mary, let's face it, whatever it is there isn't an awful lot I can do about it. He's made his bed so he'll just have to sleep in it. Maybe he misses me or maybe it was listening to Mam talking about Irish and all their achievements that upset him.' 'What do you mean Maggie?' 'I mean, Mary, Kieran must realise he has very little to be proud of. What do you think Mary?' 'I think you could be right Maggie and I think it's time I went to bed.' Struggling to find a comfortable position to lie in and listening to my husband snoring beside me, I found it impossible to sleep that night. I reflected on the evening and what a lovely time we were having right up to the final moments. Mam had liked Kieran that was very obvious by the way she had spoken freely in his company. If Mam didn't like someone, Maggie and I knew from experience that she would refuse to speak to them. But Kieran had impressed her. 'I can see' she said 'he has a lot of respect for his elders, very mannerly.'

I had never seen Kieran as relaxed as he had been earlier in the evening. There was an air of contentment about him as if there was nowhere else in the world he would rather have been at that time. It was as if we had not one, but two family members come to visit, Mam and Kieran, and for a brief time even Maggie seemed to forget that like Mam's visit, Kieran's would come to an end and once more he would be gone.

It explained Maggie's bitterness and uncaring attitude at the end of the evening when the bubble had burst and she was once again faced with the sad inevitability of the odds being against her.

Was Kieran having the same thoughts as the evening drew to a close which caused him to be upset? I certainly believe it played a major part in it compounded by the feelings evoked in him by Mam as she spoke with such pride about the Irish, who no matter where they travelled in the world, had made a positive and lasting impact. I believe that at that very moment Kieran realised for the first time how he would be remembered, and was ashamed.

The look of despair and sadness was written all over his face and the image of his face is as clear in my memory today as it was on that night twenty eight years ago. It's like when someone you know dies, you will always remember the last time you saw them and that was, the last time I saw Kieran Hennessy.

Chapter 60
BORN TO RUN

On February twelfth I gave birth in the apartment to a baby boy after twenty nine hours in labour. I had decided to have a home birth for two reasons, one because my husband and I didn't have enough insurance to cover the cost of the hospital bills and two, I took comfort in the knowledge that it would be a very private affair. No doctors and nurses parading in and out, just me and the midwife. I couldn't have been more wrong. Maggie was sitting on the corner of the bed with her friend Maura, who was also from Limerick. Both of them were drinking vodka to calm their nerves. Maggie kept telling Mam who was sitting on the other corner to stop swearing, not realising that Mam wasn't swearing but praying. And for twelve hours I listened to the midwife and my husband say 'come on Mary, just one more push!'

My son Stephen was born with a cleft lip and the midwife, after hours of pleading with her throughout the labour finally admitted that the baby and I needed to go to the hospital. Maggie was elected to call an ambulance, but little did she know at the time that when you call an ambulance in the State of Rhode Island, the fire brigade respond also. The bedroom was full of paramedics and firemen. So much for privacy, I remember thinking I might as well have given birth in 'Todd's Department Store window. But at that point I didn't care. It was a scene of chaos. My mother, Maggie and my husband were crying. The firemen and half the paramedics were sure they were in the wrong neighbourhood and listened in bewilderment to all the Irish accents. The paramedic in charge was screaming at the midwife not to touch me and that if I haemorrhaged on the way to the hospital he was going to have her charged with murder. She had fallen asleep just as I gave birth and my husband had, had to clean and cut the umbilical cord. I was the only one who was calm and kept trying to reassure everyone that I was sure the baby would be ok. As I was stretchered out onto the snow filled street at four in the morning I watched all the neighbours who had gathered having been woken by the sounds of the sirens. As the paramedics slid me into the ambulance I heard one elderly Italian lady say to another 'that's one of the Irish girls.'

In the days that followed Maggie told me that her telephone was ringing constantly, people enquiring about me and the baby and offering words of support and congratulations. There were cards and gifts and flowers from everyone, everyone with the exception of Kieran. There was no word from him at all.

'He must know you had the baby Mary,' Maggie said totally disgusted. 'I mean nothing happens in this neighbourhood Mary that he doesn't know about. It's just typical; you just can't depend on a man for anything.'

'Maybe he's embarrassed to call after the last time Maggie.'

'Embarrassed my arse Mary, no doubt he'll show up at some stage when it suits him!'

I had to admit I was at a loss as to why Kieran hadn't called or visited. He had been over the moon at the prospect of being Godfather and although you never knew when Kieran would show up, he always did. I couldn't help but feel there was something wrong, maybe I thought, Doris had found out about his visits and issued him some ultimatums?

No, I answered myself it had to be more than that, nobody in the neighbourhood who Maggie trusted enough to ask had even seen him. It was as if he had disappeared into thin air. And it was several days later that we found out that he had!

It was just approaching six o'clock in the evening and I had just put Stephen into his crib to sleep after feeding and changing him when I heard Maggie charging up the stairs, 'Mary turn on the television fast.' 'Maggie will you be quiet?' I asked 'you'll wake the baby.' Maggie ran into the living room and frantically began flicking through the channels until she reached the local news station which was reporting the main 'headline' stories and there staring back at us was a photograph of Rocco and Kieran. Maggie had to sit down and looked as if she were about to faint as we listened with horror to what the anchor man had to say.

"'Wanted' Rocco Delmonte and Kieran Hennessy on charges of conspiracy to murder, considered to be extremely dangerous' I didn't hear anything after that and it was quite some time before either of us spoke. Surely I thought there has to be some mistake as two words spun around in my mind, Dangerous and Murder!

I couldn't reconcile myself to the fact that the 'news man' who was describing a vicious criminal was also talking about the Kieran we knew, the man who I looked upon as a big brother and a person I considered to be a great friend. But there he was on the main evening news. There had to be some truth in what was being said and I remembered what little Vanessa had told us and the whispered conversations I had overheard over the years.

Was it all true? Did the mafia really exist? Did Kieran really kill someone? I finally broke the silence 'Maggie, what does conspiracy to murder mean?' 'I think,' Maggie replied 'it means that Kieran was either involved in planning a murder or he knew it was going to happen and did nothing to prevent it. Where do you think he is Mary?' 'I don't know Maggie, Boston, Florida, actually yeah; if he's anywhere I'd say he's in Boston.' 'What makes you so sure Mary?' 'I'm not Maggie, but he's often mentioned having Irish friends in South Boston.' 'Oh yeah, you're right Mary, I never thought of that. God, he's in deep shit. What a looser.' I ignored Maggie's name calling because I knew she was upset and annoyed that somehow in her mind Kieran had chosen 'that lifestyle' over her. 'Oh God Maggie' I said as the seriousness of the situation began to sink in 'what's he going to do now?' 'What's he going to do Mary? I'll tell you what he's going to do' Maggie almost screamed 'time Mary, years and years of time!'

We held my baby's christening a few weeks later and as we gathered outside the church waiting for the priest I was surprised to see Brian, Kieran's youngest brother step out of a car and approach me. He called me away from the others to tell me Kieran, who was still on the 'missing list' had asked him to come and offer apologies on his behalf for letting me down and that if I wanted, he would be happy to 'stand in' as Godfather to Stephen. I didn't ask Brian any questions pertaining to Kieran's whereabouts; I decided that the less I knew the better. But I explained to Brian that I had asked Richard Sullivan who had been a great support to myself and my husband, to do the honours.

Brian also went on to say that his brother wanted Maggie and I to know that he had told Junior Patrozzi about us, describing us as close friends and that if we had any problems we were to get in touch with him through Brian.

'You know who that guy is Mary?' Brian asked. 'Yes I do Brian,' I replied, 'he's the Godfather of Rhode Island.'

The priest arrived and it was time to go into the church. I thanked Brian for coming and asked him to tell Kieran that he was in my thoughts and prayers, and that hopefully we'd meet again under different circumstances. Before turning to leave, Brian handed me an envelope. 'This is from my brother for you and your baby.' I opened it to find a christening card and a hundred dollar bill. As I re-joined the others to go into the church Maggie whispered to me 'what did Brian want Mary?' 'He gave me a card from Kieran,' I replied unable to explain to her in full as the priest was approaching. 'God' Maggie replied 'he actually remembered.' 'Yes Maggie, with all the pressure he must be under,' I said, remembering the day that I'd asked Kieran to be Godfather and how he had smiled 'he remembered.'

Chapter 61

You've Got A Friend

A few weeks later Kieran and Rocco made headline news again. As the news reader put it 'Kieran Hennessy and Rocco Delmonte have been apprehended thanks to the tireless efforts of the F.B.I. and the State Police who tracked them to Florida.'

I had been wrong about Boston I thought, but as it turned out not totally wrong. We found out sometime later that Kieran had wanted to go to Boston, but Rocco had convinced him to go to Florida instead, and after lying low for a number of weeks in a 'safe' house in Florida, Rocco also convinced Kieran to go out for a few hours to soak up some Florida sunshine. Word had it that they were lying sunbathing on a beach when the F.B.I. arrested them. Not only were they refused bail because they were considered a 'flight risk', Kieran was immediately sentenced for violating a parole order. Neither Kieran nor Rocco were convicted on the charge of conspiracy to murder and people said if Kieran hadn't broken his parole by leaving the State of Rhode Island he would have been a free man, but because he did, he faced the next two years in prison.

Maggie was both furious and mortified, which lead to bouts of hysteria on more than one occasion. 'To think Mary, I would have married him. I mean, God only knows what people are saying. If I had known what I know now, I wouldn't have given him the time of day, he's just a common 'thug' and to think he had the nerve to dump me!'

The whole situation was coming between Maggie and her sleep and there was very little I could offer by way of consolation, but I did try.

'Maggie, I know you would have run a mile from Kieran so would I, if we had known then what we know now. Don't you think Kieran knew that, why do you think he told you in the beginning that he worked in real estate? Because he knew, just by speaking to you that you were honest and respectable, but the fact is, you fell in love with 'the Kieran' you came to know and 'thug' or no 'thug' he has always been there for you, even when you didn't want him to be and I think the saddest part of this whole scenario is, that the Kieran we came to know is the 'real Kieran', kind, considerate, loyal to the people he cares about and you must know Maggie, how much he loves you.'

'If he loves me so much Mary, why the hell did he finish with me?' Without giving me a chance to respond Maggie quickly added 'Not that I'd go out with him now if my life depended on it, I'm not having him ruin my reputation and 'good' name. I am going to make something of myself. I'm not going to college and breaking my back working God forsaken hours for the good of my health. He'll see, whether he knows it or not, I'm going places.'

Maggie paused, shaking with temper to light a cigarette. 'You still don't get it Maggie, after almost four years and everything that's happened?' 'What's there to get Mary? He dumped me and hadn't the decency to tell me why?' 'Jesus' I swore, feeling totally exasperated 'and ye call me an Eejit! Maggie, Kieran did tell you why, but at the time you understandably couldn't make any sense of it.' 'What the hell are you bloody well talking about Mary?' Maggie said almost screaming. 'Maggie, when Kieran finished with you he told you that you had a future and he hadn't. Maggie, Kieran wanted the best for you, he loved you and wasn't willing to drag you down with him. He wanted you to make something of yourself, even if it meant that he couldn't be a part of it. He did the only thing he could do to help you realise those dreams; he finished with you!'

At that moment, Maggie's tough exterior crumbled away and she cried like I'd never seen her cry before. But with the tears came a sense of relief. 'You know Mary' she sobbed. 'All those times Kieran called to see me, I knew in my heart he didn't want to leave. He would strike up such meaningless and trivial conversations or half way out the door he would decide that he needed to use the bathroom even if he had already been a few minutes before and I can't count the times I knew he wanted to kiss me but instead he would stare into my eyes, then shake my hand and walk away. It used to drive me crazy and that's why I was always so annoyed with him, but it all makes sense to me now Mary.'

'I'm glad Maggie', I said handing her a tissue to dry her eyes 'you needed some closure after all this time.' 'One more thing Mary' Maggie asked as I stood up from the kitchen table where we'd been sitting for hours. 'What's that Maggie?' 'Mary do you think if I'd asked Kieran four years ago to move to Ireland, would he have?' 'I don't know Maggie, all I know is if he had, he wouldn't be where he is now.'

With that very subject in mind and after much deliberation, I decided to put pen to paper and wrote to Kieran in prison. I kept the contents of the letter fairly casual, as I wasn't sure whether it would be opened or not by the prison authorities. I told Kieran about my baby Stephen and how fast he was growing. He has four teeth now I said and he's had three operations which were a great success.

I told him about Maggie's graduation and that she had, not surprisingly, passed all her exams with 'flying' colours. I told him how my husband hated America and I would more than likely be returning to Ireland in the next six months or sooner, if my husband had his way.

I asked him how he was doing; if he needed anything and most important of all I asked him, when the time came for his release would he consider moving to Ireland. You could make a fresh start Kieran, everyone makes mistakes I said and it's never too late to change. You and Maggie could be very happy there. I mailed the letter after signing it, your friend always, Mary. I wondered if he would get the letter and if he did, would he write back?

I didn't get an awful lot of mail in those days just the usual household bills, but even if I got bundles of it I would have recognised Kieran's letter straight away. I knew instantly it was from the prison because it had the senders address written in bold letters on the envelope.

I tore it open anxious to hear his response it read:

Dear Mary,

Thank you for thinking of me and taking the time to write. It's good to hear that you and the baby are well and that Maggie has graduated. There will be no stopping her now. I could talk to my brother Brian about finding work for your husband in construction; the pay would be much better than factory work. He could make good money Mary. I always wanted to go to Ireland but something tells me I never will. Thanks for trying to help Mary; you and your sister are good people. You always made me feel welcome despite everything. You are a great friend and I won't forget that.

Your friend, Kieran.

P.S. 'no way out.'

I read the letter over and over again. 'What did Kieran mean? 'No way out!' He was single after all, so he had no real ties, was he afraid of flying? Did having a criminal record mean he didn't have a passport? Maybe I thought, he knew that with a criminal record he'd be refused entry to Ireland.
Now many years later, twenty eight to be precise and having watched most of the block-busting movies about the Mafia, I know what Kieran meant all those years ago.
If somebody gets involved with the likes of the 'Mafia' or street gangs, which are a thorn in the side of many major cities today, like Kieran who was only in his very early twenties, they don't issue you with a contract stating the terms of your employment. It is a job for life and if that person decides for whatever reason that they want to walk away, that's when they issue the contract, that is a contract on your life and have you killed or simply disappear. The 'Mafia' does not like 'loose ends!'
I tried to imagine Kieran's predicament and understand what it must be like to be trapped in a situation with no light at the end of the tunnel. Most of us, at some stage in our lives have

worked in a job that we hated, but we knew we had the choice whether to stay or quit.

Kieran I do realise also had a choice. He was not without options. He could have quit, but in order to do this it would have meant joining a witness protection programme, which entails relocating under a new name and in return for the State providing this service Kieran would have to give evidence against the people he worked with and worked for. I could never have imagined the Kieran I knew walking away from his family. They were his whole world. Nor could I see him 'ratting' on the people he, maybe all too naively believed, to be his friends. So at the end of the day how much of a choice did he really have? Either desert his family, which would have been how he saw it, betray his friends or carry on doing whatever he was doing, live with the torment of his conscience and face God on judgement day. Loyalty to friends and family would have been number one on Kieran's list of priorities and I'm sure it was a quality that the Mafia would have found very endearing, apart from Kieran's six foot two height and strong athletic build.

Kieran caught the attention of the 'Mob' after being shot in the chest in a bar in Providence. When the police were called to the scene, Kieran who was sitting in a chair refused to give the name of the 'shooter' to the police when questioned. Kieran, like most young men of his age, was probably playing 'bravado.' But the 'Mob' knew from that moment that he 'ticked' all the right boxes.

I'm sure it was only a matter of time combined with the lure of easy money before they made Kieran on offer he couldn't refuse. The 'Mob' have a reputation for getting their own way, they certainly are not accustomed to being told 'no' and subtlety is not one of their finer points.

One example of the Mafia in action was after a robbery that occurred across the street from my apartment around the time I was due to give birth to Stephen my son. Three men had walked into the local liquor store in broad daylight and stolen a substantial amount of money from the terrified staff.

I was shocked to hear it, because that sort of thing just didn't happen on Colonial Hill. In fact, to this day, it was one of the safest places I ever lived. Elderly people walked freely to the store at night without the worry of being mugged. Cars were parked on the street with windows open and in all the time I spent there, I never had to use my front door key because the door was never locked. I listened to the six o'clock news that evening and I thought to myself, whoever the men were who robbed the liquor store, they had to be very brave or very stupid! The following day, the local news station announced that Providence police had found the body of one of the suspected thieves in a nearby wooded area and it was strongly rumoured around the neighbourhood that the body that was found was headless and had a note tied around the neck with a message for the remaining two thieves which allegedly read 'We'll get you too.'

I returned to Ireland in 1986. My husband had never settled in America and hated every moment of it, and told me so every single day. He said that he missed his mother, but I know it was that he suffered from work related allergies. That is, if you mentioned work he broke out in a rash!

It had always been my intention to return to Ireland because I too missed things about home but I had some reservations about returning so soon. One of those reasons was the lack of employment in Ireland in the Eighties.

There were certainly a lot more opportunities in America and I know that if my husband was willing to stay another couple of years there would have been nothing stopping us from returning to Ireland with enough money to buy a small home. But the most serious reservation I had about returning so soon was that my son Stephen needed a fourth operation, a procedure that the surgeons were reluctant to carry out before Stephen was two. They also had strongly advised me against returning to Ireland before Stephen had the operation and urged me to try and change my husband's mind. They told me that because Ireland was not as advanced as America in the area of Maxio Facial Surgery, Stephen might not be operated on until he was five or even six years old. There was no swaying my husband though, he missed his mother and as it turned out; Stephen didn't have the operation until he was twelve. An operation he could have had in America if only my husband had been willing to stay eleven more months.

Maggie was very sad to see us leave and I knew she would really miss Stephen. I had become accustomed every day to hearing her running up the stairs after work to play with him while I cooked dinner. Once again I knew it was going to be lonely for her on her own, and once again I would be back in Ireland waiting on phone calls from America.

Chapter 62

I Hear You Knockin' But You Can't Come In

Maggie found a new tenant for my apartment almost immediately after I had returned to Ireland which was great because she depended on the rental income to pay her mortgage each month. She had a substantial student loan to pay so it would be some time before she reaped any benefits from her new job. She continued to work part-time at the weekends as a bartender and most of the money she earned at that, she spent on updating her house. So she really started to panic when after a short period her new tenant stopped paying rent. At first he reassured her that she had nothing to worry about and he would pay her what he owed her, so she gave him the benefit of the doubt. But at the end of six months anytime she approached him in regard to his debt he would shout abuse at her and also began to 'hang around' in her back yard in a bid to intimidate her. To make matter worse she had fallen behind in her mortgage and the bank was also threatening her. Maggie was at her wits end about the whole situation. She was afraid to issue him with an eviction order in case of retaliation and slowly but surely she felt she was becoming a prisoner in her own home.

At home alone one evening a knock came to her door, so sure was she that it was the problematic tenant that she decided not to answer. Then she heard a man calling her 'Maggie, open the door I know you're home.' Recognising the voice she breathed a sigh of relief and opened the door. 'Hello Kieran, long time no see.' It was over two years since they'd met. When Kieran was released from prison a few months before he had resumed his relationship with Doris, but Maggie had accepted the whole situation and had started dating again. She was no longer angry with Kieran. He in turn never interfered with her personal life. But he never forgot her either. He always seemed to be somewhere on the perimeter of her life, watching over her.

'Hey Maggie, how are you doin'?' 'I'm ok I guess, come in Kieran.' Kieran closed the door behind him. 'Kieran' Maggie asked 'what's up with you? Is there something wrong?' Maggie was wondering what had prompted his visit. 'I dunno Maggie, you tell me,' he replied. 'What are you talking about Kieran? I'm not in the mood for a guessing game.' 'Any truth in the rumour that one of your tenants is being a wise-ass Maggie?' 'Well yeah,' Maggie answered reluctantly 'he hasn't paid any rent, but I can handle it Kieran.' 'That ain't what I'm hearing Maggie.'

'Why? Do you know him Kieran? 'Cause if you do I'm telling you now, he's a real jerk.' 'No, I don't know him, he ain't from around here, he's gonna get to know me though,' Kieran said opening the door to leave. 'Kieran, what are you going to do?' Maggie asked remembering all too vividly 'Rudi' the chef years before. 'I'm just gonna persuade him to change his mind, which apartment is he in Maggie?' Maggie watched as Kieran bounded up the steps to the back door and knew he was going to find her wayward tenant with or without her help. 'He's in Mary's apartment Kieran,' she said momentarily feeling a wave of sympathy for the unsuspecting tenant who was under the impression that she was a woman alone in a strange country.

Maggie, as usual called me the following day to tell me the minute to minute details of how the story unfolded. 'What happened then Maggie?' I asked surprised to hear his name mentioned after such a long time. 'He came out of the apartment Mary after five minutes and told me that my tenant had, had a change of heart, that not only would he be paying me my rent in full, but that he'd be moving out today.' 'Are you serious Maggie, what did you say?' 'I asked him how he knew that I was having problems and his response was 'it's my job to know these things Maggie. Just look at me as a kind of guardian angel'. 'He's some angel alright, isn't he Mary?' Maggie laughed. I laughed too, unable to picture Kieran with a halo on his head. But I was glad that he hadn't lost his sense of humour. 'So what happened this morning Maggie? Did the guy leave?' 'Oh yeah Mary, I woke to see a removal van outside the door, but before he left he limped across the yard looking a little the worse for wear and put an envelope in my mail box!' 'Was there money in it Maggie?' 'Oh yes, every dollar that he owed me Mary, Thank God.' 'No Maggie,' I said delighted for her, 'Thank Kieran!'

It wasn't so much that I approved of Kieran's unorthodox way of dealing with Maggie's tenant, I am, and always was very much a pacifist, but all of Maggie's trust and patience was wasted on that man. He never had any intention of paying the money he owed her. He was a bully and a parasite who took pleasure in terrifying Maggie. I believe that Kieran gave him the 'wake-up call' he needed, and if nothing else it may have served to make him think twice before abusing a woman or future landlord again.

Chapter 63

I Can't Make You Love Me, If You Don't

By 1987, I had a second child, a little girl called Grace and although she was delighted for me Maggie admitted that she was also a little envious. 'There you are Mary, two years younger than me with two children, most of my friends in Ireland are married and I don't even have a steady boyfriend' she would say 'what am I doing wrong? I always seem to pick losers.'

It was true, although Maggie had had a few relationships in the previous few years and even though they seemed promising they all came to an abrupt end. She seemed to have no luck when it came to men, no matter how particular she was about her choice of partner. Each man she agreed to date seemed to possess the ingredients needed for the making of a great husband. In Ireland they would have been described as a 'fine catch.' There was Alex the lawyer with his 'cave man' attitude toward women. Then there was Peter, a prominent paediatrician with his own practise. Maggie was seeing him at the time I was expecting Stephen and although she had high hopes for him I never liked him. Because although he was all smiles to her face, he was 'all smiles' to me when her back was turned and at the same time never seemed to look at me above my neck line. Maggie couldn't understand why I despised him so much and was furious with me when I refused 'point blank' to allow him assist in my baby's delivery. I didn't want to hurt Maggie's feelings by telling her what I knew and prayed that the truth would come out in the end. It did, and I was proved right. Maggie, after many months of dating him discovered that he was still having a relationship with a woman he had claimed to be his ex-girlfriend.

Maggie knew the woman's name and found her telephone number in the directory. Peter had told her he was going away on business for the weekend which I told her was a 'crock of shit.' 'Phone her number,' I yelled 'or drive over to her house, I bet you any money Maggie, he's there.' Maggie thankfully listened to my advice and dialled the number, Peter answered! It took Maggie about twelve months to get over the shock and when she did, she started dating Victor, who was a health inspector for the State. He was handsome man who kept himself fit by lifting weights. He wasn't a womaniser like Peter but he was a control freak and a pathological liar.

He lived on East Way, only a few blocks from Maggie in a beautifully restored historical home which he told her he had bought a few years earlier. He lived in a one bedroom apartment on the ground floor and although he told her he could use the extra space, he hadn't the heart to evict the elderly lady who lived on the other two floors because she had been there all her life. 'That's really kind of him isn't it Mary?' Maggie said in an attempt to boost my opinion of him. I had my reservations about Victor also but not without reason. A few days before, after dating him for a few months and because Victor had a very tough work schedule, Maggie had kindly offered to clean his apartment, not that it was dirty, 'if anything' she said 'it was immaculate', it was simply a gesture of good will.

Maggie's good intentions went unrewarded. She arrived home that evening upset that Victor had almost had a fit claiming that she had used the wrong polish on the furniture.

A few days later Maggie decided to put the dispute about the polish behind her and took it for granted I had too. She invited him to dinner. Victor who was listening to Maggie describing life in Cratloe looked almost panic stricken when she mentioned that the water supply in Cratloe came from our own well and was quite obviously imagining having to haul buckets to and from the house should he ever decide to take Maggie up on her suggestion that he go with her the next time she went home. Maggie, guessing his thoughts decided it was best to explain 'oh no Victor' she said laughing 'when I say well, I mean the water is pumped from a well into the house, we do have running water in Ireland you know.' 'Yes, I'm sure you do,' Victor replied 'but does your family have it tested regularly. I mean, is it safe to use?' Jesus, I thought, this man is a pain in the arse. If Maggie marries him I'll kill her. At the risk of him thinking that Maggie was contaminated in some way from years of using 'spring water' I said 'Not at all Victor, the water at home has never been tested. For all we know there could be cows shitting in it upstream!' Realising very quickly that Victor was a fanatic when it came to cleanliness, I had hoped when mentioning the 'cow shit' that Victor would finish with her there and then, but although I knew there was no possibility that he would ever visit Ireland, he didn't finish with her and a few weeks later in an effort to surprise him Maggie, having already established that he knew nothing about gardening, decided to buy daffodil bulbs, saying that 'they'll look beautiful in the spring when they are in bloom around his front garden.'

Armed with her bulbs and an array of gardening utensils she set off for Victor's house one crisp but sunny autumn afternoon. 'I'll have the garden all spruced up Mary and the bulbs planted by the time he gets home.'

Maggie raked all the fallen leaves into neat piles. She dug dozens of small holes all over the garden and was standing back deciding which colour daffodils to plant where, when the first floor window opened and Victor's elderly neighbour leaned out. 'What are you doing down there?' she asked Maggie sternly. 'Oh hello,' Maggie said 'no need to worry I'm Maggie, Victors girlfriend. I'm just tidying his garden and planting some spring bulbs.' 'His garden!' the elderly lady scoffed; 'it's my garden and I want you to leave it alone.' Maggie, believing that the old lady was suffering from some form of dementia said 'but it is Victor's house.' 'No,' the lady replied 'it's my house, he's only a tenant.'

'Oh my God Mary, why did he tell me he owned the house?' Maggie said horrified. 'I could have been arrested for trespassing and criminal damage!' 'I don't know Maggie' I said 'but you'd want to get rid of him.' 'Don't you think Mary; I should give him an opportunity to explain himself?' 'No I don't, just get rid of him' I insisted. 'But there might be some reasonable explanation Mary, and he is good to me in other ways. 'Your trouble Mary is you think Kieran's the only one good enough for me.' 'You're wrong there Maggie' I said 'Kieran is in no way good enough for you, do you really think Maggie, I want to see you spending your life visiting him in prison? 'Cause I don't, you deserve a lot better than that. But I'll tell you what I do want Maggie, if you give me a minute to explain; I want you to meet someone who loves you as much as Kieran did. Someone who looks at you the way Kieran did. Someone who will respect and admire you for the person you are. Alex, Peter, Victor, they have twice the education Kieran has but they all have one serious flaw and that is, they all lack respect for women. And in all the times we spent with Kieran you can never say he was in any way disrespectful.' Although Maggie agreed with me that day, it was sometime later she came to her senses and told Victor to get lost.

'Back to square one again Mary,' she said referring to the fact that she was once again single. 'Maggie, don't be worrying, you'll meet someone. The way you're talking you'd swear you were ancient.'

'I know Mary, but I'm not getting any younger, I'm twenty seven you know.' I knew Maggie really wanted to settle down and have a family.

Chapter 64

On The Street Where You Live

'Doris is pregnant Mary,' was the news Maggie called to share with me sometime in 1989. 'I guess after seven years she had to think of something to get Kieran up the aisle.' 'Do you think it will work Maggie? Do you think he'll marry her?' 'Oh yes I do Mary. Call it chivalry or just plain old fashioned, but Kieran won't see a child of his growing up without a father. What do you think Mary?' 'I think you're right Maggie. Kieran was never one to walk away from what he considered to be his responsibilities; he seems to look after more people than the Salvation Army.'

It was also around this time that Maggie decided to move away from Colonial Hill. 'What's brought this on?,' I asked hoping it hadn't upset her hearing about Doris' pregnancy, which would have really surprised me because she had come to terms and accepted Kieran's decisions years before. 'It's something I've been thinking about for over a year now Mary. I don't have to sell the house for a while. I can rent my cottage and then rent somewhere in the suburbs, a little house with a garden would be nice Mary.' 'That sounds like a great idea Maggie. You know, new places, new faces. I think a new start will do you the world of good, so have you decided to go ahead with it?' I asked. 'Well Mary, up until yesterday I hadn't made my mind up, but now I have. There's a few things I've to sort out but I'll be moving in the next few months. Mary, my friend Joey, who's recently joined the Providence Police called me yesterday.' 'What was that all about?' I asked noticing the ominous tone in Maggie's voice. 'He asked me was I still in touch with Kieran, I told him that even though I see him around, that I haven't spoken to him in months.' 'Why was he asking you that Maggie? Do you think he fancies you?' 'No Mary, you Eejit, Joey's girlfriend is a good friend of mine. He said that there's an ongoing investigation against Kieran by the police and the F.B.I. and that if I should get dragged into it for any reason, I can kiss goodbye to a career in this State. Mary, I've worked too hard for what I have, I haven't done anything wrong and I don't want people thinking I have.' 'I know that Maggie, you have to do what's best for you, so go for it.'

Maggie went ahead with her plans to leave Colonial Hill and was very optimistic about the move. Returning from her bartending job one evening about six weeks after making the decision to leave, she started packing her belongings into cardboard boxes.

It was two o'clock in the morning when she heard her yard gate opening. She stopped what she was doing, as she listened hardly daring to breathe. If it hadn't been for the fact that she knew Kieran was getting married the following day she would have considered the possibility that it was him, but Kieran would have knocked on the door and whoever was in her yard was pacing up and down. She listened quietly to the footsteps that walked back and forth outside her door. After about twenty minutes of listening to the continuous pacing, too terrified to look out the window, Maggie called the police. When the police arrived they searched the yard and could find nobody but asked her if she knew a Kieran Hennessy. 'Why do you ask?' Maggie asked nervously. 'Because,' the policeman replied 'he's been sitting in a car across the street from here all night.' 'No,' Maggie replied remembering her friend Joey's warning 'I don't know anyone by that name.'

Maggie felt very guilty afterwards for denying she knew Kieran. 'I feel like a real Judas,' she said. 'I hope I didn't get him into trouble Mary,' she continued in a sorrowful voice. 'Maggie, there's nothing you can do about it now,' I said 'how were you to know it was Kieran in your yard?' 'You know you're right Mary, it's that Eejits fault. What the hell was he doing in my yard the night before he was due to get married?' 'Do you really need to ask that question Maggie? I've been telling you for years that he loved you. If you can come up with a better reason for him to be standing in his ex-girlfriends yard at two in the morning the night before he gets married, I'm all ears. You should have been the last person he was thinking of.'

I can only hazard a guess as to why Kieran was in Maggie's yard that night and the only thing I'm sure of, is that he wasn't there to issue her and invitation to his wedding! To be pacing up and down outside her door suggests to me he was not exactly overjoyed at the prospect of getting married and if I was a gambling woman I'd be willing to bet any money he was trying to 'pluck' up the courage to ask Maggie if there was any hope for them as a couple, and I'm sure that at the very least Kieran knew that the marriage he was entering into was built on obligation rather than love. But with what appeared to be Kieran's rather ludicrous sense of responsibility for others he went ahead with the wedding.

I believe Kieran was full of regret and ashamed at the person he'd become, It wasn't a life to be proud of, nor was it a great legacy to pass onto a child and Kieran was not going to add fuel to the fire by deserting Doris and the child she was expecting.

Maggie once asked Kieran if he ever thought about his deceased father. She found it really bizarre that they could be on such opposite sides of the law. It was a desperate effort on her part to remind him where he came from in the hope that he would turn his life around. Kieran's response was 'I try not to think about him Maggie.' And when Maggie asked why he said 'I just hope he can't see how I turned out Maggie, he would turn in his grave.'

Chapter 65

What If?

Another three years were to pass before Maggie was to meet Kieran again. She did however; hear little snippets of news from Vanessa every now and again. Kieran by that time had a son and a daughter whom I have absolutely no doubt he would have adored.

It was early September in 1992 and Maggie called me to tell me she'd met him the night before. She explained that she had arranged to meet some friends in a bar in downtown Providence when at the last minute with a little time to spare she decided to call to another bar to see if an old friend still worked there. She thought she could kill two birds with one stone, so to speak. Just as she placed her order for drink with the bartender who had told her that her friend did indeed still work there but was on a night off, Maggie spotted Kieran at the other end of the bar. He as yet had not seen her because she said he was busy entertaining three women who could best be described as 'rough as a badger's arse.' As Maggie sat and watched she noticed how much Kieran had aged since she had last seen him, he was, after all only thirty nine. She said he had gained a lot of weight and was drinking 'shots' with the women. The Kieran she remembered was always a very sociable drinker and could take an hour to finish a bottle of beer. Maggie went on to say that the man standing at the end of the bar was a far cry from the handsome man he used to be and the women he was drinking with looked as if they would struggle to get served in the canteen at the local prison not to mention a bar. She said she was both saddened and disgusted at the way he had deteriorated and with the company he was keeping and decided to make a fast exit in the hope that she wouldn't be seen. She almost succeeded. She had just made it to the door when she heard Kieran's voice coming up behind her. 'Hey Maggie, wait up. It's me, Kieran.' Maggie said she turned to see Kieran smiling like a kid in a candy store. 'It really is

good to see you Maggie; can I get you a drink?' 'No thank you Kieran,' Maggie replied 'I was just leaving and anyway I'd hate to keep you from your friends.'
'They're not my friends Maggie, I hardly know them.' 'Really Kieran, you could have fooled me,' she replied sarcastically, but before Kieran got a chance to defend himself further, the women who Maggie said sounded like a bag of cats yelled up the bar 'Hey Kieran, come on already' and another 'Kieran can you call a cab?'
Maggie said Kieran went red in the face with embarrassment and yelled back at them 'get lost, I ain't goin' nowhere with you. I'm leaving with my friend here.'
Maggie had other ideas. 'Kieran you'd better think again,' she said 'you're not going anywhere with me. You're drunk and you're married remember?' Kieran, still hoping to change Maggie's mind, followed her to her car. 'Maggie,' he persisted 'wait up a minute; I got somethin I gotta say to you.' 'The next thing I knew Mary he had his arms around me and he gave me a big kiss. I was just about to slap his face Mary when he said, 'Maggie, I just wanted you to know I'm real proud of you, you did real good Maggie.' 'As I drove away Mary I looked in the rear view mirror and he was still standing in the parking lot, just staring after me.'

Chapter 66

The End Of The Road

Ten days later Kieran was shot. The phone call came early one morning in late September, the day after it had happened. 'Kieran's dead,' I heard Maggie say on the other end of the line 'it's all over the news Mary'. 'What happened Maggie?' I asked shocked and saddened. Maggie sounded sad but not shocked as she tried to explain. Kieran, she said had been out socialising with a group of friends the night before on Colonial Hill. There were two conflicting stories being told, one from the police who were saying that Kieran had left the company he was in to meet someone in anther bar further down the street and was shot on his way to the bar. The other was the one on the street, told in whispers throughout the neighbourhood, that Kieran had made it to the bar and was sitting at a table with his friend when a man walked into the bar and told Kieran there was a problem outside and asked if he could come outside and try to sort it out. Kieran allegedly told his friend whom he was sitting with who was a little apprehensive about Kieran going outside, not to worry that he'd be back in a few minutes. But a short time later it was not Kieran who walked back in but the man who had called him out. He told Kieran's friend who was waiting patiently that he needed to call an ambulance saying 'Kieran's been shot.'

The area where Kieran was shot was a busy street with bars and restaurants on both sides of the street. Normally a hive of activity yet the paramedics who arrived on the scene in the ambulance said Kieran was lying on the footpath, alone on the city street. He had been shot three times in the head. The paramedic was quoted as saying 'Kieran was unconscious but he was still breathing.' He died a short time later at a local hospital. I thought how sad it was that there was nobody there with him to hold his hand or say a prayer. No witnesses ever came forward and Kieran's murder is still a 'cold case' to this day.

He died at the age of thirty nine and I can't help but feel that it was some of the characteristics that Maggie and I found so appealing about Kieran were the very ones that brought about his downfall and ultimately his untimely death. His devotion and loyalty to the people he believed to be his friends and his sense of responsibility for others. I often wonder if Kieran ever thought how different his life might have been if he hadn't moved to Colonial Hill to be near his ailing Grandfather, and I can still remember how he'd say 'yunno Mary, crime don't pay, unless you get away!'

This is how the F.B.I. and the Providence Police described Kieran in their statements to the media.

Kieran Hennessy: Long-time career criminal and free-lance enforcer for the Patrozzi family; suspected involvement in gangland slayings, specifically the murder of Anthony DeVito. Hennessy spent time in prison for jury tampering, intimidating witnesses and counterfeit. Standing six foot two and of muscular build Hennessy was a force to be reckoned with and when on the streets of Providence he was very much the 'real deal.'

Ironically Kieran died only a few yards from where he had lived on Nimnuc St. with Rocco for many years and also a short distance from where Anthony DeVito was murdered a number of years before. Kieran had immediately been considered to be the number one suspect in the case and for good reason. It was common knowledge in the neighbourhood that there was no love lost between Kieran and the DeVito family who lived opposite him on the same street.

Allegedly the bitterness began shortly after Kieran moved into the neighbourhood. Apparently Kieran, after being told of a young boy who was being continually bullied by the DeVito boys, decided to approach the DeVito's to reason with them and persuade them to leave the boy alone. But allegedly the DeVito boys attacked Kieran who was on his own and gave him what people described as an unmerciful beating. In my opinion Kieran was not likely to forget that.

I remember well Maggie calling me to tell me about Anthony DeVito's murder. It was headline news at the time and Maggie was quite shocked because it happened next door to where she was bartending in Garibaldi's. She explained to me how Anthony DeVito had come in to Garibaldi's and called for a drink. Although he knew Maggie from the neighbourhood, unlike the majority of people who lived locally, he wasn't very friendly towards her which Maggie understood to be because of the on-going animosity between his family and Kieran. Maggie and Kieran were split up quite some time by then but DeVito would have known that they had been an 'item.'

Maggie went on to say that 'DeVito' was sitting alone at the bar a short while when a woman walked in, called a drink and almost immediately began flirting with DeVito and although he didn't appear to know her, he seemed flattered by the unexpected attention from the attractive young lady. A relatively short time later Maggie overheard DeVito agree to join the young lady next door for a drink. DeVito and the young lady left together and within moments shots rang out. DeVito had been shot dead by two masked gunmen who were described as being about six foot two in height. Were the DeVito's likely to forget if they believed that Kieran was responsible for Anthony's murder? I doubt it.

Chapter 67

Brothers In Arms

Just recently the F.B.I. having received new information from a police informer in regards to Kieran's death reopened the case in a bid to finally solve his murder. They made renewed appeals to the public which caused a flurry of media attention and they are now considering the possibility that Kieran was murdered by a known associate and fellow Irish man 'Brendan O'Grady.' In the ninety's O'Grady and Hennessy were charged but never convicted of the attempted kidnapping for ransom of a reputed mafia associate.

According to the F.B.I's informant two years later the relationship between O'Grady and Hennessy soured because according to O'Grady, Hennessy was trying to muscle in on his territory. The informant went on to say that O'Grady complained Hennessy to Berlusconi, the New England crime boss and that it was he who ordered the 'hit' on Hennessy. Berlusconi denies any knowledge of this and says the F.B.I's informant must have done a deal with the F.B.I. in return for his statement.

O'Grady has been described as a man who was capable of anything, a person who showed no loyalty to anyone and took care of number one, himself. Police went so far as to say that one word would describe O'Grady, sociopath.

If indeed, the informant was telling the truth about O'Grady then in my opinion it makes the whole scenario even more tragic. That it's quite possible that Kieran's demise was brought about by one of what Kieran would have described as 'his own,' a fellow Irishman; which begs the question, is there any such thing as easy money? I believe that long before his untimely death Kieran knew the 'real' cost of 'easy money', and ultimately paid a premium price for his wrong doings.

Did Kieran know he was doing wrong? Most certainly.

Do I believe Kieran Hennessy was wrong? Most definitely.

Now I know the extent of Kieran's criminal activity, do I like him any less? No, because thankfully I have never had to walk a day in his shoes and I'd rather leave the task of judgement to God.

Would Kieran have expected people to be sympathetic? I don't believe so.

Kieran knew he was playing a dangerous game in very much an Italian world, where for most part despite being useful, he would, I would imagine, always be considered an outsider, simply because he wasn't Italian. And I would go as far as to say that I believe he would have been hated by a lot of Italians in the 'neighbourhood' because of the power and influence he had in what they considered to be their territory. It may also explain the initial 'kinship' between O'Grady and Kieran. It may very well be that Kieran felt a certain amount of solace in the notion that he had a fellow Irish man to watch his back!

Chapter 68

I Say A Little Prayer For You

In recent years the world has become a much smaller place with the advancements in technology especially the internet which enables people to access information all over the globe by simply typing what it is one needs to know. In the decades since Kieran's death, he has, on many occasions 'popped' into my head for no apparent reason and I'd always take it as a sign that he needed a few prayers said for him. But on one of those occasions two years ago I decided to borrow my son's laptop, Google his name just to see what would happen. I was immediately both shocked and saddened.

Shocked by the amount of media coverage and saddened one because Kieran was staring back at me from his photograph and it didn't help watching the old footage of him being stretchered into an ambulance after being shot. I thought how awful it must have been for Kieran's children, the innocent victims of this story who were left at a young age with no father which is a hard enough cross to bear in normal circumstances, but to lose him in such a horrendous way must, I can only imagine, be unbelievably painful, made worse by the fact that the majority of people believe that your father was a bad man who got what he deserved, coupled with what must seem like no closure and unending media attention.

It must be I thought, for them, like having salt continuously poured on an ever open wound. But what totally un-nerved me that day was when I glanced at the calendar on my kitchen wall. I was shocked when I read the date. It was Kieran's anniversary!

It came between me and my sleep for several nights, but I came to the conclusion that there had been a reason for it, that I must have been destined to read all the bad things that were being said about Kieran and although I'm not in a position to dispute anything that has been said, it prompted me to put pen to paper and tell my story and that of my sister, of the Kieran Hennessy we came to know all those years ago, and if nothing else I thought it would be my way of saying thank you to him for being both a gentleman and a friend. If somebody asked me to describe Kieran Hennessy in two sentences or less I would say: Kieran Hennessy was a good man, who took the wrong turn at the crossroad, got lost and for whatever reason never succeeded to find his way back.

I have no doubt that people have many explanations for Kieran's violent demise.

'The hand of God is slow but sure,
Live by the sword and you'll die by the sword,
You will reap what you sow' or there's the Bible's version: 'Do onto others as you would have them do unto you'.

My 'take' on it is, be careful what you wish for others, it may also come true for you!

I do believe wishes come true and looking back now it seems that everyone involved got what they wished for with the exception of Kieran and Gerard Molyneaux. Gerard was arrested in the mid-nineties on a charge of extortion. His third felony conviction and was one of the first people to be convicted under the relatively new 'three strikes policy' he was handed a life sentence with no possibility of parole. Now in his seventies he is still in prison today. This is how Gerard Molyneaux has been described by the F.B.I.

Gerard Molyneaux, born in the Forties to a strict Catholic family, he was groomed from an early age for life in 'the mob.' He was half French but equal to a lieutenant and served under Patrozzi who controlled crime in the New England from 1952 -1984. Patrozzi was succeeded after his death by his son Junior. Molyneaux was one of Southern Massachusetts most feared criminals, whose acts included loan sharking, extortion, major hijackings and the F.B.I. also suspect he was responsible for at least seven gangland slayings. To date he has spent forty-five years of his life behind bars. What I believe to be one of the saddest revelations of this whole tale is that Gerard Molyneaux made a statement from prison recently accusing Rocco Delmonte, (the man Kieran lived with for many years and held in the highest regard) of being an informant for the police.

Epilogue

All I can do now whenever I think of Kieran is say a little prayer and ask God to look at the bigger picture. I will always remember Kieran as a friend and I will always be grateful to him for two reasons: One, for taking my sister and I under his wing and watching out for us when we were young and dumb, two Eejits in a strange country and secondly for 'letting my sister go.'

As I said I find it fascinating in a strange sort of way to look back now and realise that apart from Kieran and Gerard everyone got what they wished for. Doris got Kieran, but in a cruel twist of fate had him snatched away, leaving her a young widow with two children to support. Rocco Delmonte got Kieran's respect, loyalty and friendship until he was murdered. Maggie got a successful career, a husband who loves her, two children and a beautiful home. Vanessa went on to have a successful career and was a tower of strength and support to her three children. Mam also finally saw the light at sixty years old and left Paddy, she has never looked back. I separated from my husband in 1992 shortly before Kieran's death. I raised my two children alone and I now live in a small cottage with my dog and two cats.

The End